DON'T FOLLOW ME, I'M LOST

DON'T FOLLOW ME, I'M LOST

A MEMOIR OF HAMPSHIRE COLLEGE
IN THE TWILIGHT OF THE 80'S

RICHARD RUSHFIELD

GOTHAM
BOOKS

GOTHAM BOOKS
Published by Penguin Group (USA) Inc.
375 Hudson Street, New York, New York 10014, U.S.A.
Penguin Group (Canada), 90 Eglinton Avenue East, Suite 700, Toronto,
Ontario M4P 2Y3, Canada (a division of Pearson Penguin Canada Inc.);
Penguin Books Ltd, 80 Strand, London WC2R 0RL, England;
Penguin Ireland, 25 St Stephen's Green, Dublin 2,
Ireland (a division of Penguin Books Ltd);
Penguin Group (Australia), 250 Camberwell Road, Camberwell,
Victoria 3124, Australia (a division of Pearson Australia Group Pty Ltd);
Penguin Books India Pvt Ltd, 11 Community Centre,
Panchsheel Park, New Delhi – 110 017, India;
Penguin Group (NZ), 67 Apollo Drive, Rosedale,
North Shore 0632, New Zealand (a division of Pearson New Zealand Ltd);
Penguin Books (South Africa) (Pty) Ltd, 24 Sturdee Avenue,
Rosebank, Johannesburg 2196, South Africa

Penguin Books Ltd, Registered Offices:
80 Strand, London WC2R 0RL, England

Published by Gotham Books, a member of Penguin Group (USA) Inc.

First printing, October 2009
1   3   5   7   9   10   8   6   4   2

LIBRARY OF CONGRESS CATALOGING-IN-PUBLICATION DATA
Rushfield, Richard.
Don't follow me, I'm lost : a memoir of Hampshire College
in the twilight of the 80's / by Richard Rushfield.
p.   cm.
ISBN 978-1-59240-453-7
1. Rushfield, Richard.   2. Hampshire College—Biography.   I. Title.
PS3568.U7273Z46   2009
813'.54—dc22   2009017817

Printed in the United States of America
Set in ITC Galliard ● Designed by Elke Sigal

....

*Penguin is committed to publishing works of quality and integrity. I
n that spirit, we are proud to offer this book to our readers;
however, the story, the experiences, and the words
are the author's alone.*

For Nicole

"I've always imagined that you'd take me to some place where there lived a huge viscous man-sized spider and that we'd spend the rest of our lives staring at it in fear. And that's how we'd spend our days of mutual love."

—DOSTOEVSKY, *THE POSSESSED*

CONTENTS

CHAPTER ONE

Orientation, September '86

"I swear, man, it's not a hippie school."

"Dude." Nino looked me deep in the eyes. "It's like the biggest hippie school in the world. Hampshire is the Harvard of hippie schools."

"You can keep saying that"—I sighed—"but I've been there. I went to *parties* there and I'm telling you I didn't see a single hippie."

"Whatever, man. But if you come home wearing a poncho, don't expect me to talk to you."

I shook my head. "Don't worry about it. I wouldn't drag myself four thousand miles to be locked away in the woods with a bunch of hippies."

Six months later, I stood on line at freshman orientation. In front of me a pale-faced boy in a sagging knit sweater passed a joint to his parents, who carried his canvas duffel bags for him. Behind me, a young man in a rainbow bandana smiled when I turned his way, tossed a tiny leather bag into the air, and then kicked it into my stomach. It bounced off and plopped onto the ground.

"What's up, bra?" he asked. "You don't hack?"

I remembered the conversation with Nino, eating chili fries in his car parked outside the Westwood Village video arcade. We chewed over the specter of my living among hippies like it was the plotline of a postapocalypse zombie movie, a story in which the living dead would drain my life force with a suffocating web of Buddha beads, leaving me to stumble across the earth, more rainbow-colored corpse than human, until the end of time.

Not that we actually knew what hippies were. Between us, my friends and I owned a handful of Bob Dylan and Pink Floyd albums, which weren't bad background music, but they seemed as close to our lives as records by the Four Freshmen or, for that matter, Johann Sebastian Bach.

In mid-eighties Los Angeles hippies were, like the bobbysoxers and zoot-suiters of yore, an extinct tribe who had roamed our land in prehistoric times. Legends were passed down of how in their age they had panhandled on the Sunset Strip while Jim Morrison had invented the "rock poet" genre, of their large concerts where they smoked marijuana in protest of war. Our only direct contact with the historic peoples was in the person of our headmaster, who called frequent assemblies to remind us that at our age he and his consciousness-raised buddies had changed the world, while spoiled brats like us couldn't even be bothered to show up for last Saturday's Nuclear Freeze Forum Day. In his agonized soliloquies, it was impossible to make out *what* exactly he had done to change the world (the story involved backpacking in South America, growing his own vegetables, and reading Robert Frost), but our parents assured us constantly that our headmaster was a great man, a *visionary*. They were the longest assemblies of our lives.

So when I visited Hampshire on my prospective student tour, it was with a fair level of trepidation that I stepped in to the famed collegiate Hippie Haven. My friend Drake, a surfer with beatnik tendencies, who had graduated from my high school and come to Hampshire two years before, hosted me for the weekend. He showed me around the campus with its dilapidated ski-lodge buildings set into clearings amid the snow-dappled forest, from the giant Art Barn where he was sculpting a papier-mâché wave, to the little apartments where he lived with three others in admirable squalor. Friday night, Drake had his friends over to watch *Miami Vice*. While I tried to disguise how quickly I had gotten drunk on Drake's gin fizzes, I listened to their speculation about Crockett's new car, which was to be revealed on the episode, and their groans of displeasure when the white Testarossa was unveiled.

"That is the most clichéd choice they could've made," one friend fumed.

"This show might be losing it." Drake shook his head.

"I told you guys, we should stick with *Magnum*," said another.

"I dunno," Drake mourned. "I just thought *Vice* was above this kind of chicanery."

After the show, we walked over to a party in a little village on the other side of campus called Prescott House that looked like a giant tin ski chalet. The crowd seemed a bit like the drama scene from my high school, but more intimidating, more severe, wearing even more black, with even more dramatic eyeliner. "It's the New York kids," Drake told me.

A girl in a black miniskirt and red stockings, who looked like she'd been crying, asked me if I knew who was holding Ecstasy on campus. I told her that I was just visiting for the weekend, which made her laugh and ask, "Is that why you've been staring at me all semester in Gogol?" She grabbed my arm and made me dance with her to a Bauhaus song. We sat on the couch, where she told me her name was Malaria, and said, "Let's pretend everyone here is dead." While the music blared we stared at them and tried to picture them deceased. "You're good at this," she whispered. She said that Lewis in Enfield might be holding something and we should go check, but first she had to go to the bathroom. She stumbled off and never returned. Half an hour later, I glanced out the windows and saw her stumbling down the stairs with a guy in bondage pants and dreadlocks. I stood to follow her but Drake stopped me. "Play hard to get, Rich. That'll teach her." Two months later, when I received my acceptance letter from Hampshire, her red stockings were the first image that flashed in my mind.

On the walk back to his house, stumbling through the slush and mud, I held on to Drake's shoulder for support. I asked him, "Why do people call this a hippie school? All day here I haven't seen a single hippie yet!"

Drake sighed. "Well, it's like I told you. There's a Grateful Dead show in Hartford tonight." He had indeed mentioned that earlier and I hadn't seen the relevance then, and didn't really now. The Grateful Dead, so far as I knew, were some mildly successful 1960s group who had backed up the Turtles or something, probably played at Woodstock, I supposed. I failed to see what a concert of theirs over a hundred miles from the campus, in another state, had to do with anything.

"Well, okay," I said. "But they can't *all* be there."

"Yeah, actually they can. It's kind of a big deal." I shook my head again. You might as well have told me that the school canceled class every time Scritti Politti stepped foot in the state. And so a couple weeks later I assured Nino he was mistaken and six months after that I stood on line while a boy in a rainbow-colored bandana kicked a Hacky Sack into my stomach.

At the front of the line, a pink-faced woman in her late thirties wearing a denim dress over a gray T-shirt tapped a pencil against the top of a folding table. She glanced up and, in a tone of grave skepticism, asked my name. She responded to my answer with a deep nod indicating that she wasn't a bit surprised, and passed me a sheet of paper and a pen, like a cop ordering me to sign my confession.

"You've read the house rules?"

"*Read* them?"

The house madam, whose name, I learned, was Deb, sighed deeply. "The house rules were sent to your home."

I had, in fact, received many large envelopes from Hampshire since I had been accepted. The course catalog I set aside for bathroom reading, but the rest, filled with long lists appended with subsections and graphs, had never grabbed me. I recalled glancing at it and thinking that it was impossible to believe that anyone else going to a liberal arts college of progressive inclinations could read this stuff either. Deb glared, and not knowing what to say, I murmured, "I took a look but it didn't leap off the page."

She set down her pencil as though letting it rest before it should be called up to do the hard labor of penetrating my eye socket. "What are you trying to say?"

"Nothing," I said. "Not a thing."

She sighed, shook her head, and pushed the keys to my new home across the table to me.

The Dakin House freshman dorm was a U-shaped, three-story red brick building that leaned grimly over at a beaten-up square of grass it shared with the neighboring dorm. Jamaican flags waved from the windows; on the roof, girls in tie-dyes danced by themselves to an Allman Brothers album. I lugged my duffel bag up the staircase of the J-wing, my feet sticking to dried beer puddles on the tiled floor. Strains of drum solos echoed from the halls that ran out from either side of the stairwell. Down one dark hall, I saw a guy lying asleep on the floor, a dog licking his stomach. The soon-to-be familiar smell of moss, stale beer, and laundry detergent introduced itself.

I got to J-3 and paused. Affixed to the door with four thumb-tacks was a sign that read STUDENTS AT WORK. PLEASE TAKE YOUR CONVERSATION OUTSIDE. Inside the hall, the pungent smell from the stairwell vanished, replaced immediately by the overpowering aroma of lemon-scented Lysol. The room doors were all closed. A board showed where every resident was, with round magnets marking each person's location. On the hall. In class. Eating. At the library. Off campus. I noticed that my own name had not been written on the board.

As I fumbled for my keys in front of J-309, suddenly, the hall's quiet was disturbed by a door opening at the far end, followed by a head emerging at an angle, topped by a sweep of long blond hair, tied back into a ponytail, washing up over an incongruously steeped forehead beneath which a pair of narrowed eyes peered at me.

"Are you Richard?" the head asked. I confirmed that I was.

The head withdrew into the room and out came a young man, a few years older and, not counting the hair, a few inches shorter than myself, swaggering down the hall toward me with a magisterial air—his pomp just slightly undermined by the fact that he was wearing only a black unitard, with fuchsia stripes up the sides.

"So there's been a mistake," he said.

"Really?"

He nodded grimly. "You're not supposed to be here. It was a really big screw-up. I've been telling the housing office for four years now that their filing system needs to be overhauled, but they won't listen, and now, here *you* are." He tutted, looking me over with such barely contained disgust I thought he might at any moment start spitting to get rid of the foul taste I was putting in his mouth.

"But I sent in my tuition. They sent me the acceptance letter—"

"Yes, yes. Of course you're supposed to be at the school. The mistake is much more complicated than that. You see, the housing office placed you on *my* hall."

"They gave me a key."

"Precisely, they gave you your little key. But what you don't know, I mean how could you, is that *this* is a *quiet* hall."

"Oh . . ."

"For *older* students."

"Well, can I go back down and tell them I need to change?"

He threw his head back and roared. "Ha ha! Don't you think that if there were any way possible to not have you here, I would've done that by now!?!"

"Good point."

"The fact is, the school is overbooked, every room is full. So until someone drops out and their room opens, we're stuck with you."

"Wow. I'm sorry."

"Yes. But don't worry, we'll let you know when you're disturbing us."

"Oh, good. Thanks."

"Until then, don't get too comfortable. And by the way, if you need anything, I'm Lonnie—your SID [Student Intern Dakin House]." "I'm at the end of the hall. Don't hesitate to knock." And with that he wheeled back down to his room, golden mane waving behind.

I stepped into my room. I estimated it was about the dimensions of a medium-sized refrigerator. But at least, I reminded myself, it was a single room. The summer before, when people asked me why I had chosen Hampshire, I spoke about the progressive education system—the freedom to invent one's own curriculum that was a natural mirror of one's soul, inner depths manifested as a course outline, and all that. I would turn to the charms of Massachusetts's Pioneer Valley, tucked at the foot of the Berkshires— renowned for its brilliant springs and the poignancy of deep, rich autumns; the area's historical riches—it had once been home to Emily Dickinson and Calvin Coolidge; the five-college system, which allowed me to take my classes not only at Hampshire but at neighboring Smith, Mount Holyoke, Amherst, and UMASS. Unmentioned was the reason truly closest to my heart, what in fact, if I really stopped to question myself, may have been, apart from Malaria's red stockings, my *only* real reason for choosing Hampshire—the promise of single rooms for each and every entering freshman, just like, I frequently imagined, an all-suites hotel!

My desperate longing for a single came not from a pathological need for privacy or any inability to share—I was, in fact, unable to share anything, but that was a separate issue. The thought that loomed throughout my high school days as the clock clicked ever closer to graduation: A single room meant I was likely to be beaten up far less often than if I had a roommate. And by that thread, my choice of colleges hung.

Like Hampshire, my high school was a liberally oriented school cloistered from reality, with no gymnasium and no required athletic activity. The official selections for my high school PE class included bowling one year and bicycle rides to neighborhood lunch spots the next. Without the presence of jocks, one's chances of getting beaten up at my high school were slightly less than being electrocuted by a passing zeppelin. My high school had been founded on 1960s-inspired principles of nonviolence and social reform that losers like myself could take advantage of to roam the campus, head held high, and play monstrous pranks on our snooty socialite classmates without any fear of an ass-whooping.

But I knew this could not go on forever, and I counted down to the expiration date on my charmed life. In a vision that perpetually haunted my sleep, I pictured my roommate, the football team's star human meat grinder, arriving home after a night of keg-pounding and date rape at a Scorpions concert; he would spend the rest of the evening vomiting on my bed and pummeling me to a fine paste while casting aspersions on sundry elements of my physique. (Amazingly, this scenario played itself out, almost to the letter, on a friend who went to NYU.) So when Hampshire's promise of a room of one's own was dangled before me, it was like hearing the phone from the governor's office ring just as the warden had finished his final polish of the electric chair.

But beyond the unbelievable lure of the freshman single, Hampshire College looked to be very much a continuation of the blessedly cloistered life I had known thus far. Hampshire College had been founded as a self-conscious experiment in education by the four major schools located in the idyllic western Massachusetts wilderness of the Pioneer Valley. These institutions—Amherst, Smith, and Mount Holyoke colleges and the University of Massachusetts—conceived Hampshire as a laboratory free of the constraints of established schools, an educational institution with standards second to none, with the boldness to traipse down the paths its stodgy neighbors feared to tread. Hampshire professors were to serve without tenure, students would not have majors but create their own multidisciplinary courses of study; communal living, no grades, projects rather than papers—all this was Hampshire's promise. When the gates opened in 1970, the boldness of the experiment met the spirit of the age and the school was flooded with applications. It was campus legend that for that first year Hampshire was harder to get into than Harvard.

And for a few years the promise of looser restrictions but world-class standards seem to have held. However, by the early 1980s looseness was clearly driving the cart. Whatever the talk of world-class standards, Hampshire drew a collection of misfits and malcontents from around the globe, drawn to the school by its lack of formality and discipline. The structure of the school, intended to break down departmental walls, had become a three-tiered work-at-your-own-pace gauntlet of invent-your-own projects and concentrations. Without a static four-year system, the school was famed at this point for the high number of students who stayed on as undergraduates well beyond the half-decade mark, and for the one student who had "majored in" Frisbee. While the first-year admissions may have been impossibly competitive, by the time I applied somewhere upwards of 60 percent of applicants were accepted. And even that figure is suspect. To this day, I have never met anyone of my generation who admits to having been rejected by Hampshire.

When making up my mind, I had heard murmurs of all these legends and found them all immensely reassuring. No standards, no requirements, and single rooms; why, I wondered, didn't everyone go there?

My dorm room was furnished with a few pieces of wooden block furniture pushed into one corner and a pale-green plastic mattress leaning against a wall. Exhausted, I lowered it to the floor and climbed aboard. Rolling up my jacket for a pillow, I quickly passed into unconsciousness and, the drum solos resounding from a faraway hall, drifted to a land far away from Hampshire College.

Some hours later I awoke, my face glued to the green plastic by a sheet of hardened drool. The world was dark and I could barely make out the outlines of the room, the furniture shoved to one corner. I felt my body warring between pangs of disorientation, hunger, nicotine withdrawal, and exhaustion. Outside I heard distant strains of conversation and drumming. Someone strummed a guitar very, very slowly. I realized I had missed the orientation sessions that Deb, the house madam, had warned me I was to get myself to immediately. I turned on the light and picked up the schedule.

"7 P.M.—Hayride and new students mixer. The Red Barn." I wondered if I might find Malaria there. I threw on a jacket over the orange Hawaiian shirt I'd picked out for my first day of school and headed out.

It was a warm, still, summery night and the campus was out loafing in the damp heat. Across the dark quad, clusters of students plopped on the ground talking, some drinking. I walked by one group passing around a purple glass bong. A man who looked to be in his fifties sat on the ground taking a hit in his turn. I wondered if he was a parent? A professor? I looked around in vain for any sign indicating where the Red Barn was, or even where the main part of campus was. The paths I had taken that bright morning had vanished.

Around a picnic table a group of seven or eight sat nodding their heads gently in silence. I approached and noticed one of them picking at an acoustic guitar. Was he actually playing something, or just poking it, perhaps tuning, or inspecting its structural integrity? I stood at the group's edge with the others. No one looked up at me, so I began nodding my head, more or less in time with the others, who seemed to be keeping rhythm with some unheard melody. The guitarist gently rubbed his fingers across the strings, humming softly to himself as others grooved to the phantom melody.

After I'd been watching for a few minutes, the guitarist stopped. He cleared his throat, as if coming out of a trance, pulled his long hair back, tying it with a rubber band, and looked up, straight at me.

"Can I help you?" he asked. The others stopped nodding and also looked at me.

"The Red Barn?" I stammered. "I was looking for the hayride."

The guitarist stared at me with a look of deep sadness, as though glimpsing for the first time the sad fate of a doomed planet. "Jesus," someone else muttered. "Fucking first-years."

"The Reagan Youth are taking over." They all shook their

heads and grimaced at each other. I grinned like a halfwit. "Is it down by the road?" I begged.

A young man in John Lennon glasses said, "We don't know anything about your hayride, but if you're looking for the Barn, yes, it's down by the main road." I thanked him and walked on into the night, listening to the group exchanging whoa-what-was-thats behind me.

A sign reading New Students directed me down a muddy path through a yellowing field. In the darkness the crickets chirped and a stream burbled somewhere far off. I tried to recall how I had gotten here from Los Angeles, where I had woken up just that morning. After ten minutes' walking, I arrived at a big red barn sitting next to a cluster of clapboard buildings. Out front, a few students picked beer bottles and plastic cups off the ground. "Is the hayride still happening?" I asked one.

He shook his head and said without looking up, "It ended hours ago."

I walked inside the barn, which had been converted into a sort of assembly hall. The room was deserted but, starving, I lunged for the disheveled food tables. Even in my hunger the plates of sticky glowing cheese cubes and melting broccoli spears were too ominous to toy with. I spied, however, an unopened jug of Gallo red table wine and picked it up. Slipping quietly out the door, I retraced my way down the path toward the dorms.

Back at Dakin House, I plopped down in a lounge on the first floor. Three others sat on mustard-colored couches, glancing at each other while a Leonard Cohen tape played in a tiny cassette deck on the table between them. They gave me nervous looks as I entered. I collapsed next to a pinched-faced young woman who had her arms clasped around herself as though for protection. I opened the jug of wine and took a sip, which provided a moment of solace to my empty stomach, followed by a spasm of pain, which

I chased away with another gulp. Still no one spoke; the boy leafed through an ancient copy of the *Utne Reader*.

"Are you all freshmen?" I asked.

"First-years," said the girl next to me. "We're called first-years here."

"Right, well, are you?"

"I'm a transfer," volunteered a boy in floppy blue jeans and V-neck sweater, who looked much too normal and clean-cut to be here.

"Where from?" I asked.

"Bucknell."

"What the hell are you doing out here, then?" I guffawed.

He answered in earnest, nodding as though he'd been forced to tell this story many times. "Last summer, I picked up a book, poems by Richard Brautigan. And I just knew, right away, *that* was what I was going to do with my life."

"Write poems?"

"Write poet-*try*."

I nodded, impressed, and offered him a sip of the Gallo. He shook his head and rewound the tape to play a song over again.

The girl next to me said, "I'm first-year. I'm going to study plant biology."

"That sounds hard."

She shook her head. "It's not. It's just something you have to work at a lot."

"Did you guys go to orientation?"

They looked at me incredulously. "You missed it?"

"Was there anything important?"

The girl looked like she was about to cry. "You're going to be in so much trouble tomorrow."

"What happened?"

"Everything. You better call your advisor first thing in the morning."

I didn't feel up to asking how they knew who their advisor was, so I took another sip of the wine and, after a few quiet moments listening to the Leonard Cohen tape, noticed the room was starting to spin, very pleasantly. A few minutes later, we were joined by a guy with curly brown hair and glasses, in a denim jacket with a clock hanging from a chain. "WASSUP!!" he greeted us. "Home-ies!" We soon learned, with little prompting, that he was Ace from Baltimore, a musician of the streets, so he told us.

"Is that the same as a street musician?" I asked.

"You watch your tongue, my man." Unfolding a sheaf of lyric sheets, Ace volunteered to perform his raps for us. All of them. I gave a look of alarm to the girl, who said, to my horror, "That would be nice." I drank rapidly through my jug as the raps beat past. Frequently, Ace would lose track of his beat and have to start a song over. I remember, about half an hour in, turning over the jug and finding the wine was all gone. I have a rough memory of crawling through the halls of Dakin House sometime after this on my hands and knees, trying to get back to my room. I remember crawling past an open door and a hippie girl seeing me and calling out, "Horsey ride!" She raced out to jump on my back, but then, catching my ghastly pallor, yelled, "Oh, no!" and ran back into her room, slamming the door behind her.

A while later, I woke up in my still dark room, my face again stuck to the pale-green plastic mattress. But this time I had a horrible feeling that a nuclear warhead was about to launch from my stomach. I lunged for the door and, in midleap, realized I was completely naked. I grabbed at my jacket and, holding it, raced into the hallway, barely making it out of my room before I collapsed on the hall floor. My body, convulsing, churned up the jug of wine, every last drop of it, sending it on the return trip from my stomach onto the hall's brownish-gray, Lysol-smelling carpet.

Naked, I heaved and shuddered and bawled, amazed that the wine kept coming and coming, long after it seemed a jug, even two jugs, had been released. The thought passed through my head: *It's like the Chanukah oil.* And more miraculously, no one came out into the hall to discover me vomiting over the carpet of my new home.

When all was finally expelled, I stood up and looked down at the catastrophe I'd unleashed. I wrapped the jacket around my waist and grabbed a handful of paper towels from the bathroom. I dabbed and mopped at the sea of vomit, but its volume didn't seem to decrease. After a few more pathetic tries, I saw there was nothing to be done and gave up. Feeling much better for the purgative effect on my stomach, I plopped back onto my green plastic mattress and sank back to sleep.

In the morning, after a good night's rest, the mattress actually felt rather homey. I was able to lie on it peacefully for several minutes before the smell hit me—and the sound of voices in the hall.

I stood up, threw on yesterday's clothes again, and gently opened my door. The horrible, deathly holocaust smell rushed into my room. I gagged and looked up. Lonnie stood with ten or so others, inspecting the lake in their hall.

"Richard," Lonnie said, "did you do this?" They all glared at me, nostrils flaring in revulsion. I considered making a break for it, but then remembered I had no place to go. This was my home now. "No," I said, shaking my head. "No, I didn't."

CHAPTER TWO

The Slaves of Dakin House

A s the young woman in the lounge pointed out, entering Hampshire students are not freshmen, we are first-year students or simply "first-years." Sophomores are second-years. Hampshire's educational system at that time cast aside the hidebound tradition of the four-years-to-a-diploma frog march practiced at other schools in favor of a work-at-your-own-pace plan. In theory this meant that a diligent student could earn a diploma in three semesters (that theory was never, to my knowledge, tested in those days—I met few in any great rush to see how fast they could graduate). In practice it meant that many students stayed longer than four years, some much, much longer. Counting the years up skirted the issue of what to call a student approaching his second decade as an undergraduate; terms like *fifth senior year* becoming as unwieldy as roman numerals—not to mention all the hierarchical baggage of the freshman-sophomore-junior-senior paradigm.

Though it was not empowering to be a lowly freshman, I thought, lying on my pale-green plastic mattress, the clinical tag "first-year student" lacked romance; it failed to capture the drama of my journey—traveling thousands of miles from home, diving headlong into an unsupervised adventure in a foreign woods.

Perhaps this was why, whenever first-years gathered, someone was sure to throw out the statistic that the average Hampshire student "seriously considers dropping out three to five times in their first year." This statistic was followed by wildly varying accounts of the number who would actually do so (anywhere from 25 to 90 percent), the number who would actually graduate (almost none, one in fifty tops), and the number who would commit suicide (not less than a third—most by leaping from the Dakin House roof).

Whenever the "considered dropping out" number was offered, I found it impossible to believe that any first-year could have considered dropping out *only* three to five times. By the end of September, I'd had few waking hours when I wasn't considering dropping out.

But reexamining the statistic as it was quoted, the modifier *seriously* gave it some legitimacy; none of my dreams of fleeing survived long enough to lead to anything as tangible as filling out a transfer application, buying a bus ticket, or visiting a naval recruiting station.

Within weeks of landing on Hampshire's shores I had fallen farther than I had ever in my brief life imagined possible. In high school, I never mistook myself for "cool," but after a few years I'd achieved a certain status—if not enviable, at least definable. On good days, my clan occupied ground roughly parallel to, or even slightly above, the drama crowd. A clique of revival-movie-going, Cole Porter–reciting, self-styled intelligentsia, we somehow maintained an edge of freakishness that gave us the slightest bit of caché in *Less Than Zero/*Brat Pack–era Los Angeles. But now, in the woods of Massachusetts, I wasn't even a nerd.

I saw nerds around my dorm—they walked everywhere in one big pack, carrying stacks of books, and held hushed lunchtime discussions in the middle "quiet" room of the SAGA dining hall (named for the company that had once provided food services, although this task had long since been passed on to the Marriott Corporation). I tried one desperate day to sit with them, approaching one of my nerd hallmates as an "in," but I was rebuffed by their bearded leader with a stern "We're preparing a presentation today. This isn't social time."

Denied even nerddom, I became a nonperson. I wafted around campus, droped in the Bridge Café (so named because it was, in fact, a line of tables on the sliver of a bridge between the library and athletic buildings), eavesdropping, sipping coffee and glowering over a Jim Thompson novel checked out of the library. Through the Bridge windows I looked down on the still-summery grand lawn and watched the armies drift by—battalions of tie-dyes and oversized wool sweaters and mere platoons in black jeans and leather microskirts, like jaded refugees from Warhol's factory.

I passed long hours in my dorm room digging through my duffel bag and boxes (despite having nothing to do, I still hadn't found time to unpack), searching for my *Clockwork Orange* T-shirt, which never turned up. One afternoon, overwhelmed by a burst of motivation, I bought some thumbtacks from the bookstore and hung my *Apocalypse Now* poster. But most of the long hours I passed listening to tapes on my tiny boom box, *Ziggy Stardust* in heavy rotation, summoning comfortingly painful memories of my ninth-grade years when, new in high school, the end-of-the-world ballads had seemed pertinent to me.

I paid a couple visits to Drake, who lived a fifteen-minute walk away through the fields in the distant "mods" (modular living units). Unfortunately for me, he had fallen into a relationship with an older woman who lived off campus, and he spent most of his time at her cabin somewhere in the woods. The *Miami Vice* parties, he told me, had died out. "The switch to earth tones really hurt us."

One day, however, Drake paid me a visit. Knocking one afternoon on my door, he announced, "Grab a towel. It's time you had a sauna." One of the most celebrated aspects of the Hampshire experience was the clothing-optional sauna, famed throughout academia. Through these early days, my knowledge of the sauna had loomed ominously above my every move. It was a specter I knew I would have to confront, but nothing made me think I was ready to face that day yet.

"But, Drake," I pleaded, "I'm only a first-year! I'm not even eighteen!"

"Hampshire College is no place for boys, son," he barked. "Suit up."

We soon sat on a wooden bench, Drake stark naked, I with a towel wrapped several times around my waist, another one draped over my shoulders, another one wrapped girdle-like around my torso. Drake lay down on the upper bench and drank in the heat, describing his new fling to me. I sat at his feet, coughing violently and trying to ignore the three hippies sitting across from us. There were two boys and one girl—all even paler than myself, all completely naked. When I peeked over, my eyes locked on incredible folds of flesh—shapes I had never fathomed loomed before me like killer icebergs rising from the sea. I realized this was the first time I had seen anyone naked in person, and I thought that if this was a glimpse at what was in store, some rough and terrible decades lay ahead.

Drake asked if I'd "gotten laid yet."

"Not yet, actually."

The hippies snickered.

"Well, what are you waiting for, soldier? This is Hampshire. What else was the point of coming here?"

"I guess the subject hasn't come up yet," I gulped out and collapsed in a coughing fit, choking on the heat. Drake seemed to be falling asleep. When I recovered I asked, "So I haven't seen that Malaria girl around."

"Who?"

"Remember that girl from the party when I was visiting? The one in the red stockings?"

"Malaria? . . . Oh, you mean Malaria Grant."

"I guess so."

"Oh, right, she's hot, Rich. You should get with her. But look out for Luntz."

"Luntz?"

"The head of the Alternative Music Collective. The guy who brings all the punk bands to campus. Looks like a tank in a leather jacket."

"Ohhhh . . ."

"Don't pretend you didn't know she was shacked up, Rich, you devil."

Lonnie, my SID, was still deep in denial about my presence. He communicated with me only in scowls and murmurs implying that the wheels for my extermination had been set in motion, and that since I would cease to exist as soon as he carved through some troublesome red tape, it would be a waste of his time to acknowledge me.

After our first tentative hellos, the other hallmates greeted me with nervous smiles and glances at the floor when I tried to speak to them, as though they had been secretly told about some terrible fate being prepared for me. If they were in a giving mood, they'd trouble themselves to point at the QUIET! signs on the hall when I opened my mouth.

One afternoon, I opened a letter that had been buried deep in my orientation packet folder and learned I had an advisor; Leo

Raintree, a Social Sciences professor who specialized in health policy. I then saw that I had an appointment with him—three days ago. In a mild rush of panic, I hurried to the brick-and-concrete Franklin Patterson Social Sciences Hall and found him in his office, door open. A portly white-haired and -bearded Santa Claus type, he sat at his desk in a baggy white knit sweater applying Wite-Out to a yellow sheet of paper in his typewriter.

"We just assumed you'd never showed up!" he said when I introduced myself. "Lots of Californians chicken out."

I assured him that I was, in fact, here.

"So how's your first week been?" he asked, summoning me to join him among solemn mountains of faded statistical abstracts and legal pads.

"Well? I think. . . ." Across the room I squirmed on a metal folding chair. Leo stroked his beard and smiled, waiting for me to elaborate. "It's going really well."

"That's great. Wonderful. I knew there was no cause to worry about you." Leo nodded. "What classes are you looking at?"

"Classes? I'm not sure, um, do you know how that works?" I had noticed in the past couple days that the crowds were moving across campus with an ominous new sense of purpose. I'd even seen a few people hurrying. And the presence of books under arms was becoming undeniable. In the back of my mind I was aware that classes would form a part of my college experience. But I assumed that somehow or other I would be informed through proper channels that it was time the whole learning thing got rolling. Despite the evidence that academia was breaking out across campus like a prewinter flu, it didn't seem credible that just days after arriving, when I still hadn't even put sheets on my bed, the school was expecting me to throw myself headlong into any higher-learning rigamorole.

Leo looked concerned. "You haven't signed up for classes yet?"

"Signed up?"

"But this is the last day of shop-around!"

"Ah, shop-around. Of course."

"Ha! Wonderful!" Leo slapped his knee and leaned back, laughing. I joined in, chuckling a bit, glancing up at his poster of ripples across a pond above a Robert Kennedy quote. "You know, I get more and more first-years these days coming in here obsessed with signing up for classes, figuring out their requirements. But that's not why we came to Hampshire, is it?"

"No, no. Definitely not."

He leaned in and grew serious. "Richard, this is your chance to explore YOU. It may be the only chance you ever have in your life. And you and I know you can't do that sitting in classes." I agreed. "So whatever they tell you, take some time, explore, make mistakes, find out what moves you. Maybe get a little crazy. . . ." He pantomimed inhaling a joint.

"That sounds like a good idea."

"You bet it does. Solid." He stood and put his hand out for me to give him five, which I did.

"So . . . ," I asked as he motioned me toward the door, "I should just show up at some classes?"

"Ha, yes. You probably should!"

"And where do I find them?"

"Where do you find classes? In the classrooms!" He roared with laughter again. "But don't get obsessed with that! Remember our deal. Come back and see me midsemester. I want to hear everything. Take notes! Take pictures!"

I left Leo's office with my swagger restored. I strutted around campus, turning my nose up at the fools racing off to class with their silly textbooks. I applied myself with new diligence to hanging my *Great Rock 'n' Roll Swindle* poster and my collection of personalized California license plates, stolen off the cars of my high school classmates. In my spare moments, I took the time to get acquainted with a Galaga machine I discovered in the college tavern.

Twenty-four hours later, however, having completed several circumnavigations of the campus, gotten the high score of the day on Galaga, read through another detective novel, and listened to Hüsker Dü's two-record *Zen Arcade* three times in its entirety, I lay on my pale-green plastic mattress staring into Marlon Brando's pitiless sneer on my *Apocalypse Now* poster. Outside the Indian summer lingered and I listened to the bits of conversation that wafted up to my window with the smell of pot. I wondered what I was going to do for the rest of the day. I wondered what I was going to do for the rest of the week. I tried to wonder what I was going to do for the next four years, but like comprehending infinity, my mind refused to grasp what seemed an impossible contradiction—limitless time with nothing to fill it. I sighed and reached for the course catalog lying on my floor.

The next morning I trudged through a cluster of woods behind the library to the discreet white lodge labeled "Emily Dickinson Hall," which looked like a Radisson conference facility in some leafy suburb. About thirty students drifted into a classroom and sat around a long conference table. Through the giant picture windows, five hippies tossed a Frisbee to each other, knee-deep in an overgrown field.

From the name of the class it seemed like fate: "From Mark Twain to *Miami Vice:* Images of the American Male in Popular Culture." This was where I would find my people—in the *Miami Vice* class!

As my fellow Crockett and Tubbs scholars filed in, however, I checked the catalog a few dozen times to make sure I had come to the right classroom. Dressed identically to the rest of the campus in tie-dyes, knit sweaters, Birkenstocks, flowing skirts, and dreadlocks, the group bore little resemblance to any *Miami Vice* fans

I'd ever met. These people dressed as though *Miami Vice* had never happened.

And once again, they all seemed to know each other.

The teacher entered. Helen was a tall, fiftyish, more imposing version of the girls in the class and she had the stately air of disapproval of a Margaret Dumont masquerading in hippie garb. She announced that she wanted to start the class out with one fun session before we got "down to business." She wanted to see where we stood on the texts—how well informed we were about the issues they raised. "So just think about *Miami Vice* and Mark Twain," she said, "and write whatever comes into your mind. Don't stop and think, just write. Go ahead."

We took out our pens and the rest of the class, without a moment's pause, attacked their pages like starving men set down before a plate of butterscotch cannoli. All except me. I gaped at the page and scoured my brain for a thought. It was empty, a sea of whiteness like the blank sheet before me. I looked again. The sentence flashed in my head, "I want to be Sonny Crockett." I grabbed for my pen and I pushed harder—noting the students on either side scribbling wildly. I caught Helen looking at me. "There's no right answer here," she urged. "Any thoughts you have are equally valid. Just share with us."

Images came to me—moments from the past season. Finally, phrases dashed through my head like lightning flashes. I began to write.

Ten minutes later, Helen coughed and said. "All right, let's hear what you've got. Drew"—she motioned to the dopey-looking blond boy on her right—"would you read for us?"

Drew cleared his throat. "When I think of *Miami Vice* and Mark Twain I see Huck floating on his raft, the sunlight on his face, tapping his hands on the water. On the shore, a factory churns out smoke and identical Miami police costumes, but Huck turns his raft away and with his friend aboard, the river drifts to a time from before cities and industry. Off in the distance, they can see the nuclear missiles flying, but on the river they are free and they are beautiful."

I stifled a laugh and shot eye-rolling glances at the kids across the table. They looked away. "Perfect," Helen said. I glanced down at what I had written and a cold sweat broke out in every corner of my body.

Next to him sat a petulant-looking hybrid hippie girl/aspiring librarian (a tribe I would come to know very, very well over the next five years) with a pen tucked behind her ear and a neatly pressed gray sweatshirt from "Burlington-Managua Fellowship Week: July 14–21, 1985." She cleared her throat. "*Miami Vice* depicts the Meese Justice Gestapo disguised in pastel camouflage to hide their instruments of oppression under brilliant plumage." I restrained myself from shouting, *But they've switched to earth tones.* "Underneath their colorful garbs, Crockett and Tubbs are in fact creations of the RCA corporate machine, which is complicit in the many crimes of the Reagan regime. The war on drugs they pretend to fight is a war on the indigenous peoples of the Americas, straining for empowerment after centuries of imperialist domination."

"Very, very good, Laurel," Helen gushed when she finished. "We are *really* going to need your perspective this semester." In full panic I slid my page off the table and into my lap. "Now, who's next? What's your name?"

"Richard," I mumbled. "But I don't have anything to read."

"What do you mean?" Helen looked down her glasses at me. "I saw you writing."

"I think—I think I misunderstood the assignment."

Helen chuckled. "There was no assignment, just to share with us. There's no right answer here; no judgment."

"I just think I'd rather not."

"Don't you trust us?" Helen purred. "We just want to get to

know you." I looked around the room. The other students smiled at me, vague benign stares, poised for a group hug. "Why don't you give us the chance to show you what a safe place this can be."

I was on the opposite side of the room from the door. If I made a run for it, I would have to leap over a dozen sets of legs splayed from the second row. Alternately, if I sprang onto the conference table and if I flung myself hard enough, in one leap I might be able to fly over the heads of the opposite row and reach the door, all it would take was a little luck, perfect coordination, wind conditions . . . I sighed and pulled the crumpled paper off my lap, smoothed it on the table. "So this is just me, just like free-associating, right?"

"Absolutely." Helen nodded. "Share with us."

I mopped back a wash of sweat, cleared my throat, glanced tentatively around the room, looked down, and began. "Drop the bomb, exterminate them all. We're up the river, all right, Tubbs. Never get off the raft, never, until they're all blown away. 'Nam. Cracktown. Back with Jeff on the river. We're all orphans when the shit comes down, Jeff, and this one is gonna be bad. Warehouse full of Colombians, no air support for forty clicks and Calderón is flying out tonight. Gotta take him down, but Zito and Switek are going to need their cut. Switek—don't get high on your own supply, man. Remember which side of the river you're on. First you get the drugs, then you get the money, then you get the power, then you get the girls. It's in the air tonight, man, so don't fuck this up or Carmen ain't gonna have her girls waiting for us. Sheena Easton. Going to get her back. Do I want her back? Pastels made our name but earth tones, earth tones, man. On my sign, we go in four and don't stop firing until no one is moving. Drop the bomb. Never, ever, get off the raft."

I finished and kept my eyes fastened on the page. Around the class, I heard a silence so complete, I wondered if anyone was still in the room with me. I wondered if perhaps the entire campus had vaporized. I waited for the deep, rich, full-bodied silence to end, but it didn't. Eventually I looked up. Hippie faces are not made for strong emotion. Generally they alternate between dizzy, mouth-half-open smiles, and mouth-half-open vegetative gawks of sympathy—reserved for the sight of stumbling puppies and overcooked tempeh. So when I saw thirty of these faces pointed my way, contorted with sneers of disgust, eyes suddenly piercing from their soft, pale faces, my first thought was concern for them. *Are they all right?* I wondered.

"Well," Helen said finally, "you certainly do have some interesting thoughts. That's not exactly where this class is headed, but I suppose it's important for everyone to hear that. Where are you from, Richard?"

"Los Angeles," I murmured. Everyone laughed.

"Well, that explains it all, doesn't it?" Helen burst out laughing. My classmates howled, some doubling over their desks so heartily, even I couldn't help but join in.

"Yes," I choked out, "it really does!"

CHAPTER THREE

What Friends Are For

After a couple weeks stumbling in and out of classrooms, I found three professors still fishing for students who were willing to let me into a class on fascism, a seminar on Emerson and Nietzsche, and "The Media versus the U.S. government." The Emerson class was taught by an ancient, storybook tweeded professor, who, without a single nod or feint to the sixties, or the march of pop culture since, might as well have been a knight from King Arthur's court teleported to the campus. He had a habit during class of galloping his trains of thought off into distant mists—driving his lectures from Emerson's theories on nature to "that damned fool Godfried whose paper was just wrong wrong wrong. Imagine, bringing in Heidegger! Shameful!"

Near the end of September, I sat alone one night in the distant corner of the back room of the dining hall, puzzling over my first writing assignment—a two-page paper, due the next morning, on Emerson's quote "Faith makes us and not we it." The quote awoke as many thoughts in me as if I were reading a recipe for duck *à l'orange* in Urdu. Worse was the problem that I still had not bought my books. In fact, I still wasn't sure whether Emerson was a novelist and the professor was just reading this idea stuff into the plot or if Emerson had just jotted these big ideas down willy-nilly. Philosophy, I understood they called it.

In week three, it was still possible to skip merrily through college without books. No one had made an issue of it; I'd even joined in class discussion once. But with a paper due in twelve hours and the bookstore closed, a tiny panic began to curdle my edges. Even to those who had done the reading, the professor's ruminations had been so obscure that some speculated they might have been meant for some other class he was teaching—or had taught years before. I played with my bowl of "hunter's stew" and stared at the doodles I'd made during the lecture, hoping one of them would sprout wings and turn into a two-page essay.

And then suddenly someone said, "Do you mind if I sit here?" I spat my Coke out into the hunter's stew. These were not words that typically stood the universe on its head. "Do you mind if I sit here?" was no "Friends, Romans, countrymen" nor "The meek shall inherit the earth," "Death to the tsar," nor "The better angels of our nature." The sentence might not even have held up to "I want my MTV," but this was the first time in three weeks at Hampshire that those words had been spoken to me. By a girl, no less. They descended like a thunderbolt hurled from Mount Olympus.

The young woman who faced me had medium-length brown hair, eager brown eyes, and a suspiciously broad smile that made me suspect that I was the victim of a cruel joke. She wore sweatpants and a lightweight overcoat. Stunned, I nodded nervously, and turned back to my Emerson doodles. A few seconds later, I glanced up and saw she was looking at me while chewing on a soggy slice of the dining hall pizza.

"Is that an art assignment?" she asked, smiling bemusedly.

"Um, no. Sort of. Maybe. This is what I took away from my Emerson lecture today."

"Well, at least you went. That should count for most of it, right?"

"Yes! It should!"

Her name, she said, was Dana; she was from Rye, New York. An aspiring photo student, I soon learned. Dana had come here because her brother had graduated from Hampshire seven years before. The school, she said, was "still kinda decent then."

Dana asked why I chose Hampshire.

"Well, there's that progressive education thing. . . ."

"Oh, yeah, I love that." She smiled, with still scary enthusiasm, at me.

"Yeah. It's great." More smiling. Silence. I shuffled papers on the table.

"Do you have any pot?" she finally asked.

"No. I don't."

"That sucks." She nodded. I nodded back. "We should find some, don't you think?"

I actually didn't think so. Perhaps the biggest handicap I had brought to Hampshire, the thing that made me totally unsuited to survive in this ecosystem, was my aversion to marijuana. I had no prejudice against illegal drugs in general (as I would soon amply prove). But pot and I had had a difficult history. As an angst-obsessed high school student I'd often felt I was in a losing battle for my sanity, and marijuana had not been fighting in my corner. I had endured three very harrowing experiences with the grim reefer, the last of which had me cowering in terror on the floor of a Doom Buggy in the Haunted Mansion ride at Disneyland, and had sworn it off for good. There were also the drug's hippie connotations, which made it anathema to my friends at home—half of whom opted instead for hard alcohol and amphetamines, the other half European film. I searched for a middle ground.

If there was one disclaimer that the Hampshire admissions office in good conscience owed its prospective students, it was that marijuana aversion was not a tenable position. Pot was to Hampshire what basketball was to Notre Dame, calculus to MIT, résumé points to Harvard, and what food or oxygen were to the world at large. In the following years, never would I pass a day without being asked for or offered marijuana. I would spend countless hours nodding my head through discussions of how to deseed marijuana, the different varieties, how to smuggle marijuana in hollowed-out candles, how to get your DEA file, how to tell if your hallmate or advisor was a secret DEA agent, how to spot DEA listening devices around your room, in your backpack, even, most diabolically, it was whispered, stuck to the bottom of your bong.

All this would come in time, but at that moment all I knew was that there was a girl sitting at my table. Speaking to me. Albeit one with a demented grin plastered on her face suggesting we share an experience that terrified me to the depths of my soul. But she was a real live human who was female, no less, and she seemed to be suggesting that our acquaintance should continue after we left this table.

"That would be great," I said, to which Dana continued smiling.

We had to venture all of two feet outside the dining hall before Dana found a marijuana vendor. I forked over ten dollars for my share—beginning to panic that I would be called upon to consume it—and we headed back to her room.

It was the first Dakin room besides my own that I had been in, and I stopped cold in the doorway to absorb it. This space was so different from my own cold, still unpacked refrigerator-box of a home that I froze dead—my very understanding of the concept of dorm room shattered. I tried to understand what was so fundamentally different here from my room. First—there was that smell—like laundry detergent and soaps and vanilla. . . . And the sheer orderliness! A poster of a couple kissing on the streets of Paris hung perfectly aligned with the right angle of the walls and ceiling. The bed was made, with red and orange quilts tucked in. A giant teddy bear leaned contently against the pillows—grinning the exact same grin as Dana. The desk was set with a chair and little lamp and books neatly stacked. It seemed more like a museum than a dorm room. Was it possible that Dana, or that any human force, had done this?

And then I noticed another difference. There was so much more space than in my own room. You could dance in the middle of that floor, between the beds. Between the beds! There were two of them.

"Why do you have two beds?" I asked.

"I don't have two. I have one and Sydney has one."

"Sydney?"

"My roommate."

I shuddered, astounded. "Oh, my God, they gave you a roommate!" I nearly screamed, so profound was the injustice.

"They didn't give me one. I asked for one. Isn't it weird to live all alone?"

I had to sit down to take that in. Plopping on the roommate's bed, with increasing worry I stole glances at her as she prepared her purple bong. She took a long hit from the smoldering tube, coughed heavily, and tried to pass it to me.

I opened my mouth to explain the latent disease I had contracted on safari a few years back—nothing awful, certainly not contagious, but just something I had to live with, knowing that if it ever came into contact with inhaled marijuana, my vital organs would turn to stone.

The tale was half out of my mouth when the door flew open. With a whoop and a leap, in bounced a girl with a spunky brown bob of hair, gigantic brown eyes behind frameless round glasses, and astonishingly, in this campus of baggy sweatshirts and flowing caftans, a dangerously tight yellow sweater. This was Sydney.

"You are not going to believe what Ace just did," she announced, looking me in the eyes without a hint of surprise at discovering a strange guy in a Hawaiian shirt sitting on her bed.

"Who's Ace?" I started to ask when I saw, sauntering in behind her, the rapper/poet I had met on my first drunken night in the J-2 lounge.

"Bo-oy, it was sick," he said, looking at me, betraying no signs of recognition, interest, or surprise at finding me sitting on his friend's (girlfriend's?) bed. I wasn't sure if he remembered our earlier meeting or perhaps the question of whom he was talking to was of so little importance that it didn't merit an eyebrow raise. Sydney raced around the room, hopping up and down in excitement. I looked at Dana, bong in hand, grinning at me still, but with the merest hint of irony in her eyes.

"What was sick, Ace?" I finally asked.

"My man, you should've beeeen there. You should've witnessed."

Sydney blurted, "Ace took the mike at the coffeehouse and rapped for forty-five minutes straight. There were, like, two hundred people crowded around by the time he was done."

I wanted to ask where the coffeehouse was but instead questioned, "What did you rap about?"

He looked at me and suddenly grew very serious. "The streets, boy." He nodded. "The streets of Baltimore."

Sydney came around and patted him on the back. "Baby, you don't have to go back there now. You're safe here."

He pushed her arm away. "But my brothers ain't."

I stayed listening to Ace and Sydney rap until eleven that

night. Sydney, I learned, had been a high school drama student and veteran of many Berkshire summer workshops. She'd starred in several of the musical comedy numbers, which she restaged for us. As much as I wanted to turn away from her *Pippin* medley, the unrelenting tautness of her sweater kept me an entirely rapt audience, crying for encores after each number.

At no point did Sydney or Ace ask who was this person sitting on her bed. A couple times I started to introduce myself and offer tidbits of my own high school drama days, but was cut off and didn't insist. I spent most of the night trying to figure out Sydney's relationship with Ace—she freely jumped in and out of his lap and fished a lighter out of his jeans front pocket but didn't actually kiss him. Dana, for her part, sank into a happier and deeper cloud of marijuana as the night went on. At one point, however, she seemed to catch me gaping too openly at Sydney's sweater, and scrunched up her face to give me a look I roughly translated as *Are you weird or something?*

As Ace went into another rhyming tale of near-death in Baltimore, I gave up trying to wait him out and excused myself. Slipping back to my room, I acknowledged to myself that the night had been, by all my known benchmarks, completely horrible, but nonetheless wondered how soon it would be okay to reprise my visit.

I sprawled on my pale-green plastic mattress and wondered again what I might have to say about Emerson and faith. I scribbled, "In saying faith makes us and not we it, Emerson acknowledges that some days you wake up and feel like the world is full of sunshine, but many days you just want to go hide somewhere and even philosophy can't really help you." I reread the line, then tore the page out of my notebook and crumpled it up.

Then all at once, I bolted upright; a divine inspiration lit up in my head like a flame. *What if I just don't do this assignment?*

I tried it on for size, and found it fit like the tan Members

Only jacket I'd abandoned in shame two days into ninth grade. Bathed in a contented glow, I sank into sleep.

The next morning, I woke and briefly looked around for the essay on Emerson and faith, before the night came back to me. The bravest and most honest way to deal with the situation, I decided, would be to stay in bed, listening to the Cure's *Head on the Door* album. I stared out the window at the damp autumn morning, trying on for size various excuses for missing class, and for not writing the paper. In high school, if I hadn't shown up for class, someone would have called my home. And I wondered now from what quarter the hammer would fall. When I finally stumbled to the bathroom, Lonnie and his girlfriend, Stephanie, were standing at the mirror in their matching orange terry-cloth robes. They each gave me, I thought, extrasuspicious looks, although the high volume of suspicion in their normal looks my way made it hard to judge.

I inched out the door onto campus, looking both ways, for I wasn't sure who might stop me and demand to know why I wasn't in class. But as I went for lunch, browsed the library, got my mail, played Galaga, it dawned on me that I was free; no attendance clerk was on my trail. The weight of this sank in and I collapsed on a bench in front of the library, next to a girl sitting at a table signing people up for an "Empowerment Weekend in Burlington." I could skip class whenever I wanted. I could omit writing papers at all and no one would demand an explanation. The horizons of my world sprang open. I had been living in eighteen-inch black-and-white and suddenly the universe revealed itself in blazing Technicolor across a CinemaScope screen.

I looked around, wanting to share this with someone. The girl at the Empowerment table squinted a warning my way not to approach. Drake was out of town. Ten minutes later I stood in front of Sydney and Dana's door, knocking intensely. No one answered, but lost in thought, I continued gently tapping, almost as though

I were absentmindedly whittling away at it. A hallmate passed and I smiled, knocking away at the door and building castles in the sky to fill my new life, a land where I might let days pass without seeing the inside of a classroom. And then the door opened.

"Dana!" I said, before noticing that it wasn't Dana but Sydney standing before me. I'd rehearsed this moment a number of times on my walk over, planned how I would announce my return to their room. But in every contingency, it had been Dana who opened the door—Dana with whom I'd share my news and tolerate until her roommate returned for me to ogle. But to my shock and horror, the roommate herself stood before me, in a wrinkled *Godspell* T-shirt and sweatpants, rubbing sleep from her eyes and looking at me in bemused confusion.

"Sydney! Oh, my God," I exclaimed. "Are you awake?"

"I am now." She smiled ironically.

"It's Richard. I mean, I'm Richard from last night. I was sitting on your bed."

"Yeah. Hi."

"So is Dana here?"

She shook her head.

"Oh, um. Well, that's weird."

She stared at me and continued smiling ironically. Her eyes looked even huger without her glasses. I fell quiet and rubbed my hand along the door. Started humming "In Between Days" until I finally blurted out, "You know, we don't have to go to class!"

"What do you mean?"

"Class, it's, like, optional. Like, if you don't go, nothing happens. Same with turning in papers."

She smiled again. "If I didn't want to go to class, why would I have come to college?"

The thought had not occurred to me and I gaped dumbly in response.

"Do you want to come in?" Sydney asked, standing back from the door.

I sat down on Dana's very well made bed. Sydney climbed back in hers and pulled a blanket over herself. She leaned over to her tape deck and clicked on a Sade album.

"So you guys had a late night?"

"I can't believe you left. It got crazy." Apparently, after my departure, Ace the poet had called up two of his Baltimore friends from down the road at UMASS, and they had all driven over in Sydney's car and spent the night dancing on the roof of UMASS's eighteen-story dorm (the tallest building in the county). As dawn came, Sydney led them all in a thirty-minute version of "Good Morning Starshine," which drew dozens of other UMASSers to join them on the roof. I nursed mixed feelings: The adventure sounded like the worst nightmare I could imagine, yet I raged that I'd missed a chance to hang out with Sydney until dawn.

I sat on Dana's bed for several hours more as Sydney told me stories of summer stock, touring companies, and her plans for the Hampshire College Theatre, which "has some really, really talented people, but no one who connects with what's happening now, the way performance art has completely changed our concept of the stage."

We talked more through dinner, which we took together in the dining hall, and then up at the coffeehouse, where we sat spinning tales of high school productions. Incredibly, neither Dana nor Ace showed themselves. I held my breath, willing both to stay away. However, my glee was darkened by the thought weighing on my mind, giving me chills—just what was Sydney's relationship with Ace?

The confusion was cleared shortly afterward, however, when Sydney dropped a reference to her fiancé, who was coming to visit in a few weeks.

"You're engaged?" I asked, incredulous. I had never met an engaged person.

"Oh, yeah. We've been engaged since I was a sophomore in high school. I have a ring but I don't wear it. Devon thinks it would put a wall between me and the other students in drama." Devon, apparently, had been one of the drama coaches in her summer company and was still in the city, doing some off-Broadway and teaching.

My first reaction was a tsunami of relief that she wasn't involved with Ace, followed by a second, and even bigger, tsunami of relief that she wasn't involved with Ace. The notion of Sydney in a wedding was so hard to take in that my mind went into shock against it. But as much jealousy as I might have felt toward Devon, Ace had not touched her, and that was the critical fact here.

Platonic friend that he may have been, Ace's presence was no less overwhelming when he and Dana strolled down the bridge together, waving to us. "What up, boyie!" Ace saluted. I sunk into silence for the rest of the night as our foursome drifted across campus. Sometime after three, I finally abandoned the field and slunk off to bed.

For the next week, our quartet seemed inseparable or, from my perspective, un-pry-apartable. Together we wandered the campus and sprawled on the floor of Dana and Sydney's double, Ace and Sydney mugging, Dana grinning, me ogling and brooding off in a corner. In retrospect, given how little I contributed other than resentment and frustration, it is hard to understand why they allowed, even encouraged, me to hang out with them—other than the most obvious answer, that they were nice people and they were being nice to someone who, for his own inscrutable reasons, seemed to want to hang out. At the time, however, the last question in the world that would have occurred to me was why they wanted me around.

In their company, I saw more of campus, but the thrill of discovering new places was tainted by the embarrassment of arriving as part of Ace's entourage. One night, sitting on the lawn, we watched a parade of nonhippie types—kids dressed in black skirts, spiked hair, and punkish T-shirts trooping off down a path in the woods. I asked where everyone was headed.

"There's a band playing at the Tavern," Ace said. "Some fools from Boston. Thrasher band or something."

"Really?" my eyes lit up. "Should we check it out?"

"Not me, palsy. I've got no time for those burnouts." I looked at him. As far as I could tell, he had nothing but time. I considered getting up and going off on my own, but then Sydney said, "Maybe we should call for pizza," and I stayed.

I repeated the adventure of missing class several times more, thrilling to find when I returned that the professors didn't even mention my absences and overdue papers.

In the vacuum of space, stars can burn for eons with no force to oppose them. So, too, in the dark void of first semester of freshman year, infatuations can grow and consume every ounce of energy their host body can muster. But eventually, if not given true sustenance, the infatuation will burn out and destroy its source, and so it happened. Much as I obsessed over Sydney, the cost of trailing after them, hopelessly searching for some kind of reciprocation, became too much, and my infatuation turned to resentment. Little by little, I pushed away from the fire and back into the void. I stopped coming by their room and avoided the places where I might run into them. Dana came by my room and slid a couple notes under the door, but I ignored them and looked away when I saw her with others at the dining hall.

Eventually I went a week without running into Sydney, by which time I had blended back in with the moldings of the dining hall's forgotten middle room and library study carrels. I had even gone to class a few times, although once again, I hadn't quite been able to write a Nietzsche paper. When I finally saw her, it was from across the Bridge Café. She was with Dana and a guy I had never seen before, who I guessed was her fiancé. She waved to me and gave me a confused what's-up-with-you? shrug. I shot back a petulant sarcastic smile and turned away. I wanted to respond but I had no clue what it was I wanted to say, which made me feel worse. And then I felt bad for avoiding them, Dana especially, which made me long all the more not to have to see them. In the galaxy of relationships there are none sadder than those made in the first days of freshman year when people are randomly thrown together and give each other some comfort, but must ultimately part. For the years to come I would see Dana or Sydney across the room at a party or walking toward me down a path. By the end of first semester, we gave no sign that we had ever known each other, but the pang of regret never completely vanished as I watched them go by.

A week later, a fire alarm awoke Dakin House in the middle of the night. Standing outside in my T-shirt and sweatpants, I was for the first time in my life seriously cold, and I wondered how much worse this was going to get. The temperature, I thought, might be in the forties. Had I ever felt the forties before?

A group of hippies had started a sing-along, and soon the whole dorm joined in bellowing "Joy to the World." I slunk away and sat on a ledge, watching a dance circle form in the middle of the quad. I braced myself. Soon the drumming would begin. Across the way, I saw Sydney and Ace crooning to each other, Dana watching them benignly.

Next to me on the ledge I noticed two also sitting out the festivities. One was tall and lanky with a mop of unruly black hair, in blue jeans and a droopy sweater. The other wore a flannel bathrobe and was shorter than I was, with an impossibly boyish face and round glasses. They both gazed upon the carnival with heartwarming looks and malice. Then I heard the short one say to the taller one, "Do you think the mall is still open this late?"

As the taller one shook his head I stood and stuck out my hand. "You guys wouldn't by any chance be from L.A.?"

They looked at me in shock, like explorers in a distant land might have if, upon prying open an ancient Mayan pyramid, they looked down into a sacred sarcophagus and found their elementary-school class picture inside.

"What are you doing here?" the one in glasses asked me, as prisoners might ask, "What are you in for?"

"Single rooms, you know . . ."

They nodded. "It had the shortest application," the tall one said.

We all stared at the ground, reflecting for a moment on where our paths had led us.

"Is there anyplace to watch *Letterman* around here?" I asked.

"I have a TV in my room," the one in glasses said. My eyes widened and I offered him my hand.

Three weeks later, we loafed in Nathan's room as he made a phone call. "I'm sorry to bother you at this hour. Is Anthony in?" Nathan removed his round wire-framed glasses, wiped them, and sighed. Even making a prank call he radiated seriousness of purpose, quietly demanding respect. "Yes, it is after midnight, but I thought you'd want to know, your cat is in our tree."

Nathan patiently nodded as a voice whined on the other end, before saying indignantly, "You don't have a cat? Well, we don't have a tree!!!" Nathan held up the phone to pick up the sound of Zach and I laughing hysterically, as we heard the voice on the other end shriek, "FUCK YOU!!!! ASSHOLES!!"

"He took that pretty well," Zach said after we hung up.

"Add him to the list. We need to call him again sometime." Nathan marked a red star next to Anthony's picture in the fresh-man face book (known as the Frog Book, its cover decorated each year with images of the school's amphibious mascot).

We fell quiet and stared at the snowy image of David Letter-man on Nathan's twelve-inch black-and-white. The sound came and went until finally it was overcome by static. Nathan sat on a folding chair next to the set and played with the coat-hanger antenna, trying to restore reception. Sitting on the floor, I picked at the hardening remnants of cheese stuck to the cardboard delivery box of the pizza we'd finished an hour before. Sprawled on Nathan's bed, Zach leafed through a copy of *Spin*. "Fuck it," Zach said. "Chris Elliott's off this week anyway."

"Should we try my hall again?" I asked.

Nathan glanced out the window across the Dakin Quad. "Looks like Lonnie's light just went out again. I guess we'd better."

He dialed the extension of the J-3 hall phone. Across the quad, we watched Lonnie's light pop on and then Lonnie himself grab a robe and leap for the door. "Three—two—one." Nathan counted down, and hung up just as we heard Lonnie pant "Hello" into the phone.

"Do you think he's expecting someone? Why's he so worked up about answering that phone?"

"He needs to keep his ducks in a row," I said, imitating Lonnie's prim voice. "Business conducted on the hall phone is hall business." Across the quad Lonnie slammed his door and threw his purple robe to the floor in rage.

"Who's next?" I asked.

"I dunno. Maybe we need a break. I feel like we're recycling our material," Zach said.

"You guys going to class tomorrow?" Like myself, Zach had discovered the miracle of life without attendance slips. Nathan, however, amazingly, no matter how late we stayed up, even after the night he passed out drunk on a rock beside the school's driveway, never missed a class.

"I might," Zach said. "There's supposed to be a slide show in my South American poetry class. Someone's summer trip to Chile."

"A slide show?" I stroked my chin. "Maybe I'll check that out."

The next evening in the SAGA back room we considered the evening's options. The school had been blanketed with flyers for an "All Campus Drum Circle (for the *población salvadoreño*)."

"They might have free beer. Or food," I suggested.

"Hippies don't drink beer. Or eat real food." Nathan sighed.

"What if we turned off the power on the amps?"

"Amps?" Zach sneered. "It's a drum circle." I stared at him. "Amps are what you plug guitars into."

I reddened. "That's what I meant. Guitar amps . . ."

In the past week, we had seen every movie playing at both neighboring malls (not excluding *Space Camp* and *Jumpin' Jack Flash*), had crank-called approaching two-thirds of the Frog Book, sprinkled itching powder on our hallmates' towels, dropped water balloons off the library roof, and spiked the punch at a hippie party with Tabasco sauce.

But now we were in a rut. Even the slide show in Zach's class had been a disappointment. The poet/professor only had one slide of South America and it was of himself speaking to a classroom of ten-year-olds at an elementary school where he had somehow passed himself off as a visiting dignitary. While he displayed his one slide on the screen, he repeated his presentation to the young students—essentially a recitation of his own poetry followed by a brief call to arms against commercialism.

Several of the students in the slide appeared to be asleep. The rest looked politely confused. When he concluded his presentation, asking if there were any questions, Zach had raised his hand and asked in a voice burning with indignation, "How is one slide a show?" The poet asked us to leave.

Sitting with Zach and Nathan in the dining hall, I noticed Gideon, a quasi hippie from Connecticut who lived on Nathan's hall, carrying his tray on the lookout for an empty table, and alerted the others. The precise term for quasi hippie was "Preppy

Deadhead," which described New England boarding-school students who had adopted the trappings of hippiedom—jumbo-sized knit sweaters, dancing-bear stickers on the rear windows of their Saabs or Volvos, patchouli scentings—without committing to hippies' scorched-earth policy toward hygiene and mental health advocated by Hampshire's "real" hippies. For that reason the Preppy Deadheads—or Frisbee elite, as they were also known—were equally despised by the school's punk and hippie populations.

A week earlier, Gideon had walked by Nathan's open door and heard us playing David Lee Roth's *Crazy from the Heat* album. "Dudes," he had said, "either buy some taste or transfer to UMASS."

In response, we'd phoned every girl in the Frog Book pretending to be Gideon, said we had noticed them in SAGA and asked them each if they wanted to go to dinner with him and his parents "up from Greenwich" that night. (Three had said yes.)

Back in the dining hall, Gideon was searching in vain for the rest of his clan, likely in their rooms practicing on their desktops for the impending drum circle. I watched him with Zach and Nathan.

"Check out Valerie." Zach pointed to an intense beaky-faced first-year immersed in a textbook, sitting alone at one of the giant center tables. She lived on Nathan's hall and had yelled at us for making too much noise at least twice. "He called her, didn't he?"

I nodded. "She threatened to file a harassment complaint." We watched while, as though guided by fate, Gideon placed his tray on her table.

Agonizingly for us, she failed to look up and take notice of who had joined her, until finally, as he was shoveling the final bite of damp pizza into his mouth, she glanced at him, executed a flawless double take, and then glared as though she actually believed her eyeballs were equipped with machine gun turrets. We watched Gideon's shock but were sadly too far across the room to hear the exchange that followed. When the gale finally blew itself out, Gideon silently stood from the table and picked up his tray. He stumbled past us, pale and shaking, a shell of the Preppy Deadhead we once knew.

"That was the best thing that's happened to me since I got to this place," Nathan said.

"Maybe there's hope after all," Zach agreed.

With renewed vigor we debated between going to see *Space Camp* at the mall for a third time (Zach and I were convinced Nathan was in love with Lea Thompson) or bothering the D-2 girls' hall, where I'd heard there was a girl named Daphne who had decorated her entire room as a Billy Idol shrine.

"I'm up for that," Zach said after some thought.

My vote tipped the balance toward D-2, made especially vehement by the fact that since last night, the weather had become truly cold in a way that I hadn't thought the world could get. The one cotton sweater I was so proud of myself for having had the foresight to pack had become a laughable mockery of protection against the elements. I crumbled before the thought of waiting outside for the two buses it took to reach the Hampshire Mall, but I didn't want to ask Zach or Nathan if they had brought an extra sweater I might borrow.

"We have to go to D-2," I said. "They need our support." And so the motion carried.

CHAPTER FOUR

The Interview

One month later, Deb, the Dakin House master, leaned across her desk. Her tiny eyes clenched mine. The room was nearly dark; a tiny lamp flickered on her desk. She spoke very slowly, softly hammering each word for emphasis. "We just need you to tell us, *why* did you write that on Heidi's door?"

I stammered, "I—I really don't know what you're talking about."

"But you admit you wrote something?"

"Um, no, actually."

"Richard"—she took a deep breath—"her entire hall saw you. Ten of them ID'd your photo in the Frog Book."

I shook my head. "That's so weird. . . ."

Deb struggled to control herself. Over her shoulder, Lonnie leaned against the back wall, veiled in darkness, and sputtered, "This is ridiculous. Just have Adele expel him and be done with it."

Deb shot him a glance and then bored back into me with her

beady gaze. She tried to smile, something that clearly didn't come easy. "We know you wrote on her door. We have witnesses. I just want to help you clear up this misunderstanding. Heidi says that you're out to get her. But that isn't true, is it? You were just trying to be . . . funny. . . ."

I thought hard. To tell the truth, I wasn't quite sure who this Heidi person was. I thought she might be a round-faced blond girl from Ohio in my Emerson class; I tried to remember if I had ever spoken to her, let alone threatened her.

Then I thought back to a night weeks before. Zach, Nathan, and I had been stampeding through the Dakin halls, falling down drunk, when I had noticed a Bob Marley poster on a door, and paused for a moment to pull out my Magic Marker to scribble a witty commentary on it. After intense thought the words UMASS FOOTBALL KICKS HAMPSHIRE BUTT, followed perhaps by HIPPIE DEADBEATS, YOUR ASS IS OURS, were all that came to me. Peering deeper through the haze of my memory, I recalled capping the marker, looking down, and seeing a group of people sitting on the hall's floor, staring at me, mouths agape. I recalled smiling at them, shrugging, and stumbling away. And thinking back to that group, yes, Heidi had been one of them. But was that *her* door? Did she really like Bob Marley? Or had I been back there with my marker again later?

I looked Deb in the eye and shook my head. "That is the most terrible thing I've ever heard. I can't believe someone would do that."

Deb's nostrils flared and Lonnie looked as though he might wrap up the debate by wrenching every last inch of breath out of me with his tasseled-mittened hands. "And I suppose that's not the same Magic Marker that has defaced every poster, sign, door, and message board on our hall?"

"Our hall? That's my home! I would never!"

Deb leaned in farther, the smile gone. "We've had a major

problem with graffiti this semester. With one person's graffiti. Walls and doors have been defaced all over the House."

"Terrible . . . ," I muttered, nodding sympathetically.

"The phys plant just gave us an estimate on how much it will cost to restore everything. Do you know how much it is?"

"Seventy dollars?" I guessed.

"Eighteen thousand. It's going to cost eighteen thousand dollars to undo this damage."

I gulped. "That's expensive paint."

"So why don't you just work with us? I'm sure we can figure out a plan, so we don't have to send your parents this entire bill all at once. . . . Maybe you can work off some of the bill."

"Or we can expel you today!" Lonnie added lustily.

I remembered how on the first week of school, on a whim in the student store, I had bought a thick black marker that I had carried in my pocket ever since. That marker was, in fact, in my pocket at that very moment. I thought of all the doors and posters I had written on through the semester. Commentary, I had thought in my egomaniacally delusional seventeen-year-old way; commentary and political expression. You might even label it guerrilla theater, just like the hundreds of crank calls Zach, Nathan, and I had made. Or like on Halloween when, wearing ghost sheets, we chased those tripping hippies into the woods. Wasn't this all protected as free speech? Shouldn't I be getting academic credits instead of being treated like a monster?

And how could a few splotches of paint on a few dozen doors cost eighteen thousand dollars? Could it really take more than one can of paint to cover up all the damage I'd done? Couldn't I just paint it myself? I thought of how my parents would react if given a bill for eighteen thousand dollars, along with what was increasingly shaping up like a fairly catastrophic report card. Surviving that conversation was unthinkable. My course remained clear.

"You guys, I am so, so sorry. I want to help you but I don't know anything about this."

"Richard," Deb fumed, "we have ten witnesses. Ten. Who saw you do it."

"That is really, really weird."

Deb stood and glared at Lonnie. Lonnie glared back at her. Then they both turned and glared at me. I smiled and sheepishly waved. They turned and left the room.

In the years to come, I would learn more about the nuts and bolts of collegiate discipline. I would discover that in the lawsuit era, if a school wants to do something really vicious to a student, like expel him or sentence him to humiliation and hard labor, the school needs the student's cooperation in his or her punishment. Lacking real courts, attorneys, or due process, et cetera, Deb needed me to admit I was deserving of punishment. Unwittingly, I was protected by a loophole of college discipline that would keep me and my friends out of truly serious trouble for a good while, until things took a much more serious turn at Hampshire.

Deb and Lonnie came back into the room. Deb once again leaned across the desk toward me, the caring smile all gone. "Look. We know you did this. We *will* get you for it. But right now, we just want you out of here."

"Out of here?"

"Find yourself a new place to live immediately." Lonnie smirked.

"Where am I supposed to go?"

"That's not our problem."

"But are there forms I fill out or something?"

"You figure it out, genius," Lonnie said.

Deb sighed. "It just makes me so sad that some students feel they can't trust us. . . ."

———

I threw myself on my bed and began to review my options, seeking inspiration in the bedlam on my *Great Rock 'n' Roll Swindle* poster. The wisdom of Johnny Rotten had seemed especially profound on the nights of the past few weeks when Zach, Nathan, and I careened across campus like exhaling balloons. But now that the question was "How do I find a place to live when I hardly know my way around campus?" Rotten's bleating cartoon image offered little guidance.

I went to the hall phone and called Drake, whom I hadn't seen since our sauna.

"Wow, Rich, that sucks. Where you gonna go?"

"I don't know. How do you get a room in one of the mods?"

Hampshire College was divided into two types of living quarters—the two four-story brick institutional dorms, occupied mostly by freshmen and social misfits who, like my current hall-mates, had never left the Lysol-scented nest, and the mods—three houses of shared condolike apartments, each containing groups of four to ten. I knew moving into a mod involved some sort of interview/selection process, but how that worked was still shrouded in mystery. Drake, unfortunately, was able to shed little light.

"A room in the mods? Well, that's tough. You know, you've gotta like interview and work it out, you know?"

"Is there a form I fill out?"

"Nooo . . . It's more like something that just happens."

"There's nothing I can do to, like, make it happen?"

"In the middle of the semester . . . do you know anyone who has an open room in their mod?"

I tried to think if I knew anyone who had a mod. Drake's was the only mod I'd even stepped foot in. He broke in. "Rich, Tanya is calling. We're going go take an ice bath. Freezes and refreshes both. Amazing for the pores. But let me know what happens, man."

I hung up and sat down in the tiny unlit closet where the hall phone lived. I wracked my brain to think of anyone I remotely knew who I might call. I thought of the few people whose faces I'd come to recognize in classes and at the cafeteria. Going over the few people whose names I could say I even knew after two and a half months, almost every person on that list had entered my life after warning me to "keep down the noise" or had given me an unsolicited lecture on how I could forget about everything I'd learned in Los Angeles. A few others had by turns sneered at me in public places or expressed their disgust that Hampshire was letting in people like Zach, Nathan, and myself. None of these little exchanges seemed to imply that they were just waiting for me to ask if I might live with them.

And then it occurred to me: Maybe there was someone I could call. . . . Back in my first week at Hampshire, Lonnie had taken me aside, in his characteristic manner that was the more terrifying for its seeming concern that he was anxious for my safety, and warned me that there was a group of evil, despicable people at the school. Horrible, dreadful, terrible, he said, spitting adjectives until he was gasping for breath. He didn't want to scare me but he had reason to believe that these people, who called themselves "the Supreme Dicks," might try—he kneaded my shoulder with a caring hand—might try to *talk* to me. You see, he continued, he had noticed that I bore a resemblance to one of them—one of their leaders who had left the school after, Lonnie went on, eyebrow arched, his brother had died.

"How did he die?" I asked.

"Believe me, you don't want to know," Lonnie said. "But because you look like the older brother, they might try to talk to you."

My heart raced. Weird people, with some tragic secret, will want to talk to me?

He shook his head. "Don't worry, when they do, you tell me and I'll speak to the House Office and take care of it."

After being told that the evil terrible people were going to try to talk to me, for my first two months always in the back of my mind was a desperation for them to get on with it already. I searched for these supposed Supreme Dicks but as Lonnie refused to supply any more details, I had no clue what to keep my eyes peeled for. Zach, Nathan, and I discussed them. Zach had heard people cursing these Supreme Dicks in the dining hall one night, but didn't catch why. I asked a couple older students in my classes about them, but they looked as though they wanted to punch me in the face for bringing up such a distasteful topic. One day, sitting in a library toilet stall, I looked up and saw, carved into the metal door, the words "Supreme Dicks Rule OK!" Someone else had tried to scratch out the words, scraping away slashes of paint, and someone else had written below it, "NO THEY DON'T," and someone else, "Go back to your fucking spoiled mothers you fascists!"

And then, on Halloween they materialized—more or less exactly as Lonnie had foretold they would.

Hampshire Halloween, aka Trip or Treat, was the school's annual contribution to the liberal arts legacy. From the first days of the semester, I had been warned not to eat the food in the cafeteria on Halloween, that every last tofu pup was dosed by the cafeteria workers.

On Halloween morning, Hampshire went into lockdown, with a checkpoint established on the main road into campus. A week before, all students were required to submit the names of their visitors to security—a maximum of five guests each. In town a group of Amherst guys had stopped Zach and offered him a hundred dollars to put their names on the list. He took the money but had lost the napkin they'd scribbled their names down on.

By noon a line of cars beginning at the security checkpoint stretched far down the highway running in front of campus. (The cordon on the main road left only the back entrance and the

three miles of woods and farmland surrounding the school unde-
fended for those who were turned away and wanted to try to cross
the border illegally.)

By midafternoon the school resembled a flamboyantly dressed
refugee camp, with costumed students from across the East Coast
flooding the lawns and wandering through the dorms trying to
stock up on drugs. Nathan quoted a statistic that the campus dealers made 40 percent of their annual profit on this day alone. Lonnie prepared for the day by posting a large sign at the entrance to
J-3 that read WE ARE NOT SELLING DRUGS! But though he may not
have been selling, even Lonnie and the hall drones were not impervious to the spirit sweeping the campus. The entire hall ditched
class and spent the day in Lonnie's double room sewing lines of
glitter threads into black cloaks, painting their faces, and—my
nose informed me—honoring the occasion with a day-long marijuana binge.

At one point, Lonnie wandered into the wall, giggling, and
told me, "Today, I'm not going to give you any warnings at all!"
And then exploded in laughter.

As dusk fell over Hampshire, the campus echoed with the
sounds of a twenty-piece jam in the dorm quad, and hippie cackles
drifted from the Hampshire woods. On the lawn, ignoring the
bracing cold, gangs of people in capes and wizard gowns danced
or rolled on each other.

I had pulled a blue sheet off my bed, cut eye and mouth holes,
and wandered the campus incognito—not that anyone recognized
me even without a sheet over my head. People were beginning to
remove their clothes. One hippie girl grabbed my arms and started
dancing with me; the jam-style of dancing—which resembled jog-
ging in place while waving your arms over your head—proved difficult to execute in a sheet.

The song we danced to, which seemed to be entirely drum
solo, went on for minute after long minute until I had trouble cal-

culating how long we had been dancing. I tried to leave but the hippie girl, who showed no signs of fatigue, held fast to my sheeted arms. Was it possible the song had been going on as long as it seemed, or had I accidentally picked up the wrong drink somewhere today? Was I tripping now?

I felt a pair of hands on my shoulders pull me out of the melee. Nathan, dressed as a vampire, and Zach, dressed as himself, ripped me free from the hippie girl.

"Can your girlfriend score us some 'shrooms?" Zach asked.

"What the hell is with that song?" I panted.

"It's not a song," Nathan explained. "It's called a space jam. Some of them can go on for five, six hours. One song can continue over a dozen bootleg tapes."

We walked into the dining hall. In the back room a performance-art collective dressed in long robes and scarves fluttered across a stage while some sort of Syd Barrett harmonic chant blasted and a hippie read verses of Rilke into a mike. The ensemble looked like a tribe of Bedouin traders playing a game of Red Rover. On the linoleum floor, some fifty hippies writhed and rolled on top of each other, occasionally clasping each other's face between their palms. Zach, Nathan, and I stood in the back of the room frozen in horror.

"Are they going to do it?" Zach finally asked

Nathan shook his head. "They're too drugged out to think about sex."

We considered pulling the fire alarm, but then Zach had the far more efficient idea of spilling fruit punch on the floor, making it sticky and gross to roll around in. We were debating how we could steal jugs of punch from the cafeteria storeroom when I caught sight of something out of the corner of my eye.

About three feet away, someone was staring and gaping at me with a demented grin that seemed to swallow his entire face. With his tiny frame, dressed in a giant sparkly shawl that hung to his knees, a purple scarf, and pointed velvet boots, he looked something like a medieval court jester. At the sight of his grin my mind was ripped away from the discussion with Zach and Nathan, and I squinted back at the staring jester as he grew closer.

"What is your name?" he asked me. I told him. "You're name isn't Moser?" he pressed. I denied it. "Are you related to Billy and Stan?"

"Who?"

"Amazing!" he said, and let out a terrifying cackle that for a moment drowned out the Syd Barrett and the Rilke. And then he turned and scampered from the room in a flash.

"What was that about?" Nathan asked. I shrugged, and we returned to plotting the fruit punch heist, our minds elsewhere, until two minutes later, the jester returned, leading along three others. If the rest of the room was animated by an airy spaciness, this little group shuffled in a dark, stagnant void that looked as though they might, with their very presence, snuff out all the light in the room. At the lead was a largish, round-shaped lug with a quizzical expression, wearing a moss-colored mohair sweater and a gabardine overcoat. Flanking him was a Sid Vicious type, a hulking character in a black leather jacket whose disgust for the hippie congregation looked so acute he seemed he might actually be sick, and a girl in a floppy dark dress with a mop of black hair covering her face.

"See!" cried the jester, pointing at me. "It's him!"

"Oh, my God!" the lug at the front of the group answered.

"He doesn't look like Stanley!" the girl said.

"Are you crazy?" the lug responded. "Of course it does." They all gaped at me for a few moments more. Zach, Nathan, and I gaped back until I felt obliged to say, "Umm, I'm Richard."

The news seemed to stun them and snap the group out of their reverie. The lug stepped forward. "Oh, right. Hi. I'm Jon. You just look like somebody."

"Are you guys, by any chance," I asked, "the Supreme Dicks?" They glanced at each other, eyebrows raised.

"We're some of them." The jester introduced himself as "Friar Tom" and then continued sotto voce, "But there are others. . . ."

"It's kinda a big organization," Jon explained.

A new song came on. The Doors' "Peace Frog." A cheer went up from the floor. "Maybe we should dance," Jon said.

The girl with hair in her face replied curtly, "I'm leaving," and walked out. Jon looked confused.

"Is that your girlfriend?" I asked, trying to think of something to say.

"Girlfriend? Noooo. . . . We're celibate."

"Really?"

"It's like a Reichian thing. . . . It's hard to explain."

Friar Tom burst in. "I'm not celibate."

"But you're not really a Dick," Jon answered.

"That's true," he admitted. Our chat was shortly interrupted by two campus security guards, led over by a hippie who pointed us out to security, screaming, "There they are!"

"Jon, what the hell are you doing here?" a guard asked.

"Just rocking to some groovy tunes," Jon answered. He giggled, rocking back and forth on his heels while Sid Vicious to his right glowered.

The guard shook his head. "Come on, this isn't your scene. What're you kids up to?"

"But they're playing my song, Officer!" Tom, the jester, began prancing around to the strains of "Peace Frog," grabbing a hippie boy and twirling him in a waltz.

"Okay"—the guard pulled himself out of Tom's embrace— "out of here. You're disturbing the party."

"Half of the people here are on, like, acid and PCP, and we're just standing here and we're the troublemakers?" Arthur, the punk, asked.

"I'm not going to explain it to you. You know what I'm talking about." He then whirled and turned to me, Nathan, and Zach. "And you kids, do you know what they were up to?" We shook our heads. "What are you doing hanging around with this bunch?"

"We're also enjoying the groovy tunes," Zach said.

"Hmph. Lemme get your names," he said, and made us each show our college IDs, writing our names down on a little pad. Zach, Nathan, and I looked at each other nervously.

The Dicks group was escorted to the door but before they left, Jon gave us their extension number. "You guys should come hang out. Extension two-four-five."

"Do *not* do that!" security said. "Do yourself a favor and forget that number."

I didn't forget the number but I didn't use it either. I jotted it on a napkin, which sat on my desk. Numerous times over the following weeks I looked at it and considered calling, but wondered what I would say. "Hi, I'm the guy who looks like the guy you used to know . . ." or "If you all aren't too busy, my life is a living hell at this school. Would you mind coming to save me?" Instead of calling, I waited to run into them somewhere on campus. Now that I knew what they looked like, how long could it be, in a school of a thousand students, before I saw one of them? But mysteriously as they had materialized, they had vanished again into the Hampshire mists; not once in our wanderings did I catch a glimpse of any of them. I was like Wendy and Peter back in London, gazing into the fog and babbling insanely about the Lost Boys and Neverland.

Back in the phone closet, after the ultimatum from the House Office, with nowhere else to turn, I dialed the extension. After fourteen or so rings, a girl picked up.

"Is Jon there?" I asked.

"I'm not really sure." Pause. "You know, it's kinda hard to say."

"Whether he's there?"

"I mean, he should be, but he could be anywhere, you know?"

"Yeah." I nodded to myself. "Totally." I hung on to the phone and we sat in silence for a good minute.

The girl broke the spell. "Hey, who is this?" I told her. "I don't know you. Are you sure Jon knows who you are?"

"Maybe. I mean, I don't know. I met him at a hippie dance."

"Is this Rich? Rich from the dorms? The guy who looks like Stanley?"

"Yeah, I guess that's me."

"You missed your dinner!"

"What?"

"You were supposed to be here for dinner last week." She went on to explain that after meeting me, Friar Tom had told the house that I was coming for dinner the following night. They had actually cooked and everything, the girl on the phone explained, but I hadn't shown up and no one knew how to get in touch with me.

"I think maybe he forgot to tell me about dinner."

"That's cool. It wasn't very good anyway. So what's going on?" The girl, whose name, I learned, was Meg, and I got to talking. While I sat on the tiled floor of my hall's phone closet, we whiled away nearly an hour. She told me that things had been crazy at 21. (Mod 21 was their address.) The administration was trying to break the house up, she said, had been reading their mail, listening in on their calls. "They're probably listening now . . . ," she whispered.

"No one can live in peace around here," I whispered back, and told her about my own housing dilemma.

"That's amazing," she said. "You should come live here!"

"You have an open room?"

"I guess so. There's always a room, isn't there?" I agreed

there was. "But you've gotta talk to Susie. You should come on out." I said I'd rush over and was given some very vague directions to Greenwich House. "In the woods behind the library," she told me.

The red brick and concrete library/gymnasium/administration triad occupied the highest ground on campus and the geographic dead center. Paths to the various plots of campus radiated in spokes from this spot; the design gave a big piece of evidence to the group of students that believed Hampshire College, from its inception, was not a bold experiment in education reform but a plot by dark forces within the U.S. government to lure subversives to one place and then snare them in an airtight riot-control net.

Stemming from the back of the library, one spoke led straight into a dense patch of woods, and somewhere within, I had been told, sat Greenwich House. I stood behind the library, shivering in the still November night. No life was visible down the path, nothing except the clump of icy, bare trees.

I tiptoed along, cursing the cold that had really begun to work us over in earnest. I was now wearing a cotton sweater, a hooded sweatshirt, and a raincoat and still I was cold. Surely this was some kind of joke, I thought.

As I followed the path into the trees, the library behind me disappeared from view. I squinted through the night and saw up ahead what looked like five dilapidated flying saucers made of rotting wood, which had apparently thudded to earth in a small clearing. The circular, two-story structures lay in dead, idiotic stillness before me. I wandered toward the first, trying to figure out how they were numbered. Close up, they looked like doughnut-shaped, broken-down condo complexes, with gray and white peeling paint, their slushy lawns strewn with plastic beer cups and rotting concert flyers. A naked mannequin hung by its toes from a tree. I thought of Colonel Kurtz's camp in *Apocalypse*

Now. On each porch hung a number, 8 being the first I saw. I circled several looking for 21, not seeing a person alive through the drawn shades. Finally, facing toward the deeper woods and away from campus, I heard guitar sounds pulsing from behind one door; with no identifiable melodies or vocals, the noise thudded through the empty frigid night and I stood frozen, listening to it for a moment, unsure whether I felt drawn to or terrified by its harsh, unlovable radiations.

I climbed up to the porch, stepping over a car transmission and a ventriloquist's dummy and treading on some broken bottles ground up in the slush. Black curtains were pulled tight across the glass doors. I knocked. There was no response. I knocked again, then turned the handle and walked in.

One foot through the doorway, the smell washed over me—an aroma alive and vital with decay. The air overflowed with the afterbirth of a million cigarettes, human sweat, incense and, I thought, rotting vegetables. I fought my gag reflex and peered through the red light that lit the space. It was a small living room, about the size of a moving van, with low ceilings and walls that seemed to lean over on top of the inhabitants. The room was furnished with a couch, two armchairs, and a couple stools and a dozen or so people sitting stuffed together, crammed into open spaces between piles of debris. Like the bunch I'd met in the dining hall, this group was a mix of types, belonging to no clear tribe—a couple of punks, a few hippies, several in what I'd later know as "old man clothes," and a decidedly preppy woman in polo shirt, cardigan, and pearls. As I opened the door, I heard someone say, "Cockroaches are my friends!"

The discussion stopped for a second as everyone looked up at me. I nervously smiled, braced for someone to ask what I was doing there, but they showed no surprise or curiosity about my sudden appearance and turned back to their conversation. "Ox," a girl pleaded to a frail young man in an overcoat, bouncing anxiously from one foot to the other, "they're everywhere. They're in the shower."

Ox shook his head. "What's so bad about sharing your shower? Cockroaches wouldn't exterminate you."

I stood listening, ignored by the group. I looked around the room, strewn with discarded garments, plates of food, and people crouched in every corner. As they discussed them, I saw the walls were alive with a dance of cockroaches rhumbaing happily from floor to ceiling. The music thudded out of a little turntable on the counter. A banner heralded BOB WEINER FOR CONGRESS. On the opposite wall, a framed photo of three Apollo astronauts grinned maniacally. I considered edging back out the door, but at that moment conversation hit a lull and I found the nerve to ask, my voice squeaking with anxiety, "Does anyone know if Meg is here?"

The crowd turned and looked at me with tired amusement. No one spoke until the one they called Ox, short for Daniel Oxenberg, said, "I'm pretty sure she's in Boston." Others murmured agreement. I was about to protest when Jon suddenly tumbled down the staircase at the other end of the room. Stumbling forward, he saw me and said, "Rich. You're here."

"Oh. Jon, hi! How's it going?"

"Pretty good. Pretty good. How are you doing?"

"I'm great." The conversation had reached an impasse and we stood smiling at each other, Jon's hulking roundish figure bobbing up and down. The rest of the room watched us, nodding and smiling, as though they might very pleasantly doze off at the spectacle our dialogue presented. Finally, I steeled my nerve and blurted out, "I talked on the phone to some girl named Meg and she said it might be all right if I lived here!"

At this many started out of their stupor and bolted upright; the cockroaches on the walls danced a bit faster. "Oh, really?" Jon said. "Oh, right. Definitely, you should. For sure." He gave me a knowing look, like we were acting out a prerehearsed script; I wondered what my next line was supposed to be.

"It's just—I'm getting kicked out of Dakin." The room murmured its approval.

"Oh, wow. Then you have to live here." Several nodded in assent and my heart did a little skip, while I remained absolutely terrified and confused.

"But he's gotta talk to Susie," someone said. Others agreed. "Let's bring him up to Susie."

"And we all get to interview him!" a girl with dark bangs said fiendishly.

At once, the room broke the rust free from their joints and rose to their feet. "Let's take him to Susie!" Jon turned to rummage through the refrigerator as I was herded up the stairs and into a large bedroom that seemed so different from my dorm room, it was as though I had stepped through a portal into another universe.

If the downstairs air greeted you with the stench of death, one step into this room and an aroma of thick, stagnant sweetness ran you down like an eighteen-wheeler. The room glowed in a deep purplish-red light, hung dense with willowy draperies and furnished with tattered Louis XV armchairs. A half dozen more people, all of whom appeared on the verge of fading from consciousness, slumped on the floor and in chairs as a scratchy Bessie Smith album played on an antique turntable. The effect was like entering a Gilded Age New Orleans brothel that had been ransacked by a very unmotivated band of Huns.

On a great billowing bed, covered with cloudlike comforters and rags of old blankets, sat Susie. At the sight of her ironed-out blond hair, and confronted by a face full of makeup sufficient to repaint a medium-sized cottage, I was first roiled by an overstimulation of the senses—as in a room that had been decorated within an inch of its life. But on second glance, a slightly maniacal but sweet and comforting smile lit up her face and indeed the entire room, at once putting me at ease and making me want to instantly confide all my cares and woes to her.

"Susie," someone said, "this is Richard. He wants to move in here."

"Oh, really?" She sat up. The others around the room stirred slightly.

"Deb threw him out of Dakin."

"Oh, my goodness. Well, then, of course you have to live here," she said.

"Is there even a room open?" Ox asked.

"There's always a room." I nodded but found this very hard to swallow. As I came upstairs and looked around, there seemed to be at most two bedrooms downstairs and three upstairs, and there were no fewer than twenty people in the house just at that moment.

"If it's too crowded," I stammered, "I can just, um . . ."

"Don't be silly! There's Steve's room. Nobody's seen him for two months. Is he even enrolled next semester?" she asked the room.

"Was he enrolled *this* semester?" someone else asked.

Ox's head started bobbing uncontrollably as he slowly spat out words one at a time, taking a huge pregnant pause between clauses, his eyes lighting up to savor the many secret meanings. "I . . . got a message . . . from Laura . . . who said she hung out with him . . . in Florida."

"What's he doing in Florida?" someone asked.

"And she said," Ox continued, "he was talking . . . about coming back . . . for Ken's Hermeneutics."

"When's that?" Susie asked. No one seemed to know. "Well, I don't think Steve's been enrolled for at least two years. It's fine, you can have his room."

"But he needs to interview!" The crowd had gathered around the bed and pushed in.

"That's right," Susie said. "We need to interview you. You don't mind, do you?"

"Not at all." I shook my head, panicking in mortal terror.

"Good." She patted the bed beside her, motioning for me to sit down. "Who has questions?"

People stared at me, or glared at me, in contempt and boredom, I thought. "Do you have a name for your penis?" asked a heavyset girl, standing in the doorway wearing clunky black boots.

"Oh, be quiet, Jeanie. Can't you see he's still just a baby?"

"Yeah, right," she spat, seeming indignant with the whole thing. "Okay, then, tell us the names of all the girls you've screwed since you got here, cowboy."

I looked for Susie to intercede, but she stared at me benevolently, waiting for my answer.

"Ummmm . . . I've really been focused on my work this semester."

Everyone stared aghast, and then in unison broke out laughing. "You're a virgin!" someone shouted. "That's perfect." I turned dark crimson. Jon reminded me, "Don't worry. Supreme Dicks are celibate."

"You are really?" I asked.

Ox said, "Yeah, that's very important. And vegetarian."

In one corner, an emaciated man with stringy black hair, named Brian, was cutting up lines of cocaine on a full-length mirror that lay on the floor. He looked at me. "I'm sorry," he said in a tone of great courteousness. "Do you want a line?" I nodded and scampered across the room. Grabbing a rolled-up five-dollar bill and ignoring the fact that flecks of blood dotted the rim, I leaned down and, trying not to be greedy, sucked up the smallest line on the mirror. I bolted upright and felt the shot of blood leap through my brain.

"Put some on your gums." Brian showed me how. In seconds I felt excited to continue the interview. And suddenly the idea of moving in here seemed overwhelmingly great. "I really want to live here!" I yelled to Susie.

In the hours that followed, a cast of thirty or so drifted in and out, taking turns asking me questions. It was never clear who actually lived in the house and who had a vote as the questions flew from every corner. I was asked about why I was being thrown out of the dorm; there were many questions about Lonnie, whom they all seemed to know. Several, rather than asking questions, directed long speeches at me, warning me that if I moved in, the whole campus would hate me. "There's no going back," Ox said. Friar Tom appeared and gave a soliloquy about how the Supreme Dicks were about love, which was violently booed down by the room.

Sa'ad, a twenty-year-old black man sporting dreadlocks and a blazer with little mod pins and an English accent that came and went, sat down on the bed and asked me what sort of music I listened to.

"Ummm . . ." I stalled, struggling for an impressive answer. "Bowie . . . Velvet Underground . . ."

"Of course." Sa'ad nodded. "But have you listened to anything *lately*?"

"I like Hüsker Dü?" I said, more as a question than a statement.

Sa'ad chortled. "You really listen to them? Don't you find them completely derivative?"

I nodded, carefully. "Yeah, sometimes . . . but not maybe their last album . . . ," I said, wondering what *derivative* meant. "What do you listen to?"

Sa'ad fixed a braid in his hair. "There's some Joy Division I can stand. I used to like the Swans, but I'm getting bored with them. Psychic TV are geniuses, of course."

"Of course."

"Do you really think so?"

I nodded solemnly, praying I wouldn't be asked to name one of their albums. Sa'ad fell silent a moment and looked me deep in the eyes. "So how long have you known that you're gay?" he asked.

"I, um, well . . ." I looked around the room for support, but the others stared blankly at me, waiting for an answer. "I'm not sure. . . ."

"Oh, stop it," Susie mercifully interrupted. "Sa'ad thinks everyone is gay."

"Are you saying he's not!?"

"Of course he's not. He's just a nerd! Look, he's wearing a Hawaiian shirt under his sweater." I didn't know if this defense was helping my cause, but I kept silent. The discussion soon drifted back to the house's celibacy strictures. "It's Reichian," Ox explained to me. "It's important for your orgone energy."

Susie disputed this, saying, "Celibacy is just the line they use to get laid. You guys know that sex is the best thing in the world for your orgone."

"Susie!" Ox looked genuinely shocked. "I can't believe you're saying that. I know *my* celibacy is very serious." As the night wore on, everyone seemed to forget about my interview. Once the coke ran out, the crowd thinned as people trailed away or just fell asleep where they sat. The clock on Susie's nightstand read six A.M., and I was having a very hard time keeping my eyes open as the celibacy debate continued. I sensed that asking if the interview was over or if I had been accepted would be tactless, so I sat quietly and tried to follow the conversation about campus figures I had never met and books I'd never read.

I jerked upright and realized I had fallen asleep leaning against the wall. The clock read ten A.M. The room was quiet, with several people dozing. On the other end of the giant bed, Susie sat up writing in a crepe-bound journal. She noticed me shudder awake. "Hi." She smiled. I smiled back. The face that had seemed so jarring twelve hours before now looked like the warmest, most caring on earth.

"Ummm . . ." I struggled for words. "Is the interview over?"

"Congratulations. You can have Steve's room."

"But, uh, what if he comes back?"

"Then you'll have to fight him for it." She smiled benevolently, but with no sign that she was joking. She told me I could move in immediately. I struggled to my feet, realizing I hadn't eaten since lunch the previous day. My skull felt on the verge of implosion, and when I swallowed, my mouth seemed to be filled with vast quantities of rotting-vegetable-flavored quicksand.

"It was nice to meet you," I said.

"It was really good you found us. You belong here." Susie turned back to her diary. I beamed at her as I struggled my way down the stairs.

CHAPTER FIVE

Cold Turkey

On Thanksgiving I returned to Los Angeles for the first time and my family gathered to celebrate the holiday with the family of one of my high school best friends, also named Richard. In high school, Richard was perhaps the most noted figure of our generation. Typically dressed in overalls, white-collared shirt, and bow tie, he was given to flamboyant spectacles such as the day when he stormed the roof of the administration building in pirate costume and threw tortillas ("food for the masses") to the campus below, setting off a day-long riot.

After a semester at NYU, however, his semicrazed, mischievous swagger seemed shaken. His head was shaved and he muttered the phrase "The city, man. It's real," over and over. He said he had been arrested by the NYPD for chalking drawings of Ubu Roi on the subway walls and had spent a night in jail. I wondered how both of us had graduated from high school under the illusion that graffiti was a socially and legally acceptable form of expression.

Richard's first roommate had been a basketball player who, one night with his friends, brought a semicomatose girl to their room and dropped her on the bed. They were in the middle of discussing which of their group should assault her first when Richard leapt from his own bed and attacked them with his lacrosse stick. The girl momentarily came to her senses and raced for safety, leaving Richard alone with a group of unsatisfied, drunk basketball players, who stopped just short of inflicting upon Richard the assault they had intended for the girl. A week later, the roommate was expelled for attacking a campus security guard. His replacement was a student from Taiwan who Richard nicknamed Homeboy and who spoke no English—at least none directly to Richard. On a couple of occasions, however, Richard had walked into the room and was sure he'd heard him speaking perfect *anglais* on the phone, which he abruptly dropped when Richard entered.

"The city, it's just real," he repeated again as we drove away after dinner toward Ricki's house. If we had gone to a normal high school, Ricki would have been our queen. Perched atop a clique of the wealthiest, prettiest L.A. teens, in a just world Ricki wouldn't have even known our names. But in our world, every year after Thanksgiving dinner, she heard a knock on the door and found Richard and me standing on her front stoop waiting for her mother to invite us in.

Keeping up the tradition seemed to put Richard in a better mood, carrying him back to his old mind-set.

"Oh. My. God," Ricki exclaimed when she saw us. "You are so not here. This is *college* now."

"Now, be nice, Ricki," her mother tutted. "That's so sweet of you boys to stop by and say hello. Would you like some pumpkin pie?" We pushed past a slack-jawed Ricki to take our places in the living room. Over pie, we talked about our first months at college and Richard recounted tales of Homeboy, who had taken to feeding the mice that infested their dorm, leaving bits of food around on the floor. Ricki had gone to college in Colorado and was mildly impressed with the fact that the students there were "less judgmental" than people had been in L.A., and she claimed the film program to be decent.

I tried to explain what I'd been doing at Hampshire, tried to tell them about my new housemates at Dick House/Mod 21, where I'd moved just before leaving, but I couldn't get out much more than "They're really interesting people. Like really focused on, like, the arts and stuff." When I threw out the question "Do you have to, like, go to classes at your schools?" their giggles reinforced my idea that the facts of Hampshire life were better left unspoken here.

In the days before Thanksgiving I had carried my belongings across campus an armload at a time into Mod 21. After avoiding J-3 for days, I moved under the cover of night, hoping to avoid confrontation with Lonnie and the hallmates. Ox and Friar Tom had offered to come and help. At two A.M. we crept onto J-3. "I can't believe you live here," Ox said, looking in awe at the Dakin stairway. "I haven't been to Dakin in years."

"Has it changed?"

Ox peered through the dim hall light onto J-3. He glanced at Lonnie's many warning signs posted at the entrance to the hall.

"I guess there wasn't any such thing as a quiet hall back then."

"I think this hall's sorta a special place."

"Oh, my God." Ox's head bobbed up and down and he hopped from toe to toe, as though a surge of excitement was struggling to break through the fossilized layers of apathy he had blanketed himself in. "J-three. That's where . . . Adrian lived."

"Who was Adrian?"

Ox's nodding grew more frantic. "Adrian, oh, really. Yeah, Adrian . . . She was a New Wave monster."

Friar Tom ducked into the lounge, discovered a tub of hummus in the refrigerator, and brought it back, along with a long wooden spoon. "Be careful, Rich," he warned. "Don't let him start having flashbacks to his hippie days or we might lose him."

"Her father was the Grateful Dead's road manager." He stared wistfully at the door to J-307. "Of course, this was all before I was celibate."

On cue, Lonnie emerged from his room, indignant in fluffy robe, hair tied back with a scrunchy. "What is—hello, Tom. . . ."

"Lonnie! Well well well well well."

They stood in silence, looking at each other. "I think they were friends when they were first-years," Ox whispered. They stared each other down like gunmen preparing to draw.

Friar Tom drew first. "So do you still do the joogie dance before you go to sleep?"

Lonnie turned dark red. "Tom, you need to leave my hall. Richard, what do you know about these people? What are they doing here?"

"I'm moving in with them."

I won't swear that steam actually poured out of Lonnie's ears and that his eyes leapt from his head, but within moments it felt as though the hall had been enveloped in a cloud of smoke.

"How—how did this happen?"

"Just one of those things, I guess."

Lonnie exhaled, dropped his head, and looked defeated. "Do you realize who these people *are*? Have they told you the *things* they've done?"

Friar Tom grinned broadly and raised his eyebrows. Ox was still studying Adrian's old door. "At the Limelight, there was a table named after her. . . ."

Back at 21, we carried a load of blankets and my duffel bag into the living room.

Ox asked, "Does anyone know if there's a key to Steve's room? I mean Rich's room?"

The crowd looked blank. "Rich," Ox said, "I think you're going to have to just card it."

"Oh, okay." I nodded, and followed him down a tiny hall off the living room. At the second door, Ox stopped, took out his student ID, and ran it down the groove between the door and the jamb with a twist, forcing the knob to turn free. "It's pretty easy, really," he told me.

The room smelled intensely of cat urine. The floor was carpeted with old clothes, album covers, beer bottles, papers, and candles that had burned down and melted into the floor.

"Is Steve going to mind me stepping on his stuff?" I asked.

"Oh, really? Is Steve back?" Ox said, looking surprised. I threw my rubble on top of the rest of the rubble and plopped on the bed, a single, monastic-looking futon with a blanket tossed over it. On the wall was tacked a quote from Bertrand Russell, "Life is nothing but a competition to be the criminal rather than the victim," written in dripping fountain pen on a piece of parchment paper, a print of the Munch painting *The Dance of Life*.

"Welcome home," Ox said.

We walked out into the living room, where Ox announced, "So I guess Rich is living in Steve's room now." The group stirred slightly and looked up at me in befuddlement.

"Just so long as you don't stay in the bathroom all day," said one with a knot of waxed hair and giant Coke-bottle glasses.

"I'll try not to."

"Steve goes in and stays forever. We timed him at over six hours one day."

I laughed but they all nodded back at me, straight-faced. "What does he do in there?"

"What Steve Shavel does in the bathroom is the Supreme Dicks' most closely guarded secret."

For much of that first night I sat in the living room trying to puzzle out who actually lived there and what they were talking about. The revolving cast seemed equally at home plopping down on the floor or going through the refrigerator. The talk whirled between the latest moves by the Supreme Dicks' enemies around campus, the effects of deadly orgone radiation (DOR), which was said to be taking hold across the Pioneer Valley, and gossip about other campus and local bands, little of which made any sense to me but which I struggled to follow as if for an immersion class in a foreign language.

Much of the conversation focused on various facets of "orgone energy," the life force. A theory of Austrian psychoanalyst-cum-scientist Wilhelm Reich, orgone had become the cornerstone of the Supreme Dick worldview, and Reich the group's guiding philosopher. Wilhelm Reich had been, early in his career, a protégé of Sigmund Freud's, but he eventually took his master's ideas in esoteric directions, theorizing that all life was fueled by a force known as orgone energy, which in its purest state was a deep blue. When individual lives were dominated by anger or went out of harmony, their orgone became blocked, poisoned, and red. Reich eventually designed a machine, an orgone accumulator, that aided the flow of orgone in individuals.

Late in his career, Reich moved from Austria to the tiny town of Rangeley, Maine, where he founded a commune and built a massive orgone accumulator gun with which, he claimed, he created rain showers and shot down an invading alien spacecraft.

Although Reich had insisted that orgone energy could be released by the power of the orgasm—which he defined in fifty-three stages—Supreme Dick philosophy argued that in contemporary corrupt society (suffering from "the emotional plague"), sexuality had become colonized by the state and consequently orgasm was no longer an efficient mechanism for releasing orgone energy. And thus, it was argued, celibacy was the only solution.

Around eleven P.M., Marilyn and Arthur tumbled in the door

with a paper bag filled with food, which they spread out on the coffee table for everyone to grab at; cheeses, a pasta salad, bread, olives, hummus, a half-eaten block of tofu were all quickly devoured.

"Those fucks in Forty-three wouldn't go out," Arthur cursed. "And I know they made lasagna last night."

"Where did this all come from?" I asked Meg.

"It's called mod shopping. We try to keep our food supply re-stocked at least once a week."

"Other mods give it to you?"

"Sort of. . . . They give it to us when they go to sleep and we go into their mods and try to fill our shopping list."

Around one A.M., a call came from Tim Fall, up at Prescott.

"Tim thinks we should play at Mod Eighty-nine," Jon announced, hanging up the wall phone.

"Eighty-nine!?" some exclaimed. "Those guys are so wasted, they won't even notice we're playing. Will the party even be going by the time we get there?"

Jon shrugged. "I dunno. Tim says it's pretty happening."

Slowly, the room shook off the crust of stationary hours and rose to their feet, wrapping themselves in moth-eaten jackets, scarves, and hats; reaching for guitars, amps, and drums lying around the room. I knew, as I'd been told constantly, that the Supreme Dicks were not just a social collective but an actual rock band, but until now, that idea had never sunk in.

As we filed out the hall and into the snow, I asked Ox, "So this is like a gig? This mod invited us to play?"

"Not really. . . . We are kinda booking it ourselves."

"So it's okay to just show up and do a show?"

"Ohhh, really?" Ox nodded. "I don't think so. Is it?"

Wrapped up from the cold, we made our way across campus in a long line, sliding across the icy paths, each of us with an instrument in hand. This was my first return visit to Prescott House, the collection of three-story tin-lined ski chalets, since I had partied there as a prospective student. All year, the little village had loomed in my imagination as an enchanted fantasyland, a nonhippie sanctuary on the campus. But somehow I had never found my way back to Prescott. In fact, by November, I wasn't quite sure where the tin village was, never having noticed the little path leading into another clump of trees behind the Science Center.

Our group wandered into Prescott like a pack of refugees, schlepping our belongings in our arms. A distant XTC song filled the canyon between the buildings and we followed it to its source, a mod at the far end, at the top of a narrow red fire escape. We tripped our way up the metallic steps, slippery in the frost, struggling to hold the railing and clutch our equipment, pushing through revelers packed tightly together in the cold.

The mod itself was a dark, low-ceilinged room, maybe twice the size of the 21 living room but cramped and airless with a hundred or so people packed in, the only light coming from the open refrigerator. After the bitter chill outside, the party felt almost furnacelike, the room stuffed with people like a cattle car. On one side of the room, a cluster swayed back and forth to a Replacements song playing from a stereo that was perched dangerously on a much-jostled stool in the corner.

Like a rugby scrum pushing against a rival mass, we surged with the instruments through the crowd into the far corner of the room. Jon, Ox, Tim, Arthur, and others took out their instruments, plugged into various outlets, and began, very slowly, to play. At a glance, I counted nine guitars in the ensemble.

The concert sounded, to my untrained ears, more or less like the band was tuning up. The rest of the room seemed totally unaware that a concert was beginning. A couple of people shot disturbed looks at the band. But slowly the discordant, random chords held for painfully long moments evolved into something else—much louder discordant, random chords held painfully long.

Jon and the others stared intensely down at their instruments and strummed in almost slow motion. The sounds soon overwhelmed the music from the stereo as, around the room, people looked up with confusion and then horrified grimaces of recognition.

"Get the hell out of here, you assholes!" Boos resounded from across the room but they were soon drowned out by the strumming of the guitars, somehow increasing in volume while still preserving a sense of lethargy, as though a negative intensity were swallowing the room. Cold air flooded space as people fled out into the night, their faces twisted in anger.

The din of the instruments surged into something that at moments was almost melodic—like an orchestra tuning up occasionally in unison. Jon, Ox, Tim, and the others stared at their guitars with a focus I'd never seen from them in weeks of loafing on the 21 couch. While their collective strumming didn't cohere into anything identifiable as music, the growing intensity had a power that was almost beautiful.

The fleeing crowd, however, clearly did not hear the hidden charms. The party's hosts were soon standing in front of the band screaming at them in vain, their voices swallowed by the music. One of them, in parachute pants with a safety pin through his ear, crawled down at the base of the wall and unplugged Jon's and Tim's instruments. When he crossed the room to pull the plug on Ox and Arthur, Jon and Tim broke out of their trances and nonchalantly leaned over and plugged themselves back in. He raced back to pull them out again and Ox and Arthur revived their guitars. Minutes later, the mod pushed and shoved the group of us out the door and all the way down the stairwell. We stumbled on the icy steps, grappling with our armfuls of amps, guitars, and drums. The crowd from the party lined up on the fire escape, booing and shoving us as we went down.

"You Dick scum are destroying this school!" one young man shouted in my face.

At the bottom of the stairs, faces flushed from excitement and shivering in the cold, we all stopped and looked at each other. "I think that was our best show ever," Ox said.

The next morning I was awakened by what sounded like the clacking of an electric typewriter in the room. I glanced around. It was hard to make out the room in the weak dawn light streaming through the trees outside my window. I noticed two people—Meg and Sa'ad, I thought—sleeping on the floor, half-buried under old clothes and magazines. Nothing moved in the room, other than a few odd bugs traveling up and down the wall, but the sound of the typing seemed to echo in my head. Then I realized the sound was coming from inside my head, that it was the sound of my teeth chattering.

It was cold in this room. Very cold. Even when I wrapped the wool blanket around me it was laughably, hilariously cold.

And the room smelled even more violently of cat urine.

But on my floor, the two shapes slept soundly. From the living room, I heard someone playing "In-A-Gadda-Da-Vida" on an electric guitar.

The pale-yellow light streamed in. I wrapped the blanket tighter around me and, teeth chattering, drifted contentedly back to sleep.

The night after Thanksgiving I had met Zach and Nathan for coffee at Dolores, a twenty-four-hour coffee shop in West L.A. The macabre waiter with long fingernails who'd served me many times before seemed to have forgotten me in the three months I'd been away. I gave him intense, meaningful looks, digging for a burst of recognition, but he took our orders with a deadpan stare. I had been erased from the Dolores's family.

"So are you guys going back?" Nathan asked.

Zach and I picked at our chili fries. "Do you think there's any way to get a refund on our plane tickets?" Zach asked.

"No, I already checked. You have to request a refund two weeks in advance."

"Terrific." They both looked glum. I thought back to the mod. Three days earlier, on the Tuesday afternoon before Thanksgiving, duffel bag over my shoulder, I had set off for the three buses and one taxi ride that would take me to Bradley Airport outside Hartford. As I left, the crowd was flopped around the 21 living room, listening to Jon play a tape of what sounded like a single note on a guitar held forever.

"That's brilliant," Monica, a girl incongruously in pearls, said. "It's like, a call to something."

"You guys aren't fooling anyone." Sa'ad snorted. "It's a game to you. Not music."

Ox blurted out, "To me, it sounds like a beautiful lullaby."

Everyone cracked up and Sa'ad fumed until Jon broke in, "Rich, where are you going?"

"Oh," I stammered, "I mean, aren't people going home for break?"

The room looked up. "What break is it?" Monica asked.

"I think, maybe Thanksgiving."

"Oh, really?" Ox nodded. "Wow. Really. So you're going someplace for that?"

"I guess, like, home pretty much." I stumbled for some way to make it sound less pathetic. "I guess there'll be a lot of food."

"Oh, wow," Jon said. "Amazing, Rich. That sounds really cool."

"Really?"

"Yeah, totally. Food is awesome."

"Supreme Dick Rule Number One," Ox said. "Never turn down a free meal."

"Okay, then. I guess I'll see you all. So it's okay to just leave my room?"

"Yeah, Steve's room. It will be fine," Monica answered. "You didn't lock it, did you?" She looked suddenly alarmed.

"I don't have a key."

"Oh, good. No, it's cool, then."

At Dolores's Zach and Nathan stared down glumly, contemplating their return. Zach picked up a chili fry and studied it. "Do you think it's really so hard that the whole East Coast can't make one of these? Three months back there without a damn chili fry."

I looked around the diner. The few patrons mostly sat alone, and under the fluorescent lights they seemed to be eating in slow motion.

"I guess it might be fun when we get back," I said.

Nathan gaped at me.

"Whaaa . . ." Zach asked.

"At Twenty-one. You guys should hang out. I think it'll be okay. Maybe . . ."

CHAPTER SIX

Mohair Days, Lithium Nights

The tension settled over the 21 living room like the damp mist that clung to the campus and seeped into your bones each day until well into the afternoon. Everyone was aware of it; I could feel it lapping at the edges of our conversation in furtive glances and terse replies. But no one was going to say anything about it. I certainly wasn't. After a week back at 21, I had learned one thing well: Never, ever, be the person to bring up a problem.

We chattered about our outrage that the Dicks were the only major campus band not asked to play the upcoming show at SAGA, but the conversation grew stilted; the knowing looks deepened. I glanced at Meg and she glanced back at me; she seemed to be outraged that I wasn't saying anything. Even the cockroach walking across my foot seemed unusually tense in his gait.

Predictably, it was Sa'ad who at last spoke up and laid the

whole matter on the table. "You guys," he said, "I'm fucking hungry."

Several people sat up straight in anticipation. Jon looked at Sa'ad and tilted his head from side to side as though the comment had gotten stuck in a pocket of water in his ear. Finally he said, "Really, Sa'ad? Wow, that's crazy."

Sa'ad glared back indignantly, his minidreadlocks quaking. "We've been sitting here all day. There's no food in the house. It's dinnertime. Let's eat."

"Dinnertime," Jon repeated, taking that in. "Like sitting with your family?"

Tim said, "I didn't realize you were so into traditions, Sa'ad."

Charles, one of the punks, jumped in. "I think dinnertime means it's time to *be* dinner."

Chortles erupted around the room and then Ox said, "I think Luntz banned us from the jam because he was afraid our orgone levels would upset his equipment." Meg agreed with the non sequitur and offered that Luntz, the head of the campus's Alternative Music Collective and thus one of the Dicks' mortal foes, was now in a state of all-out warfare against us, since the last show when the Dicks had refused to relinquish the stage. The punk band from Marblehead Luntz had booked had apparently stormed out in disgust.

The conversation again heated up, speculations as to Luntz's motives flying. Sa'ad slumped in a corner, started to cry, and threw a boot at Jon, who ignored it and played with his unplugged guitar.

Months later, Steve Shavel would explain that Supreme Dick conversation was based on the Buddhist allegory:

Q: Does the dog have the Buddhist nature?

A: Mu.

That is, all our conversation was diabolically nonsensical to outsiders but to those initiated in the secrets of our world, completely transparent. For myself, I had discovered that asking direct questions or suggesting action would only bring frustration, or worse, make you look anxious and thus uncool.

The conversation drifted from the evils of the Alternative Music Collective to a warning Susie had received from the Greenwich House office, where she held a part-time job, that apparently the college president had passed down an edict that this was to be the Supreme Dicks' last year at Hampshire.

"Good," said Tim Fall, a tall, red-bearded ringer for Shaggy. "I'm sick of this place. I've been stuck here six years already." Tim was at work on what was considered around the house to be the most monumental project ever undertaken by a Hampshire student—a pixilated film history of Hampshire parties, 1980 to the present. Anytime more than five people gathered on Hampshire soil, Tim appeared and, with his antique Super 8 Bolex camera, snapped half a dozen shots of the festivities. It was said that his Division III (the Hampshire equivalent of a senior thesis—the one final massive project that students spent their last year or so working on before they could graduate) committee had seen the work, pronounced it brilliant, and offered him a diploma several years earlier, but out of a perfectionistic sense of duty to the project he had declined and stayed on to see it through, presumably to the party's end.

Michael, however, who sprawled in a corner in his ochre Krishna robes, was not so sanguine. "Easy for you to say but if we get thrown out, where am I going to go?"

"You're not even a student here," said Monica, the preppy Radcliffe transfer.

"It's my house as much as it is yours! It's not like you go to class!" The previous year, Michael had fled a Boston Hare Krishna tribe and hopped the bus out west to Northampton. He had met Susie in a coffee shop and she had invited him to come live with us.

"Maybe we should stop using the phone," Ox offered. Although almost certainly untrue, it was common legend that our phone was bugged, supposedly confirmed by a late-night visit Jeanie had made to the Security Office, where she claimed to have heard them laughing at one of Ox's calls home.

The topic of the Dicks' enemies' closing in was so huge and multifaceted we could only scratch its surface in any one conversation. Hunger pains soon enough reasserted themselves and private anguished looks were traded around the room.

Eventually, it was Jon who, after pushing the eating topic off the table earlier and letting it sit there on the floor until the room had been driven mad trying not to touch it, gently, obliquely, brought it up again. "Have you guys heard about that Denny's?" he asked. No one had. "Yeah, they opened one in Chicopee." The words hung in the air. Chicopee, many calculated, was down the road past Mount Holyoke, forty-five minutes away.

"Wow." "Cool." "Denny's." "I wonder what that's like?" Expressions of vague interest wafted through the room as we contemplated the distant specter of Denny's. No one, however, dared taking the thought beyond the theoretical, since suggesting action would open you up for ridicule.

"Do you think we should go there sometime?" Ox finally asked.

"Really?" Jon sounded stunned by the notion but let it sink in. "Yeah, maybe. I guess it would be cool to check that out." The room lapsed into reflection again. Jon plucked on his guitar. Several long minutes later, he looked up. "Did you mean, like, tonight?"

A shiver ran through the room. All eyes turned back to Ox. "Wow, tonight . . . I don't know. I mean, I guess so. Really? Okay. Could we do that?"

Somehow, many murmurs later, we finally arrived at an articulated agreement. It would be cool sometime to check out the new

Denny's and if there wasn't anything else happening and no one cared what we were doing tonight it wasn't really any different to be at Denny's than it was to be here so if we had to be somewhere, we might as well maybe at some point go.

Once we crossed that bridge, however, another issue loomed like a hostile and heavily fortified army on the far shore—how in the hell could we get to Denny's, twenty miles away into the neighboring county beyond the reach of the five-campus bus system on a bone-chillingly cold night? Enthusiastic murmurs of agreement with the scheme dissipated into another thoughtful silence until Jon volunteered, "I guess we could take my car."

Jubilation again; again dissipating into silence. "The Dickmobile" was a two-seater—an early-seventies Volkswagen Bug convertible with a tiny crawl space in the rear. On drives into Amherst I had squeezed in with three other people. It was plausible that someone could also sit on the lap of the passenger in the shotgun seat and another very, very small person could sprawl across the backseat, which would in theory cram six people in. A quick count of the room showed somewhere upwards of thirty present, all of whom stared expectantly at Jon, awaiting a solution to this riddle.

Instead he returned his attention to his guitar and said quietly, almost whispering to himself, "I guess we'll have to figure out who should go, then." Around the room we looked at each other with now barely concealed animosity, wondering whom we should throw off the lifeboat first. I looked at Angela, the girl perched on the arm of the sofa next to me. "Are you going to go?" I asked her softly.

"Yeah, I guess. I mean, it's Denny's?" she said, as though asking a question.

"Yeah, I guess I will too. You know, just to see what it's about. Maybe we could share the front seat?"

She shot me an are-you-crazy? look and, without a word, got up and walked upstairs to Susie's room. *It's hard to believe*, I thought, watching her leave, *that just a few hours ago I lost my virginity to that girl.*

The earth had shaken for me the night before when around ten o'clock, aching from hunger and with no sign of an impending food run, I had, for the first time since I'd moved in, done the unthinkable; I left the group. Without explanation, I had walked out of the mod. I thought about asking whether anyone wanted to come, but rehearsing the question in my head, I couldn't find any way to phrase it without sounding hopelessly pushy and lame.

I ended up back in Dakin watching *Letterman* and eating pizza in Nathan's room. Slipping back into the dorms now that I was a disgraced ex-resident, I felt a chill of danger and skulked the halls like a secret agent. After *Letterman* ended at one-thirty, I urged Zach and Nathan to come back to 21, promising that people would still be hanging out. But, still on dorm time, they began drifting off to sleep.

"Why would I want to stay awake any more than I have to at this place?" Zach asked, although soon he and Nathan could be drawn in and find themselves spending many early morning hours still loafing on the 21 couches.

When I returned to 21 I was amazed to find the living room empty. I searched the bedrooms, but not even Susie was around. There was not even anyone passed out on the couch. I grew alarmed and plopped down in the living room, taking in the unnatural quiet, all still but for the cockroaches, who seemed to enjoy having the place to themselves.

A few minutes of silence and the door flew open. In stormed Angela, in a black leather jacket, miniskirt, and black combat boots. Her thick brown hair flew in every direction and she glanced wildly about the room.

"Are they here?"

"Everybody's gone."

"But Michael and Susie? Are *they* here?" I could barely understand what Angela was saying as she stumbled over herself to tell what had happened. She explained that they had gotten a call a couple hours earlier about a hippie gathering in the woods and everyone had gone up to it. They had fought their way through the muddy paths to find a little tribe of hippies ("Not actually hippies, though, those fucking Frisbee assholes," she explained, meaning the more hateful quasi-hippie tribe of the Preppy Deadheads, aka the Frisbee Team) huddled around a little campfire and, it seemed, tripping. Seeing them from a distance, someone had the idea to break into a war cry and rush out of the woods at them. The whole group had followed, and the gang around the campfire, no doubt overcome by drug hallucinations, fled. The Dicks settled in and, despite the cold and drizzle, rather enjoyed the campfire, and the food and bourbon the Frisbee people had abandoned. Twenty minutes later, however, a few of them returned and started pelting the Dicks with clumps of mud.

At that point, bedlam broke out. Angela had fled back into the woods with Susie and Michael (the Krishna escapee), who, as best as I could understand, started trying to make out with her (Angela) against a tree. That's what I thought she was saying, but as the story progressed and whatever she had consumed kicked in, her words became more scrambled and impossible to make sense of. I was able to gather that she had torn herself free of the makeout attempt and run away, which caused Susie and Michael to violently mock her as she fled.

"They said those things! Why did they say them?" she asked me.

"What did they say?"

She looked directly at me in a way that made me shudder. "You are so sweet to pretend you don't know."

"Okay."

She kept looking at me. I felt myself becoming intensely uncomfortable, like something I had eaten hours before was just going wrong in my stomach. "You're the only person here who actually listens," she said. "You're not a freak like the rest of this crowd."

I am too! I wanted to protest, but I noticed her face moving closer to mine. I had never seen a face up so close before, like the face was blocking the sun, eclipsing the world. The quiet of the room became a roar of silence, an intensity of antisound. I thought I heard the footsteps of a cockroach stopping to scratch himself on the opposite wall. And suddenly, there she was. And the walls that had seemed impregnable, looming over my life for so many years, came tumbling down.

At some point just before dawn, while Angela slept in my bed, I heard people shuffle into the living room. They murmured to each other, like a weary defeated army, and collapsed in piles around the house. I braced myself for someone to barge in and catch us there, but mercifully, on this night, no one did.

I lay awake all night, in the hours following the brief bustle of activity. Did I feel different? I examined myself and thought, on the whole, my spirit did seem a bit lighter. I had stepped through a door that I had given up hope of ever stepping through, but on the other side found a world that looked almost identical to the world I had left behind.

Would Angela have expectations of me now? Watching her sleep, I assumed she would, but what could they be? And how would this be explained to Susie? Angela was one of her best friends. Would she be angry? Were we supposed to get permission? And what of the rest of the group—the Supreme Dicks' code of celibacy was often invoked (although still unexplained), and as best I could tell it was actually followed.

The words *boyfriend, girlfriend,* and *relationship,* if invoked at all in 21, were seen as some distant—and laughable—phenomena, like the fox-trot or the SALT II Treaty. "Dates" and "dating" were artifacts of some lost culture, as close to our lives as sock hops and village yentas.

There were, here and there within our group, examples of various forms of attachment, but if explained at all, they were termed "hanging out." Jerome generally crashed in Monica's room, but Jerome wasn't, as he often said, a Dick; he was in the band that was the most closely allied with the Dicks, the Loneliest Christmas Tree. Tim Fall, it was said, hung out with a girl who lived in Prescott House, but Tim, with his documentary missions, was very much an iconoclast within the house and in any case, whoever the girl was, no one ever saw her. Arthur, the angry punk, lived with a woman in a house off-campus, but he was too much of a raw force to be affected by philosophy, whatever the philosophy behind celibacy was.

As I started to panic about how I would break the news that Angela and I were now—what? Going out? Hanging out? Friends?—the person in question stirred. Through the dawn light she looked up at me and said, "Hey, do you mind? I sleep alone."

"Oh, right. I wasn't really sleeping. . . ."

She sat up. "I need the bed," she snapped.

"Oh, sure." I backed out onto the floor. "Right, I'll just, I guess, see what's going on."

"Cool." She instantly fell back asleep. I quietly dressed and crept out of the room, and stepping over a few sleeping figures on the living room floor, I slipped out of the mod. Outside the ground crackled from the morning dew frozen on the sidewalk. The campus was still bitter cold. I wandered around, wondering how many hours it would be before Zach and Nathan awoke and I could tell them what had happened. I ended up sitting in the Bridge Café, trying to make sense of Nietzsche's *The Birth of*

Tragedy and reflecting that all in all, I did, in fact, feel very much a different person, although I couldn't quite say how.

When I returned later that morning, my bed was empty. I went up to Susie's room to see if Angela might be there, but the second floor was still. I didn't see her again until five that night when Angela slunk into the living room and flung herself down in the only unoccupied spot available, on the arm of the couch next to me, without a glance my way. As she slumped against the wall behind me, saying nothing, I studied the faces around me for any glimmer that someone else noticed that the fabric of my universe had been torn open, but no one registered a thing.

Later, as Angela stomped up to Susie's room, the journey to Denny's still hung in the air, resisting all of our attempts to change the subject and remaining at the front of our minds. But even as Denny's seemed the only solution to our growing hunger pangs, the fact loomed that there were only five seats in Jon's car and there were twenty-nine of us. The thought must have occurred to many that we would need another plan, but having put an idea on the table we were powerless to alter or even abandon it. Suggesting a solution to the problem would have made one appear all horrible things at once—anxious, nervous, practical, out of sync. So the wet clay of the Denny's trip hardened, its impossibility paradoxically sealing its dominance.

Finally, it was Ox who offered a solution. "I think only people with pure blue orgone should be allowed to go."

There were ahhhhhs and nods around the room. "Totally." "That makes sense."

"But how"—a brazen fit of curiosity impelled me to open my mouth—"how do we know what color everyone's orgone is?"

Ox nodded and stared at me. "Right. Right. Really. Well, everyone who has been militant in their celibacy and vegetarianism should be blue, or mostly blue."

I gulped, wondering if that had been directed at me. But Liz broke in, "Well, Tom can't go, then!"

"And Angela's door was locked last night!"

Accusations flew of failed celibacy and hamburger sightings. As the conversation grew heated and fingers were pointed, several stomped out in anger. Susie sneered that celibacy was just some joke Jon had thought up because he was afraid of girls. Friar Tom announced that he had never claimed to be celibate and none of us understood anything, that "Reich was about love," and much more importantly, Brooke from the Black Light mod was having a photo show in the library and he was going to check it out all by himself and if he ended up in anyone's bed, we'd see whose orgone was stronger tomorrow.

As Friar Tom left the mod in a swirl of scarves and sequins, I counted the number of people remaining; we were down to twenty-five. So I had a one-in-five chance of getting a ride to Denny's. But could I go without Angela? I still wondered.

While I contemplated, a hush had fallen over the room. Next to me on the couch, Meg muttered, "I didn't know Brooke Jennings was having a show. . . ."

"Is she good?" I whispered.

"The Black Light mod, they are all these really rich New York club kids."

"Ahhh . . ."

"So they always have really good hors d'oeuvres."

I looked around the room. Everyone seemed lost in contemplation. "I mean, really good," Liz said. "Like this artichoke dip with baked Brie on top. . . ."

One by one, people silently rose and began the long work of

layering on sweaters, jackets, scarves, hats, gloves, overcoats, leg warmers, boots, and face masks. By this time, and after a few trips with Jon and Ox to the Salvation Army store in Northampton, I, too, was wrapping myself up like a middle-aged vagrant in Depression-era New York.

Looking like a runaway breadline, two dozen of us staggered and slid over the frosted path. We spilled into the library building's downstairs gallery and found the party well past its height. A few disdainful double takes greeted us as we drifted among the crowd dressed uniformly in black miniskirts, black jeans, black scarves, black tights, black leather jackets, and black leather shoes, quietly chattering, sipping white wine, and studying the black-and-white photos of what appeared to be body parts—knees, earlobes, and I thought I made out a tongue, blurry in intense close-up.

Our group marched directly through the room straight to the hors d'oeuvre table. As we climbed over each other to grope at the remaining vestiges, conversation halted completely, the only sounds coming from the New Order album playing on a boom box in the corner. Locustlike we quickly demolished every bit of food left from a spread that, to our disgust, turned out to be only carrot and celery sticks and cheese cubes.

The hush was broken as Tim Fall finally called out, "Brooke, where's the baked Brie? This show sucks!"

A nervous titter ruffled the room. I tried to ignore the stares of annoyance, but my friends seemed to be enjoying the spectacle. "If you can't afford a decent spread, you shouldn't be showing your work," Arthur barked, his mouth full of carrots.

Brooke, the artist, slinked her way over to Jon. Petite and elegant in a black microminiskirt, leggings, a baggy black sweater, and pixieish asymmetrical blond hair, she had poise that made her seem like a creature from another planet, or another generation at least.

"Jon," she said. "So lovely to see you."

"Hi. Great art, Brooke."

"Tell me, Jon, darling, haven't I always stuck up for you guys?"

"Totally. We just wanted to support your opening!"

"Uh-huh."

"Yeah, we love art."

Brooke looked exasperated and stared at him. Jon smiled and reached for a handful of celery.

Struggling to maintain her air of nonchalance, she smiled up at Jon, holding his gaze. He smiled back, his hulking frame, bound in an overcoat and several sweaters, towering over her.

"Enjoy the party. Thanks for coming, really. Really, I mean it," she finally said.

"Oh, really? Thanks, Brooke. Oh, actually we were just about to leave. I guess you don't really have much food here." Jon giggled.

"Oh, no. Please, stay. Come, let me show you around." She proceeded to give us all a tour of her work, describing, one by one, the motivation behind each piece. "In this one, I wanted to decontextualize Man Ray. To be Man Ray's gaze, without being Man Ray, if you follow me. To show that the ownership of the gaze, separated from its artistic pretensions, derives from a fascist impulse to colonize that which it beholds. Do you love it?"

Five minutes later we filed upstairs into the Airport Lounge, which in the winter was the school's central (and only) common area. Located just outside the library and snack bar, the Lounge was so named because it resembled a circa-1973 TWA waiting area one might find in the Evansville, Indiana, airport. The lounge was built around a conversation circle of orange foam couches, which we flung ourselves on, shedding layers of clothing and scaring off the half-dozen people who had been there studying.

"Can you guys be quiet?" one girl hissed at us.

"Who studies at nine o'clock on a Saturday?" Liz asked.

"Who studies ever?" Arthur said.

"I'm still hungry," Tim moaned. Heads nodded. The snack bar where we could buy (or "liberate" in the pockets of an overcoat while the student clerk read a magazine) cellophane-wrapped tempeh burgers and tofu pitas, we quickly noticed, had closed. People glanced nervously at Jon, having a harder time now disguising their growing desperation for a solution.

"I guess we could go to Denny's," he said softly.

"Yeah, definitely," many agreed, while no one stirred from their place.

"Maybe we should vote for who gets to go in your car," Meg suggested.

Election fever swept the lounge as everyone agreed this was the most equitable system. "All right," Ox announced. "Who votes for Meg?"

Meg's hand went up. "You guys suck," she spat, grabbed her coat, and stormed off.

"How many vote for Michael?" Michael's hand went up.

"How many vote for Angela?" I considered for a moment raising my hand in support of her, but in the end let her nomination go forward with only her own vote. She made no acknowledgment of my betrayal, which confused me all the more.

At the end of the balloting, we were all tied with one vote each, except for Tim, who got no votes after having given his own to Friar Tom, who had stormed off hours before and wasn't there to vote for himself. We broke into bickering about how to conduct another round of voting before conversation drifted to the topic of Steve Shavel's return. Jerome had heard a rumor that he had been spotted in Northampton, supposedly having dinner at Beardsley's, the town's expensive restaurant, with a table of Smith girls and, it seemed, their parents. While it was considered possible that he was hiding at Smith, people were incredulous at the idea that he would so brazenly wander around Northampton.

"He really does love Beardsley's," Ox said.

The discussion was interrupted by the appearance of Annette, a second-year who was universally noted as the most beautiful girl at Hampshire, famed for her resemblance to Cleopatra. Annette lived in the Critical Theory Mod, and her group, along with the Black Light kids, was one of the few still more or less tolerant of the Dicks. Despite her renown, Annette, for some reason probably having to do with her perpetual air of disgust with life itself, was friendly with us and had even dropped in at 21 on occasion. If you thought life was that miserable, Steve Shavel later theorized, where better to spend it than with us?

"Are any of you going to kill yourself tonight?" she asked, looking us over with approving distaste.

"Maybe. It's looking like we're never going to eat, so we might have to," Jon answered. "What about you, Annette?"

"I've vowed never to kill myself before midnight. That way I won't have to wonder if the day could get any worse."

Annette told us that there was a "truly horrible party" going on in Prescott, and suggested we go play music there.

"Really?" Jon asked. "Are they Dicks fans?"

"I'm sure they despise you."

"We should check it out, then. I guess we can head to Denny's after that."

Everyone nodded at the good sense of the plan, hunger notwithstanding.

An hour and a half later, having been ejected with our instruments from yet another party, we huddled at the bottom of the Prescott canyon as tiny flakes tumbled down from the sky. Next to me, Angela was panting from the stumble down the stairs, her face flushed with excitement.

"I've never seen snow before," I murmured to her.

She stopped smiling and looked me dead in the eye. "I don't really need for us to talk now, okay?"

"Yeah, totally."

We all stood and looked at each other, arms full, shivering and unsure of what to do.

"I guess we could go to Denny's, maybe," Jon said.

But before we could revisit that question, we marched back through to 21 to drop off the instruments. By the time we unloaded, it was half past one and I noticed now that I was really, truly hungry. The adrenaline of the past hour had masked my empty stomach, but now I was aware of a deep pain and looked vainly around the room for food, seeing only plates of half-eaten tofu scrambles perched on the edges of sofas and the floor. By now I had learned better than to look in the refrigerator or cupboard for food—having been attacked by the creatures dwelling inside more than a couple times.

I glanced around the room and caught others with looks of unease on their faces. It occurred to me that the dining hall and tavern were now closed. And there were *still* sixteen of us.

"Well, I guess we probably should think about going to Denny's now," Ox said. We all nodded and then sat down to reclaim the seats we'd been in when the Denny's subject had first been raised seven hours before.

With a solution still impossible to conceive, random topics again drifted through the room. The hungrier we got, the more ridiculous it became that we weren't moving, and the harder it became to resolve the issue. The more desperate the cause was, the more anxious one became about it. That anxiety caused an inversely proportional need to keep your mouth shut so as not to allow yourself to look at all anxious. The room was engulfed in manic chattering about school gossip while we fought to steer clear of the subject on our minds.

As we discussed Susie's upcoming meeting with her advisor (the first in a year; in her third year at Hampshire, Susie was widely celebrated for never having completed a class or a Div I), I began to feel I might be going insane. The thought of getting to Denny's gnawed away; I could feel the hunger circulating around the room, and yet no one would mention it.

Finally Jon said, "Well, I don't really need to go to Denny's. It's cool if you guys want to go without me."

"Nobody wants you to come, but we need your car," Marilyn reminded him. Jon would never in a million years let anyone borrow his car.

"Oh, right. I guess so." He sat thinking. Eyes turned attentively to him. "You guys know Larry Ogletree is going for the world's hot dog eating record?"

We had heard that. Larry Ogletree was the immensely large (six-foot-three and many hundreds of pounds) bearded fourth-year, famed for the vast trays of food he demolished at the dining hall every night. He had recently declared his intention to break the world's record for most hot dogs consumed in a minute. The local Stop & Shop had been signed on to sponsor his heroic attempt, hosting the event in its parking lot and supplying the hot dogs.

"He's doing it tomorrow. We should check him out," Jon continued.

"Don't you think he's sleeping before the big day?"

"He's probably up training all night. . . ."

Slowly we rose again, gathering ourselves for a trip to the Merrill House dorm where Ogletree lived.

"Maybe if he's training, there'll be a lot of leftovers around . . . ," Ox threw out.

"Yeah, but what are we going to do with hot dogs?" Monica said, referring to our vegetarianism.

"Yeah, that's a good point." Ox nodded. Inexorably we redressed ourselves for the cold and filed out the door.

At two A.M., all was quiet in Merrill House. We caused a sizable racket climbing the stairwell, as the fifteen of us stomped in, in our boots, laughing and hooting. When we filed into Ogletree's hall, C-3, we were amazed to find his door closed and no sign of life anywhere.

Our group barely squeezed in, and the noise of our titters and embarrassed chuckles resounded off the walls, making the space roar like the Indianapolis Speedway. We squeezed in to stare at Ogletree's door. No sound came from within. We stood in silence for a moment, searching for a next move. Finally, Ox solved the problem by knocking.

From behind the door, we heard what sounded like a stampede of miniature buffalo. And then a deep, booming bellow called out, "What the hell is it?"

"Ogletree!" Jon said. "Are you up?"

A minute later the door flew open. Ogletree, a blanket wrapped around his massive frame, stood panting before us, looking a bit like the animated version of Bluto from the *Popeye* strips. He eyed us with such hate, I started to back away toward the door.

"What are you fucking doing here?"

"Oh, Ogletree." Jon smiled. "We thought you'd be training."

"Training? I'm sleeping! Tomorrow's the day!"

"Well, we just wanted to come and support you."

His hallmates began waking up, hollering at us to get out or they'd call security. Ogletree, set off balance by Jon's forward manner, invited us in to hang out and hear about his preparations. Six of us squeezed into the room with him while the rest stayed in the hall, bickering with the hallmates.

"Don't you guys have anyplace to go?" one girl in a bathrobe yelled.

"Oh, no. Not really," Ox said. "Our mod is really depressing."

The girl looked at me with a face wrenched up like she was

about to spit out the sour taste in her mouth. "You assholes are pathetic. Why didn't you all kill yourselves with your friend?"

I recoiled and glanced at Ox, hoping he'd explain what that meant, but he merely nodded and said, "Oh, right. We should. Definitely."

About ten minutes later, two members of campus security pushed their way into the hall. A Tweedledee, Tweedledum pair, both shortish, with faces bright pink from the night air, they nodded sagely to each other when they saw us. "Where's Jon?" said the shorter of the two.

We directed them to Ogletree's room, which they somehow shoved inside. "I shouldn't get my name taken again this semester," Marilyn said, and walked out of the hall. A couple others followed.

"What happens if they take your name?" I asked Angela, who was again standing beside me, having rejoined the group.

"You've never had security take your name?" she cooed. "Oh, this is exciting!" She gave my arm a little rub and I looked at her. She smiled at me and I became very confused.

From inside Ogletree's room we heard security arguing with Jon and Tim. "Why do you guys always have to start something? Why can't we have just one night without trouble from you?"

"We're just being supportive!"

"You think Larry needs this kinda support? You think seeing you freaks in the middle of the night is gonna help him swallow any more dogs?"

Ogletree vaguely defended us but the rest of his hallmates looked ready to riot. "Get them out of here!" someone yelled.

The security officers eventually herded us all, step by step, down the stairs and out of the dorm. As we shivered in the cold they made us show them our campus IDs and they recorded our names in a little notepad. About two-thirds of us didn't have IDs, which, in the case of Jon, Dan, Jim, Angela, and some others, was not a problem, as they were already on intimate terms with the officers, whom they called Paul and Mike. "You know you have to carry your ID at all times on campus?"

"Totally, Mike. We will."

"Then why do we have to go through this every time?"

For the rest, however, the request set off a series of confusions that took at least half an hour to sort out. Their questioning revealed to me, for the first time, who among us actually went to school here. We turned out to be a fairly even mix of unenrolled students, ex-students, visitors from out of town, and, it turned out, two punks who went to Amherst High. This produced long queries of "Who's responsible for this one? Whose guest is he?"

Our non-Hampshire student majority were warned that they should not step foot on campus again without first registering with security and having someone sign them in. By the time Paul and Mike came across the high school kids, they were so flummoxed and put out at the thought of having to call their parents that they let them off with a warning to never ever come back again.

When it was finally my turn, Paul and Mike took my ID and looked me up and down. "You're a first-year. What are you doing with this lot?"

"They're my friends." I shrugged.

"Well, you need to get new ones." Paul put his face close to mine, the mist of his breath wafting across my skin. "Listen, the days of the Supreme Dicks are over, kid. The school's had enough of these assholes, and by next year they are all gonna be gone. Do yourself a favor and don't go down the tubes with them."

I nodded and looked at Jon and Ox. "It's true, Rich. You better run."

For the next couple hours, we stood outside the dorm in the

cold, again debating how we might get to Denny's, semiplausi-
ble schemes derailed by a new topic and each conversation running down another rabbit hole. Every few minutes an irate voice
would yell, "SHUT THE FUCK UP!" from the dorm windows
above.

By four-thirty cold and mounting exhaustion urged me to
walk away—as some others had done—and go back to the mod.
However, the thought of appearing anxious, of missing any of the
action, made quitting unthinkable, as deeply painful as this journey had become. There were seven of us left standing in the cold;
our number had been whittled down but we were still too many.

The first traces of thin, reedy light appeared behind the quad.
I winced as the world became disturbingly visible. The trash-
strewn, patchy Merrill House lawn we were standing on looked
unspeakably tawdry in this first light. We all fell silent. Jon finally
said, "I guess maybe Denny's was a bad idea."

No one said a word. Then Angela spat, "Fuck you, guys," and
stomped off, giving me, I imagined, an especially accusatory
glare.

In the dawn light, we watched her walk out of the quad, across
the main campus road, and down the path behind the library leading to the Greenwich House woods. As she disappeared from
sight Ox murmured, "I guess we could fit in Jon's car now. . . ."

Ninety minutes later, at around seven in the morning, with
Marilyn lying across our laps in the back and two people squeezed
into the front passenger seat, we pulled into Denny's in Chicopee.
A couple of trucks idled in the parking lot, steam pouring from
their exhausts. The restaurant was a quarter full with men in jackets, ties, or work uniforms sitting alone and reading newspapers.
After the standard million or so questions to the waitress from Jon
about what was made with animal fat and what was cooked on the
same grill as the meat, we ate our bowls of cornflakes in silence.

Finally Ox spoke up. "This was definitely worth it. I'm really glad we came."

The night after our Denny's trip word drifted back to 21. We learned that Larry Ogletree had failed to capture the world's record for most hot dogs consumed in a minute, falling short by a single heartbreaking dog.

CHAPTER SEVEN

The Legend

I n dribs and drabs, around the living room and during nights spent talking over cardboard cups of drip coffee in the Bridge Café, the full story of the Supreme Dicks began to emerge.

The conversation always started with my question "Why do people hate you so much?" In my first months I began to sense an empty space in Dick history. Somewhere in all our conversations was a void that the residents of 21 often walked right up to but then scurried back from with an uncomfortable giggle.

At first there were references to "after what happened last year" and allusions to three members of the group who were no longer present, Billy, Stan, and Joel, who had once played a huge role in Supreme Dicks life.

But nothing I had heard explained the intensity of the hatred that punched us in the face every time we left 21. Clearly the group had bugged many in its time. Their refusal to take anything even a little bit seriously got under the skin of the school's more earnest sorts—the activists, the alternative music nerds. But in these days, the earnest activists still remained a minority; the only thing the bulk of the campus took with true seriousness was comparing the seed levels of different marijuana strands.

By the end of the semester I had managed to piece together the full story; the curtain fell from Dick history and I began to understand that I had fallen in with a group that wasn't just unpopular but despised on a primal level by a school otherwise dedicated to peace, love, and apathy.

The Supreme Dicks had come together three years before I arrived, somewhere around 1982–3 (dates varied according to the telling). By all accounts the group began gathering in an earlier mod where Jon, Ox, Tim, and Arthur had lived. They came from different tribes—Jon had been a New Wave skateboarder when he first landed on Hampshire's shores, Ox a devout Deadhead, Jon a hippie avant-gardist, Arthur a working-class punk. The group was rounded out by Joel Jacobs aka Joel Joel, a roly-poly jester, whose gigantic, perpetual broken-toothed grin had the power to unnerve all who looked upon him, leaving them shaken for days as if they had walked away from a car crash. Joel Joel lurked around campus in tandem with Stan Moser, a dark, brooding, mop-headed, emaciated native of the Amherst area.

The group initially came together as a loose conclave, united by a low-grade destructive impulse, a lack of ambition, and nocturnal schedules. None of these traits was particularly remarkable in Hampshire of the early eighties, when the school was dominated by a checked-out breed of hippies, the angsty dregs of the last days of punk rock, and a smattering of rich New York downtown types. The group coalesced around a disdain for any organized anything (movements, seminars, parties, schedules) and a common aesthetic—layers of secondhand rags later described as "old man clothes." Their early jam sessions were flailing attempts at postpunk intensity, undermined by a common lack of willingness to take basics such as rehearsing or learning songs seriously. The musical side of the group was augmented by Joel Joel and Stan's merry pranksterism, which was initially limited to merely bugging people around the dorm halls.

With the addition of Steve Shavel, the movement began to take on philosophical underpinnings. A tall, lanky philosophy student, Steve was a notable figure around campus in his unvaried attire of gray cardigan sweater, white oxford shirt, skinny tie, and red Converse high-tops.

Steve came into the Dicks' life one morning when Ox wandered into the lounge of Dakin Hall and found Steve asleep on the couch with a young waiflike girl. For the next several mornings, Ox awoke to find this strange older person (Steve at this point had already been at Hampshire well more than the traditional four years) asleep on the tiny lounge couch, head to toe with the same girl, and he'd give the slumbering pair a nod as he took his tea with soy milk back to his room. On the third day, Ox was mixing his tea when a deep and sonorous tone called from the couch, "I say, that's not Lapsang souchong by any chance?"

"Oh, yeah." Ox tried not to stare at the half-dressed girl at Steve's feet. "It is."

"Say there, could I get a cup of that? With sugar and just a tiny bit of half-and-half, please? And not too hot."

Ox fixed Steve his tea and they chatted as Rose—Steve's friend—slept. When Ox got around to asking why the pair slept every night on a threadbare, tiny, dilapidated couch that was uncomfortable to even sit on, Steve explained that he was a follower of the teachings of Wilhelm Reich. He had taken a vow of celibacy and was enjoying, as he described it, a "spiritual friendship" with the sleeping Rose; together they had committed to a path of "problematizing" his celibacy. "It's very dangerous work. We're walking right on the spiritual razor's edge. One has to stay above suspicion." And thus they only slept together in public places so there could be no doubt that Steve's celibacy was beyond reproach.

Steve was then in his fifth to seventh year at Hampshire—although he claimed that even to keep track of such numbers was to accept a hierarchic system where abstract notions of time were used as instruments of control. Since his first year, Steve had devoted himself to philosophy, only taking classes from Hampshire professor Mark Adler, who conveniently held his classes at night. For the past several years, Steve had been working on his Div III, a paper on Ludwig Wittgenstein's *Tractatus Logico-Philosophicus*. He claimed his work had been slowed by the fact that there were no decent translations available in English, and he read very little German.

Steve soon became a regular among the still loose confederation (and lost Rose to several of the group who hadn't yet taken any vows of celibacy), joining jam sessions with his tabletop slide guitar and devising a philosophical rationale for the increasingly cantankerous, discordant sound coming from the jam; shortly after Steve's arrival the group began expressing their formula of sexual sublimation through music.

Since Dick philosophy held that it was impossible to achieve Wilhelm Reich's orgone-energy-liberating seven-stage orgasm in corrupted modern society, those desiring orgone purification had no choice but to seek other outlets. Somehow in these conversations, the Dicks determined that the music thrashed out in their jam sessions—musical throbbings that were becoming increasingly turgid, wordless, and melody-neutral—was in fact a sublimated expression of the stagnant orgone energy within the band members; Dick music was the only acceptable way to regain the flow of orgone. The more discordant it was and the more it sounded to the untrained ear like random noise, the more it tapped into those spiritual/physiological needs. So went the theory.

The late-night jams in Jon's living room grew louder. Some say that the early jams actually sounded like songs, but by the end of their first semester together the music had evolved into "pure noise" (although, it was said, the truest adepts could hear the songs within, like a Magic Eye painting, and the harmonies were audible to a chosen few). The music was not quite a random cacophony; the various players worked toward a common throbbing sound that could not be dismissed as random, but neither could its intent be discerned or explained.

The cacophony grew so loud that it drew what may have been the first noise complaints in Hampshire College history. The early visits by security seemed merely amusing oddities and inspired the group to play all the louder at ever more obscure hours of the night. The security drop-bys, however, soon turned into notes from the house office, which became meetings with the house office and escalating tensions between red-faced administrators and the smirking Dicks, who claimed not to understand what the problem was.

Wanting to extend their influence beyond merely annoying their neighbors, the group soon began to perform around campus. They would set up in the dorm laundry room, the Art Barn, or anyplace where their presence would ultimately become obnoxious, drawing the usual call from campus security. The various tellers of this tale reminded me that at this time in Hampshire history for people to call campus security "was, like, insane." Campus security, as far as anyone knew, existed only to help people who were locked out of the rooms and too stupid to know how to card the door. The Dicks had found a way to get under Hampshire's skin, by bringing out the one side of itself it liked to pretend didn't exist—its uptightness. It was an uncomfortable feeling, for a campus full of apathetic loafers, hippie dreamers, and nightclubbing hedonists to find themselves suddenly phoning security and demanding peace and quiet. (Soon enough, though, calling up security crackdowns would become many students' proudest moments.)

Once the band members stopped playing and began wandering the campus together, they began to get into ever more colorful chases with the campus law. Most famed of these was the Great Bell Theft of May 1984. The school was still just a decade old and the students poured all their yearnings for tradition into the Division Free Bell. Donated by an early alum who had stripped it from his family yacht, the bell hung about twenty-five feet in the air between two concrete pillars in front of the library. After turning in his Div III project, each Hampshire student would take a final meeting with his advisory committee, which would either pass him and thus grant him his diploma or ask him to return for another semester of work. (In my years at Hampshire, I can count on one hand the number of times I heard of the latter occurring.)

As the student sat nervously in his final meeting, his friends would congregate outside the library with champagne, saluting him as he appeared at last to ring the Division Free Bell. The bell was treated with a mystical aura; anyone who rang it prematurely was said to have cursed his chance to graduate. One night in our first semester, Zach, Nathan, and I decided to ring it, "just to practice." Within moments half the library poured outside, security appeared, and we were bodily pulled from the bell rope seconds before a riot erupted.

Two years before I arrived at Hampshire, Steve Shavel decided to steal the bell. It was a week before the 1984 graduation, the height of bell-ringing season, when Steve noticed a stack of platforms sitting on the lawn outside the library, waiting to become the graduation stage. Late that night, a dozen or so members of Dick society crept out under the cover of darkness and began stacking the platforms on top of each other, until they were able to scale the entire height of the columns and climb up to the bell.

They later recalled the superhuman strength summoned in the final stages to pass the heavy platform hand-to-hand some twenty feet to the top. Several times they dropped platforms from the heights, setting off thunderous explosions when they hit the ground, but remarkably security never appeared. When they reached the bell, Arthur brought his tools and wrenched it from its housing.

The next morning, the greatest manhunt in Hampshire history began; in fact it was the first manhunt in the history of the heretofore anarchic campus. With the donor alum about to make his annual trip to visit his bequest, the dean of students rounded up the usual suspects, summoning, so legend goes, the campus's most conspicuous characters, and demanded that they find and rat out the bell thieves or be expelled themselves. Jon, Ox, Steve, Tim, Arthur, and the rest were one by one brought into the dean's interrogation chambers (his conference room) and they recited their denials under withering glares. Meanwhile, hidden inside a bass drum, the bell was smuggled off-campus to a friend's apartment in Northampton just as the house-to-house searches began.

Inevitably, with so many people involved in the theft, Steve's name was passed along to the authorities. When he realized the dean knew the entire story, right up to the bass drum, Steve switched from denial to a proud defense of the heist, claiming the bell was a symbol of the hierarchical oppression that Hampshire had been created to fight.

Sadly for Steve, the uprising he had hoped to provoke was drowned out by the outraged voices of students who had been denied their turn at a bell-ringing party. Ultimately, the bell's return was negotiated but the adventure was the first of many that the Dicks would pull off, achieving the unheard-of feat of enraging the administration and the students simultaneously. Many more such milestones would follow.

In the fall of '85, once the musical element of the Dicks society had begun to get under the school's skin, the group's theatrical wing, led by Joel Joel and Stan Moser, began to stir up feelings of outright revulsion. Hampshire had a closed-circuit TV station and a small studio in the library basement that broadcast to In-Tran, the school's internal cable channel, which fed into every mod and dorm lounge. (The school's founding documents included many futuristic elements that in the eighties still smacked of overindulgence in sci-fi utopianism. Leading among these was the plan to hook every room in the school to a central computer network. All dorm rooms on campus were wired to this network a full decade before a single student would own a personal computer.)

Joel and Stan broadcast a weekly show called *Top of the Two,* which tested Hampshire's boundaries of taste with gruesome stunts and theater pieces. It was an upleasant awakening for a school that prided itself on a blasé shock-the-bourgeoisie attitude to suddenly learn that it was capable of being shocked and even offended. This all the more increased the growing hatred toward those who brought the limits of their tolerance to their attention.

While the TV show could be turned off, Joel and Stan began spreading their message off-screen. One afternoon, with his roly-poly Cheshire-cat grin, Joel Joel appeared at dinner in the dining hall's back room and announced a special *Top of the Two*/Supreme Dick political action. That week, he wheezed, the show would sponsor a telethon—to be specific, a spermathon—for South Africa, a benefit concert wherein students would be encouraged to bring their ejaculate to the show, which Dave would drink in support of the suffering people living under apartheid. And to demonstrate his point, he produced a clear plastic bag containing, to all appearances, semen, climbed atop a table, and drank it.

Had such an incident occurred three or four years before this time, it would have been laughed off. Three or four years later, Joel would have been shoved into a gunnysack, taken to the nearest bridge, and dropped into the river, his dorm room contents donated to Goodwill. But in 1985 the school had no provisions for this type of emergency. And so, several weeks later, Dave was able to stage a sequel, climbing on a chair in the back room of the dining hall and announcing *Top of the Two*'s Shitathon for the Contras.

When one looks back at the trail that led up to these disasters, one can see individuals, groups, nations careening down roads that clearly lead to nowhere but catastrophe. Taking stock, most of the people I knew in that era seemed, on any typical day, headed for disaster. But more often than not, the disaster never arrived. Friends whirling out of control somehow took another fork in the road at the last second, or managed to just keep plummeting downhill forever, never to fly off the inevitable cliff, never to hit the rocky bottom.

While in retrospect, it seems clear that something terrible had to come from the trajectory the Dicks were on, by all accounts they had no reason to think that something terrible actually *would* happen. What now seems predetermined would have at the time seemed a ridiculous notion; they were young, away at college, stirring things up as youth will do. What bad could happen? But disaster did come, and in a much worse form than even the Dicks' worst enemies would have predicted.

All through the 1985–86 school year tensions mounted between the Dicks, the administration, and a vocal anti-Dick segment of the students. The Dick jams grew louder. The complaints grew more frequent. The spectacles more disgusting. The Dick mods, 21 and Jon's in Enfield House, were placed on probation.

Each member was called regularly to the offices of the deans of students and housing on various infractions and the threats grew stronger. Until, finally, the event occurred that abruptly and forever ended the game.

Stan Moser had a little brother named Billy, a senior at Amherst High, who frequently visited the Dick mods and had become something of a mascot to the group. On an April episode of *Top of the Two,* Billy stepped forward and announced that he wanted to make a speech. Cameras rolling, broadcasting live to the campus, Billy decried the school's Gestapo administration and its oppression of his Supreme Dick brothers. Proclaiming solidarity against Dick persecution, Billy announced that he would drink a glass of cyanide-laced Kool-Aid and end his life.

Thinking the speech was a joke, the others in the studio laughed and cheered Billy on as he lifted the glass to his lips. They continued applauding, and the cameras continued rolling, as he dropped to the floor and writhed around in what they thought were mock seizures. Within moments the applause died, as Billy's body stopped spinning and settled motionless in the middle of the studio floor.

The aftermath was the biggest PR spectacle the school had ever known. The campus was flooded by TV crews from around the world who picked up the bizarre story. The Dicks, on orders from the administration and the local police, stayed off-camera and away from the reports, which were filled with tales of a mini–Jim Jones drug cult and weeping images of the traumatized students who had watched the show live.

When the media fury died down and the TV vans left, the Dicks suddenly found themselves alone on a very isolated campus with a very angry administration and a thousand students who looked upon them no longer just as annoying miscreants but as fratricidal inhuman freaks. A zero-tolerance regime fell into place.

When the band tried to play under the solar panels, security was there before they could plug in. When they made noise in the mod at night, security instantly materialized. The Enfield House office documented every health-code, cleanliness, and "community standards" violation. When they showed their faces in the Airport Lounge, conversation stopped and they were greeted with angry glares.

And then came Spring Jam. Halloween and the spring concert were the High Holy Days of the Hampshire calendar. For a full day each April, a giant music festival was held and every Hampshire band was given a slot to play on a stage behind the library. The entire campus assembled, along with thousands from neighboring schools and the surrounding area. It was held that this was an era when Hampshire produced giants of alternative music. That spring, the lineup included the greats: Beatrice, the Lonely Moans, Five Dumb Broads, Jersey Slim and the Prescott Playboys, the Loneliest Christmas Tree, and Jambone were all on the bill. As were the Supreme Dicks.

It still was not yet in Hampshire's DNA to quash anyone's ability to speak or perform in public. The need or desire had never come up before. And if eyebrows were raised by the Dick name in a prime-time late-afternoon slot on the bill, no one dared suggest that the school should not let them play. That, people would have said, would be fascism. And *that* still lay in the mists of Hampshire's future.

And so at five P.M., the Dicks climbed to the stage. It started out as a fairly typical show, discordant noise, disparate strains of melody. Jon barely audible, gulping out the words to the Dicks' one actual song, "I'm in Love with a Vegetable," a tribute to life-support cause célèbre Karen Ann Quinlan. And then Stan came to the stage.

At first it wasn't clear, over the music, what he was hollering about. But as he repeated his refrain and the words "Billy died for you," the crowd erupted in horror and revulsion.

The semester quickly lurched to a close. Joel and Stan were removed from campus. Jon's mod was disbanded. And the Dick joke became no longer a public spectacle but a weird, underground, whispered-about dirty secret.

CHAPTER EIGHT

Jan Term

"So you're saying passing only two classes is good?" My father stared at my evaluations, held them up to the light, turned them over, and inspected their backs, searching for something more to show for a semester of college.

"I'd say it's pretty good. Not stupendous, but very respectable, certainly." My father looked at me. "You have to remember with the Hampshire system, the vast majority of what we do never shows up on paper." I went on to explain the subtleties and nuances of our academic model—the Divisional requirements, the personal relationship with your advisor, the premium placed on exploration, ultimately leading to a final project into which I'd pour all the vast accumulation of my Hampshire years—not just in class but, far more important, my life experience.

My father rubbed his eyes and shook his head. "Well, at least this Emerson and Nietzsche professor seems to be pretty excited about you. . . ."

"Yes, we really hit it off." I didn't have the heart to tell him that that professor thought he was writing an evaluation for someone else, or to fill him in on what a stroke of ridiculous luck it was that I finished even two classes; in fact how close I had come to not finishing any.

Back at 21, as first semester entered its final days, a vague apprehension seeped into the corners of our lives, as a steady trickle of rumors reached us about the administration's rapidly deteriorating tolerance for Dick Nation. "They've driven us underground," Arthur reported. "Now they'll spray the poison."

Monica, who had, amazingly, transferred from Radcliffe and thus sometimes, it seemed, alone of the group still had a foot rooted in reality, had taken me aside one night and asked me if I had been going to class at all. "You know, you might want to try and finish one if you can, just to, like, show them you're trying?" she said. "That might help later."

"But no one else seems to care about that."

Monica nodded and looked solemn. "Well, you know, Rich. Most of these guys are in their, like, fifth or sixth years. Most of them know they're never going to graduate, they're just hanging out until someone figures out where to hang out next. But it's different for you. This is just your first year." She looked at me. I looked at my shoes and nodded. I didn't want it to be different for me.

"What about you?" I asked.

"Oh, I'm outta here at the end of this year."

"Aren't you only a third-year?"

"Yeah, but I've had enough. This place is getting really lame."

A week later, a letter arrived from my advisor. "Don't you think it's time we checked in again?"

The ground was frozen solid, the paths covered with a sheet of ice over which I scurried to meet with Leo, my advisor. In front of the Social Sciences Building people huddled close in little groups of three and four, hopping back and forth on their feet to keep their blood flowing. A class had just ended, and the emerging students raced to get out of the cold. I drew back, horrified at the specter of people bursting from class, diligence furrowing their brows, like a rabid phantom army I'd managed to hide out from for so long I thought they must've died off. But here they were, still alive and flourishing.

I had spent the night before fretting about how I would wake up in time to get to my eleven A.M. appointment. I ransacked 21 and the neighboring hippie mod searching for an alarm clock, but the only timepieces available were an antique grandfather clock in Susie's room and Jerome's Casio digital watch, both of which, it turned out, hadn't worked for years. I canvassed the house to find someone who would be up the next morning but was met with blank stares. Finally, I just stayed awake all night.

Behind his beard, nestled in corduroy, Leo managed to look both amused and concerned. "So I understand you've made some interesting friends."

I slumped into the metal folding chair reserved for students. "I guess so. . . . Can I ask, how did you know who I hang out with?"

"Small campus, Richard." He tilted his head and looked at me over his glasses. "Very, very small. So how are your classes coming?"

"Classes? I mean, good."

"And are you going to complete all four that you signed up for?"

"Well, yeah, I mean . . ." I gaped at him, dumfounded. "But I thought we agreed, you said to focus on finding myself. That was kinda the plan we discussed."

"It looks like you've done a bit too much of that, haven't you?"

I stared at the floor.

"Richard, I'm not going to tell you who you can and can't be friends with. But I have to warn you, the choices you make have a big impact on the community."

"The community cares who I'm friends with?"

"The community cares that people can feel comfortable here. And you have to accept your responsibility for your part of that. I don't need to tell you, things are going to be changing around here."

"Um, really?"

"So how is it coming with your classes?"

In the remaining two weeks of the semester, I returned to class on a nearly regular basis. Waking up obscenely early, I'd sneak out of 21, muttering excuses about going to visit Zach and Nathan. My European Fascism professor did a slight double take the first time he saw me in his classroom, trying to figure out where he knew me from, but continued without questioning me, no doubt thinking that if someone wanted to sit through a discussion of Mussolini's relationship with the Italian peasant class, who was he to stop him?

By my second visit, however, I learned that since I had turned in a couple short papers at the beginning of the semester, I was, in fact, amazingly still in the running to complete the class. All I needed to write was one giant ten-page paper on "the ways the fascist mind-set enters the consciousness of the masses." One night, I locked myself away from the junta in the living room and madly skimmed a copy of Wilhelm Reich's *Mass Psychology of Fascism* that Steve Shavel had left behind.

Three nights later, the night before I was to fly back home for break, I tore myself away from the group again, sat down on the floor, and put my typewriter on a milk carton and wrote the following: "Studying the economic and political factors which lead to the rise of a fascist regime can only take us so far. To truly understand what turns a mass of people to fascism we must look at the deeper subconscious conditions of their lives." At four A.M., having waxed poetic about the subconscious repressed sexuality of the German people, by way of Reich, I paper-clipped ten sheets together and attached a note to the professor reading, "Sorry to be so late. Had trouble finding a new typewriter cartridge. Hope you enjoy!"

Completing my Emerson and Nietzsche class was a bit more challenging. Returning, I found that I had missed eight of the weekly papers—and done none of the reading. The ancient white-bearded professor showed no sign of recognizing me, but then it didn't seem he had ever recognized anyone. The class was deep in a discussion of *The Gay Science,* on Nietzsche's views of man's instinct for self-preservation. After class, he stopped in front of my desk and said, "Andre, I appreciated your thoughts on the Übermensch very much. It is a parallel to hermeneutics after all!" He chuckled heartily.

"Who would've thought?" I joined in, laughing.

I decided not to go back to Emerson and Nietzsche. When my evaluations arrived in Los Angeles three weeks later, my evaluation read, "Richard's class participation was pointed and inspiring . . . his papers articulate and profound." I gasped, wondering if at that moment there was an Andre in the class who was in tears reading the most blistering evaluations of his life. Grinning madly, I brought the envelope to my parents, eager to share my two glowing reports (or one glowing report and one so-so one, to be precise). I hadn't expected that the *quantity* of my evaluations rather than the quality would catch their eyes.

After spending December in the eternal night of Mod 21, I felt like a vampire facing the sun for the first time since the Middle Ages. The neon hum of Los Angeles's shopping streets, ominously balmy even at eleven at night, the manicured housefronts, the quiet, order, and cleanliness of my parents' house, all seemed to point an accusing finger my way.

My first day back my parents tried to hide their anxiety when I slept until five. The second day, I slumbered past six, awakening as my father came home from work. They shared their concerns.

"It's the time change," I explained.

"You sleep until three at school?"

"How do you get to class?"

The Hampshire system, I wearily explained once more. You can't judge it by your hidebound, Old World notions.

The next day I woke up at two and sat in front of the TV, flipping between *F Troop* reruns, *Donahue,* and soap operas, fixating on Stacey Q's midriff in the "Two of Hearts" video. On my parents' wall calendar I counted forty-three days until I was to return to school on January 30. I called Northwest Airlines and learned that for a mere twenty-five dollars I could move up my return to January 3.

Between fall and spring semesters, Hampshire held a special month-long session known as January Term, during which students could take classes and workshops taught by other students. Whether motivated by pity for the students who would otherwise have to endure the below-zero temperatures or, as more commonly rumored, by a desire to save money on the school's heating bill, attendance at Jan Term was not only optional but tacitly discouraged. At the time it was estimated that only two to three hundred of Hampshire's twelve hundred students showed up each year. Still stuck in some of my pre-Hampshire thought processes, I cringed at the notion of "extra school" and so hadn't given any thought to returning—until the day before I left for L.A., when I heard the crowd in 21 speaking of Jan Term in ways that fired my imagination.

"Really weird things happen," Susie told me.

"Like what?"

"Campus is empty. It's so cold that you can't go outside. It's when people go crazy, they just lose it," she said, her eyes lighting up at the memory.

The room nodded and seemed shocked that I wasn't planning to return.

Three weeks later, I flew back into Hartford at five o'clock on a Tuesday evening. As I stepped out of the airport, I gasped at the cold. Three weeks in L.A., and had I forgotten this? I jumped up and down, duffel bag on my back, waiting for the Peter Pan bus. Even on the bus, where the heat blasted in blazing gusts, I still felt cold. Cold lodged itself between my toes and under my legs like a parasite. I shivered violently in my seat on the empty bus, peering into the darkness, trying to make out traces of the Connecticut River. In the seat across from me, a metalhead in a puffy blue windbreaker air-drummed to the Poison album he was listening to on his Walkman, which I could hear clearly where I sat. When he caught me glancing at him, he stopped the tape.

"What's up, man?"

I shook my head.

"Wanna score some wicked crystal?" Tempted for a moment, I nonetheless declined.

The rest of the buses I had to take were nearly empty along my route. Even the normally humming Springfield Peter Pan station was abandoned but for a few homeless people shivering on the benches, wrapped in layers of blankets. In Amherst, I waited on the deserted main street for the Five College bus, which the schedule informed me came only every two hours in January. Arriving on campus just after ten, I didn't pass a single person as I shuffled down the icy trail, past the looming concrete library and campus center, into the Greenwich woods.

I stopped and stood still as I entered the cluster of wooden doughnuts. I didn't hear a sound anywhere in the world. Greenwich sat deserted, as though it had been evacuated ahead of a marauding army. The lights were out in every window. The tree branches were bare and coated with ice.

Outside 21, slivers of light peeked from behind the black sheets on the doorway and reflected off the snow. From Susie's window upstairs, Bessie Smith warbled out into the night. I climbed onto the porch, trod over the snow-covered broken bottles, the ventriloquist's dummy, and the car transmission, and, taking a deep, frigid breath, opened the door.

In the living room, Meg, Tim, Ox, Jon, Sa'ad, Marilyn, Michael the Krishna, Monica, Jerome, Susie, and a dozen others sat talking. Meg was saying, "I can't believe you don't like the Butthole Surfers. You're such a fucking hypocrite."

Jon giggled and said, "Just another Supreme Dick cover band, if you ask me. Rich, what do you think?"

Everyone looked up at me, waiting for an answer. I put down my duffel bag. "I guess I kinda like them."

Meg and Sa'ad hooted at Jon. "You see!"

"Rich, I can't believe you're saying that." They dove back into their fight. I stood in the middle of the room. No one gave a hint of recognizing that I had just returned, or that I had been gone. In fact, looking at them, sitting in the same places in the same outfits, I realized there was no evidence that anyone had even left the living room or been off the couch in the three weeks since I'd been to California and back. There was nothing, in fact, to indicate that the last three weeks had actually happened and weren't a hallucination of mine.

My room was freezing cold and smelled more than ever of cat urine. Someone had opened a window to smoke, which I gathered from the heap of cigarette butts stubbed out on the sill. I pulled out a Camel, lit it, and sat down on my bed. On my *Sid and Nancy* poster someone had drawn X's over the protagonists' genital regions and written SEX KILLS. FUCKING IS FOR FUCKERS. I pulled a blanket around my shoulders over my overcoat and listened to the chatter from the living room. I looked out the window into the dead night. Somewhere out there, Zach and Nathan were still warm in Los Angeles. I shuddered and went back out to join the crowd.

During Jan Term the whole campus seemed to give in to our way of life. It wasn't even a question of our being unmotivated to move—there was no place to move to. In the few hours of thin daylight, we wandered shivering through the arctic cold across a deserted landscape. The library was open only for a couple hours a day. The snack bar and Tavern were closed. In the dining hall the few people who dotted the back room in little islands spoke in whispers, afraid to disturb the hush. Even security couldn't be aroused when the band set up in a Merrill House hallway. During our two-hour recital, three students wandered by, encased in dozens of layers. They peeked out under the brims of their hats, and wandered past without a word.

At night, the group, or breakaway clusters of three to six of us, ventured up to Prescott House, where every evening the hundred or so people on campus packed into a mod and shivered together. The drink of choice at these gatherings switched from beer to bottles of Jack Daniel's and Maker's Mark, which passed freely through the crowd. By eleven o'clock several people would be vomiting off the fire escape, the Joy Division album skipping unattended on the turntable. Some hippie girl would be making out with a Mohawked punk in a corner while the hippie boy she came with stood up on the counter and wept that our souls had been destroyed by the Reagan War Machine and we were too blind to see how fucked we all were.

After a few of these parties, I noticed that between the gazes of emptiness and dread, under the looks of longing that people stared each other down with, there was another element flying between people's eyes. I caught it first when I saw a guy named Carl, in a leather jacket, emerge from a bedroom in the back of one of those mods. Around the room, I caught a dozen sets of eyes fix on him with a slightly terrifying intensity. While most of the room was stretched on the floor, singing along, or bellowing at the top of their lungs, with "Bela Lugosi's Dead," which creaked out of a boom box, Carl adjusted his motorcycle jacket and strolled into the midst of the room, feigning nonchalance while twitching almost imperceptibly. He caught the eye of one girl who had been staring at him, nodded to her, and she sprang up, and together they scampered back to one of the bedrooms. I noticed the little tableau soon repeat itself, in other mods, with other people emerging from the back rooms.

A couple nights later I pointed this out to Susie and asked her what was going on. "They're buying coke. Everyone here is completely buzzed. It's really gross."

I looked around and noticed a more than average number of people talking to themselves beneath the music and pacing in corners. Even the few people pogoing in the center of the room to a Cramps song seemed, now that she mentioned it, a little too anxious about it.

"Coke makes people so boring, don't you think?"

I agreed it did. "But not like pot, I guess."

"Nothing is as boring as pot. Last Jan Term was all about Quaaludes. That was so much better. Well, I'm sick of watching this. Did you want to try some?"

"Oh, really?" I shook my head. I hadn't done any since my interview that first night at 21. "I mean, maybe." Susie smiled, got up, and beckoned me to follow. She walked us around a corner to the double room, outside of which six people stood shivering in a line. Susie vamped her way past them, shooting them shriveling looks, and pushed open the door. A deep voice yelled from within—"GET! THE! FUCK! Oh, hi, Susie."

Kneeling on the floor, Carl was measuring out tiny Ziploc baggies from a heap of white powder for a club kid dressed in black with a blue streak in his hair. In the back corner, three girls sat on a futon, focused intensely on a mirror coated with white dust and finger trails that lay on the floor beside them.

"Carl," Susie beckoned. "Rich here has lived too sheltered a life with us. He needs some coke."

"All right, but I gotta charge a hundred fifty a gram. It was a huge hassle to get it this time of year."

"A hundred fifty? You know we don't have money."

"But, Susie"—Carl looked at her as though he'd been dreaming of throttling her for ages but was unable to make his body respond to his wishes, so instead he went from threatening to whiny—"Susie, this is, like, my job!!"

"Don't be silly. We hardly need any at all. Why do you bother selling coke if you're going to be such a pain about it?" She snatched the baggie out of his hand. The club kid across the table whimpered in protest. We plopped down on the futon with the three girls.

"Hi, Malaria," Susie said. "Do you want some?" I looked up and noticed to my horror that the girl by the mirror was the girl I'd danced with as a prospective student. Her jet-black hair was now orange. Then she had looked impossibly grown-up and adult; now she looked understandably grown-up, sitting on the futon, resting on the shoulders of two death rock girls, her heavy makeup smearing her face as she wiped away the trails of snot seeping from her nose—still, to my eyes, the picture of glamour and mystique.

"Malaria . . . ," I whispered as Susie beckoned me to a narrow white line of powder on the mirror. I put the rolled twenty Susie handed me into my right nostril and leaned forward. I felt an explosion of blood to my head and wanted badly to laugh, or at least giggle.

"Rub some on your gums," Susie ordered.

The metallic taste numbed my mouth in a surprisingly pleasant way and I ran my finger over the mirror, searching for more. "Malaria," I said, "you're the reason I came to this school."

Conversation stopped. The two death rock girls whispered something to each other. Malaria looked at me, eyes wide, as though she were about to make a run for it. "You're not going to hit on me, are you?"

I convulsed. "What? I mean, no. I mean, what I'm trying to say is, you danced with me."

"I do that sometimes."

"When I was a prospective student. I was taking the tour, from my friend Drake. And we went to a party and you danced with me and you really wanted to talk and I thought you were the coolest, like, grown-up woman who had ever talked to me." I heard the words flooding out and tried to stop them, but the tide would not be held back, my brain now spinning too wildly to have any influence on my tongue. I considered throwing my hands over my mouth to shut myself up, but my hands were waving in the air and couldn't be reined in and the horrifying words were coming still. "And then you left with some guy and I came back to school here to find you." Susie, Malaria, Carl the drug dealer, his client, and the two death rock girls stared at me, I thought, not completely unkindly.

"Well, here I am. But you know, I'm a dyke now."

"Yeah, I know, I mean I didn't know. But that's not what it's about. Do you ever just feel like you're talking and you want to know somebody but it's like you're talking to somebody else and it's not really them listening?" *Shut up, please shut up,* I pleaded with myself.

Malaria inhaled a line and nodded. "It's the mind/body problem. We want to talk to people's bodies but only their minds can hear us."

"Exactly! The mind/body problem!"

"Yeah, universal incomprehension is a drag."

"You're the first person who understands!"

"And it's like that Cure song. You know, 'I'm alive. I'm dead. I'm the stranger.' We're all of that. Totally just ripping off Camus, but it's so true."

The death rock girls—Elizabeth and Lucy were their names—perked up at the mention of the Cure and offered that Robert Smith was the only artist who understood that love is the harshest form of murder.

It was after seven A.M. when I finally shivered my way back across campus, grinding my teeth and trying to manage the explosions that reverberated through my skull with every step. Rays of sun poked through the darkness and slammed into me like rubber bullets. The pasty yellowish sky over the Farm Center made me want to cry. I realized I didn't feel anything for Malaria anymore and it occurred to me that, in fact, I would never love anyone ever again.

A week after my return, Monica announced that the air in Mod 21 was becoming dangerously unhealthy. Indeed, even as she mentioned it, half the room was too absorbed in coughing fits to hear her. The normally vigorous fog of cigarette smoke, sweat, rotting food, unwashed clothes, incense, and Susie's perfumes no longer merely hung over the room but clung to every pore. No one could recall the last time the windows had been opened. Whenever a new arrival entered, he or she spent a half hour or so doubled over wheezing, while acclimating to the environment.

Monica suggested we open the windows and doors and air the place out, "just for five minutes." "And maybe take out some of this trash," she added.

We glanced nervously at each other. The temperature outside was right around zero. If she opened the windows, we'd have to leave the room, at least to get our jackets.

"Maybe we should focus our orgone on purifying the air," Ox suggested.

"I'm serious. I can't breathe in here."

"Are you sure this is about the air?" Jon asked. "Or is it that you're sexually frustrated?"

Monica screamed at Jon and a fight broke out, which, we all happily realized, eliminated any immediate threat of a window-opening upheaval.

Taking advantage of the commotion to change the subject, Sharon, a pint-sized rocker, the lead singer of the Dick-friendly group Five Dumb Broads, said, "Flavio told me he talked to Steve Shavel in Northampton last night."

"No way." "What's he doing?"

"He said he's living in some dorm at Smith. They have a guest room."

"Why doesn't he come back here?"

"He said he's planning a production of *The Tempest* on the island in Paradise Pond." This sounded credible to most. *The Tempest* was, I was informed, one of Steve's favorite plays and in the winter, when Smith College's great pond froze, he was known to stroll out to that island with whatever Smithie he could lure and hold impromptu philosophy seminars.

"What if he comes back?" Meg, sitting next to me, said. "What will you do, Rich?" She looked at me and I shrugged, suppressing a flash of panic.

Much later that night, after most of the crowd had moved into various rooms and I sat on the couch reading and trying hard to like a Kathy Acker novel Meg had recommended, the front door creaked open and I looked up to find Elizabeth and Lucy, the death rock girls I'd met in the back room at the party. They glanced around and nodded in approval. Amazingly, both seemed impervious to the smoke, breathing freely.

"So this is the Supreme Dick mod," Elizabeth, the red-haired taller of the two, said.

"How's it going?"

They looked at me, or glared in suspicion. "You live here?" Elizabeth asked.

"I guess so. You didn't know that?"

"We didn't know *who* you were," Lucy said.

"We thought you were from the library." They walked in and nodded some more at the plates of food on the floor, the backlit photo of three Gemini astronauts, the Velvet Underground album playing, the cockroaches strolling the walls.

"This place is cool," Lucy, the shorter, blond one, said. They both plopped down in the armchairs across the room and stared at me. I looked back in silence. They waited for me to say something.

"So you're first-years too?"

They nodded in unison. "Yes, we're first-years." They looked at each other and both burst out laughing.

"I guess I didn't see you around the dorms. When I was living there . . ."

Elizabeth leaned forward and said slowly, pausing significantly after each word, "We don't socialize much."

"No. I mean, me neither. I just mostly hang out."

"So do you have any more coke?" Elizabeth asked, staring deep into my eyes.

"No. . . . No. Just what we did there."

"Maybe we should go get some more." Elizabeth looked at me so intensely, I dared not refuse. A few minutes later, bundled up in a couple hundred layers, we stomped across campus. Elizabeth and Lucy explained they were from a small town in Ohio, had been best friends since they were born. I asked them how they'd ended up at Hampshire. I had begun to notice that every Hampshire student had a funny story explaining how they got here. Flunking out of another college, expulsion from high school, bizarre dedication to some obscure corner of the curriculum like animal husbandry; it was like asking prison inmates how they'd ended up behind bars and hearing the convoluted tales of mistaken identity and oppression at the hands of corrupt authorities. Elizabeth and Lucy, I learned, had come to Hampshire after a high school senior year road trip in search of affordable LSD, which had inevitably led them to an Enfield House mod.

"So do you guys, like, go to class?" I asked.

They looked at me. Elizabeth said, "Why, do you?" Lucy, I noticed, seemed not really to speak.

"Not much. I mean, I've been."

At the Prescott Mod, where the party had happened, ten or so nervous-looking people sat or paced around the living room. We started to walk back to Carl's room but the assembly erupted at once. "You've gotta wait your turn!" Carl stomped out moments later and beckoned someone back into his room. We waited our turn, while the girl with blond dreadlocks, who had previously been back of the line, took hers. I tried to make chatter with Elizabeth, who was busy whispering something to Lucy, who seemed angry at her and turned her head away every time Elizabeth neared.

We were finally summoned into Carl's room. Between us we had forty dollars, for which he measured a very small bag of white powder. He looked me in the eyes as he handed it to me. "You better stay away from that Susie, bra. She'll ruin your life."

He looked very, very serious about what he was saying.

"I live with her."

"Oh, man. You are so screwed."

"She's been really cool."

"Right. Totally cool. Just don't let her know you think so."

As we left, Elizabeth asked me, "What did he mean about Susie? Is she dangerous?" Her eyes widened.

"I guess so."

"Susie is amazing." Elizabeth clutched her arms around herself.

We approached the Greenwich woods. Lucy, opening her mouth for the first time in over an hour, suddenly yelled, "I'm going home," turned around, and stomped off back toward the dorms.

"Lucy, no!" Elizabeth yelled and ran after her a little ways. When Lucy kept going, she stopped and we both watched her small shape, flowing in black overcoat, scarf, and boots, pound down the path into the night.

Elizabeth rejoined me and we continued walking back toward Greenwich. "What's wrong with her?" I asked

"She's just really difficult sometimes." I saw Elizabeth was crying. We didn't speak until we got back to 21.

We set up on the floor of my room. I didn't have a mirror, so Elizabeth expertly cut some lines on the cover of a cassette tape. At first she still didn't want to talk.

"Did I do something to upset Lucy?" I asked.

"Not exactly. She's just—grrrrr! Why is she being like this?!" She told me about her friendship with Lucy, a saga that had involved frequent periods of nonfriendship from the time they were children together. Elizabeth swore that she was through with putting up with this behavior, but "isn't she just perfect? Isn't she the most beautiful thing you've ever seen?"

I thought to say, "No, you are," but wasn't sure whether she would storm out of my room, so instead I said, "Yeah, she's cool."

When the coke took hold, I summoned the courage to ask, "Is Lucy upset that you're hanging out with me?"

"What?" Elizabeth scrunched her face. "No, not you. Susie."

"Susie?"

"She can tell I'm in love with Susie."

"Really?"

"I mean, of course. She's amazing, isn't she?"

We lay on my bed together, dressed in our overcoats and snow boots. "You know, everyone says you guys are all going to be expelled," she told me.

"Do you think they can do that?"

"I dunno, but that's what people say. Are you scared?"

I thought about it for a moment, tried to picture being expelled. "It's kinda abstract, you know?"

We turned out the lights so we could listen to the instrumental side of David Bowie's *Low* album. We listened to it once and then rewound the tape and played it again. "If you don't understand this album, you don't understand Bowie," Elizabeth said. I listened intently to the lyrics:

> *Don't look at the carpet,*
> *I drew something awful on it*
> *See*
> *You're such a wonderful person*
> *But you got problems oh-oh-oh-oh*
> *I'll never touch you*

I looked at Elizabeth to see if she saw the significance of them. She looked at me and nodded, as though, it seemed to me, she had heard my thoughts. I watched her round deep eyes focus on a sputtering candle; her brow furrowed intensely, and her full lips pursed. I realized I was staring at her and tried not to, but found myself unable to stop.

"He's saying," I took a deep breath, "that we are vandals to art, and beauty. We dessicate it when we touch it."

"Maybe," she nodded and stared at me with a look I filled with horrible meaning.

"And he means, we do that when we touch people?"

Elizabeth smiled at me, what seemed a malicious mocking, and turned away. We focused hard on the instrumental tracks.

When the album ended the second time I said, "He's saying, if music can come from machines, then what makes us real?"

Elizabeth didn't respond. I propped myself up and looked down at her, through the darkness. She had fallen asleep, her lips curled in a menacing sneer. The urge to kiss or touch her was over-whelming, so I lay back down and stared at the ceiling, spending the next few hours listening to my heart beat as I came down from the coke. I wondered if it should be beating this fast. *That can't be right,* I thought, taking short gulps of breath. Outside, a bird started to chirp, the loudest bird I'd ever heard. I tried for hours to sleep, but the combination of the excitement created by Elizabeth's body next to me, and the very real possibility that I was going into cardiac arrest from the drugs, kept me wide awake.

Hours later, sleep had just begun to touch me when I heard a noise from the window. Someone was trying to force it open. I sat up in bed, too terrified to move or speak. The person on the other side seemed to have grabbed a trick tree branch with which he'd pried open the window a tiny bit and was forcing it to yield further. Finally there was one great shove and a grunt and the window sprang open entirely, its hinge snapped. I gasped and rose up in bed. A small canvas knapsack flew in through the window, followed by a figure who leapt in, crashing to the floor and yelling in pain. He lay cringing and grabbing his ankle. Poking out from a camel overcoat, I saw a pair of red Converse high-tops.

"Steve Shavel?"

He jumped to his feet. "I am. And who are you and what are you doing in my room? With a woman, no less!"

Elizabeth snoozed in oblivion. "We're just sleeping. See, we're fully dressed. Our shoes on, even."

Steve stood over the bed and looked at us. "Ah, so you are."

"We're problematizing our celibacy . . . ," I said, recalling the term.

Steve nodded. "Very admirable. Well done, then."

"Thank you."

"But what are you doing in my bed? Are you Susie's Krishna?"

"No. I'm Richard. I'm a first-year. I was thrown out of the dorms."

"Sorry to hear that but all the same, I'm not running a boardinghouse here. This is completely unacceptable."

"No one knew if you were coming back. Or even if you're enrolled. . . ."

"No one knew? Why wouldn't I come back? This is a travesty. Sasha!" he bellowed. As he threw open the door and marched up to Susie's room the entire house awoke, stirred from their futons and crevices on the living room floor, shook themselves off, and followed him up to Susie's room.

"Sasha!" Steve yelled, throwing open her door. "This is an outrage. What's the idea of giving away my room?"

Susie rubbed her eyes and sat up. "Calm down, Steve. No one knew where you were."

"Well, where did you think I was? I went down to talk to a *Tractatus* expert in North Carolina, then by amazing luck I stumbled into an estate auction and won a humidor of pre-Castro Cuban cigars for two hundred dollars. So I had to just pop down to Florida to smoke them. And then I came straight back here, just going for a few weeks to the transcendental workshop in Vermont, and I find you've given my room away and allowed this interloper to problematize on my bed."

"Oh, and maybe you stopped for a month or two at Smith?" Ox asked.

Steve shot up, straightening his spine. "Where did you hear that?"

Everyone laughed.

"That is not true. I just visited a friend who had a first edition I needed to see in her room, and it got late and so I needed a place to stay."

"It got late for a month?"

The bickering continued as the gray dawn filled the house. Steve eventually admitted that he had been "working with some girls in Comstock House on their orgone issues" and he had been persuaded to stay there, for the moment, as he "probably should do a bit more work before I let them loose on their own." The fact that he hadn't been, and didn't seem to have any intention of becoming, an enrolled student didn't enter into the discussion on whether or not the room was still rightfully his.

I was struck, never having had a nonofficial conversation with a thirty-year-old, by how young he looked. With his spiked hair, skinny tie, and buoyant energy, he actually seemed ten years younger than most of the lethargic inmates of the house.

While he brought a new effervescence to the mod just as we'd seemed on the brink of descending into the mold, his presence also added a new wrinkle to life in 21. Every afternoon, Steve strolled in from wherever he was staying at Smith and proceeded directly to the downstairs bathroom, where he would stay for two, three, and one day even five, hours, causing havoc as the other thirty of us had to share the one remaining tiny bathroom upstairs.

What Steve did in the bathroom was a constant topic of speculation. Autoerotic activities were, of course, suggested but always refuted by the fact that "it doesn't take four hours to masturbate." Spiking the hair with his Brylcreem certainly could account for as much as fifteen minutes of the time, a bowel movement another fifteen to twenty. But this still left hours unaccounted for. It was a mystery we would debate until the end of my Hampshire days, without ever coming close to solving it.

My life, however, also took on a new wrinkle as I started to pay nightly calls on Elizabeth. Together we rounded up what money we could gather and dropped in on Carl for our baggies of white powder. Often we would end up passing out together around dawn, but the sleepovers remained, to my deepening confusion and frustration, fully dressed and entirely chaste.

Elizabeth spent much of our time together puzzling over the unconscionable behavior of Lucy, who continued to blow hot and cold, and listening to the Cramps, the Cure, and Christian Death and debating their meaning while I privately fantasized about her.

These fantasies remained tightly sealed away despite the fact that one night, Elizabeth initiated a conversation about our relationship.

Five lines of coke into an evening she suddenly said, "Do you think we should sleep together?"

I nearly choked on the Jack Daniel's I was gulping and stammered, "We, I mean, we do sleep together. Like every night."

She smiled wryly and condescendingly at me. "I mean have sex."

"Oh, right." I tried to break free from her gaze. "Right, I mean. Is that what you want?"

"I don't know. I mean, I guess it's not that important to me either way. Do you think about it?"

I broke down coughing. "I think," I said, finally pulling myself together, "I think about everything. But, you know, I try not to, I mean, we're celibate."

"Right, celibate." She looked me deep in the eyes and smiled. "So you're saying you don't want to?"

"No, no. I mean, I'm not saying anything. I mean, you're my friend, right? So you can do things with friends?"

"I think it might be interesting. But it might be weird."

"Yeah . . . I can see that. Totally. But it might be like a bonding experience."

Elizabeth inhaled another line off the mirror. "Do you want to go and score some more?"

We didn't have sex that night, nor on any of the following nights of Jan Term, although we sporadically discussed the matter. Our actual celibacy did not, however, stop the chatter in 21 about my whereabouts.

"Oh, Rich," Jon asked one day. "You're spending a lot of time hanging out with that Elizabeth girl."

I nodded. "I guess she's pretty weird."

"Oh, really. Wow, well, does she know you're celibate?"

"Of course. She respects our lifestyle."

"That's cool. . . . So you guys are doing a lot of coke?" Jon looked at me sideways. I couldn't figure out whether he was expressing disapproval or curiosity, but I felt immediately defensive. Curiously, Mod 21 was the one place in Hampshire College where drugs were rarely seen. It was a gesture that seemed to infuriate our enemies all the more; the world assumed our behavior could only be explained by some bizarre combination of drugs, but when they learned that Jon, Ox, Steve, and the rest were behaving that way sober—a state more or less unknown on the rest of campus—that information often pushed people into frothing madness.

That night Elizabeth and I sat on the floor of my room. We were a couple lines into a half-gram when the door flew open and Steve Shavel stood before us. "Ah, Richard. Right, I forgot that you're borrowing my room."

"Oh, sorry."

"Oh, I say, is that cocaine you're doing there?"

Elizabeth hunched over the mirror to defend our diminished supply.

"Could I trouble you for just a line or two of that? I've got this Div Three I have to finish, you know."

Steve joined us, sprawling across the floor, smoking cigarettes by the light of the giant candle Elizabeth had brought over that was melting into the ragged carpet. Steve insisted we turn off the Siouxsie and the Banshees album we were playing, selecting instead the Rolling Stones' *Aftermath*.

He sat with us for the rest of the night, trying to explain Wittgenstein's *Tractatus* to us.

"To ridiculously simplify it," he said after a long exposition, "when I say I have a headache and you say you have a headache, we have no way of knowing whether we're talking about the same thing."

"But we both know what our heads are," Elizabeth said.

"Yes, but what is an ache? How do I know my ache is your ache?"

"What else could it be?"

"In the world of subjective experience, it could be anything."

We sat staring into the candle considering that, listening to the Stones pound out "Paint It Black." "Wait a second," Steve said when it was over. "Play that again."

I rewound it. The coke was almost gone and I knew any minute it would start getting light out. I hated being awake when the sun came up. "Rewind it again," Steve said when the song ended. He seemed to be deep in a train of thought. Elizabeth and I, coming down hard though we were, waited anxiously to hear what he was thinking.

After the eighth time we played it, he stood up. "It's about . . . his girlfriend's funeral."

Elizabeth and I looked at each other, confused.

Steve said, "He talks about a line of cars all painted black . . . and my love never to come back."

"Ohhhhhh." A chill went up my spine. How had I never seen that?

Steve continued. "And what about looking into the setting sun, where he says my love will laugh with me before the morning comes."

Elizabeth and I laughed. "Wow, it is." We played the song back and over again, giddy with revelation. And suddenly, laughing in the middle of it, Elizabeth and I clasped hands and as Steve explained on, she traced one finger down the side of my face. That night, lying in bed together fully dressed, we stared at each other and somehow our faces came together and we kissed for a very long minute before she said, "Good night," turned over, and went to sleep. I thought, *This is the moment I've been waiting for my entire life.*

Little did I see that almost within moments, other shoes would start falling from the sky like snowflakes in a western Massachusetts blizzard.

CHAPTER NINE

Rites of Spring '87

I n the spring of 1987, Zach and I got a radio show. One night, Steve Shavel had told us about a clause in the five college charter (the covenant that bound Hampshire, Amherst, Mount Holyoke, Smith, and UMASS together) that required each school to open a portion of their facilities to students from the other colleges. This meant, we learned, that each of the other college radio stations had to open up a small number of their DJ slots to Hampshire students, which alone of the schools did not have a station.

First thing the next morning (meaning two in the afternoon), Zach and I called WAMH, the Amherst College station, and made an appointment with Todd, the station manager. Later that day, we walked across the Amherst campus, with its stately neoclassical buildings, well-manicured hedges, and trash-free paths, eyeing the well-manicured and trash-free students who bustled buoyantly along to class, even cheerfully, making the frozen landscape seem like more a winter carnival than the canvas of death it appeared at

Hampshire. In our dark, ragged overcoats, we leered nervously at the cheery scene, like prisoners released from solitary confinement and suddenly thrust into a tea party.

The studios of WAMH were located in a dorm basement deep in the center of campus. When we walked in, Todd was sitting at a desk in the outer room, focused on sorting through a milk crate full of records. In a booth to the left, a DJ was playing an early Genesis song. Humming along, Todd stared at the cover of a Warren Zevon album and then wrote something in a tight hand on a yellow index card, which he placed near the back of a card file, under *Z*. When he caught sight of us, he perceptibly winced, before quickly pulling himself together.

"Oh, hi, guys. You must be the fellas from Hampshire."

He motioned us to some chairs and we sat down in front of his desk. "So tell me what kinda radio show you were thinking of."

"One about music . . . ," I said.

"And community," Zach added.

"Right. That's great." Todd nodded. "Music is pretty much what we do. What kind of music are you guys into?" He eyed us skeptically.

"Mostly . . . ," Zach said carefully, "mostly . . . progressive music."

"We love progressive here. That's our big thing." He motioned toward the speakers pouring out midperiod Genesis.

"I'm kinda into sorta postpunk stuff, too, kinda," I said, emboldened.

"Aha. I love it."

"He means gothic," Zach shot back. "Rich is really into gothic."

"It's not gothic. It's death rock."

"That's why you bought that Siouxsie and the Banshees album yesterday?"

"They are not strict gothic. That's punk crossover, mostly. The Birthday Party isn't gothic."

"Why don't you just wear a cape?"

Todd, looking increasingly alarmed, broke in. "Hey, guys. That's great. I'm totally into experimenting and exposing the campus to some new things."

"Awesome." Zach nodded.

"But we have to always remember, while it's good to mix some of that stuff in, we are serving the whole Amherst community. You can't forget also to play the stuff that people want to hear."

"Oh, really?"

"Not commercial stuff, I hate that crap too. And we're never going to compete with the fifty-thousand-watters in Springfield, but, you know, cool *college* music. But, hey, I love punk too. And I think the direction it's going now is amazing. You guys must've just died over the Iggy Pop album."

"I guess so." Zach and I looked at each other.

Todd started singing "Real Wild Child" to himself. "Well, you'd probably be surprised to hear that Amherst students actually loved that album."

"So can we have a show, then?"

"And lucky for you, there's a slot that we haven't been able to fill yet. How would you guys feel about Sunday morning?"

"That sounds great."

"From three to six A.M."

Back at 21, the living room was in a pensive mood, everyone rapt in private contemplations. Jerome leafed through a copy of *New Music Express*. Ox pasted letters cut out from magazine headlines onto a sheet of paper, making a flyer advertising "600 Dead Tapes, 1969–present. For sale or rental. Cash only. Grass not accepted."

Sprawled across the armchair, Jon talked quietly on the phone. "I dunno," he said. "I guess I feel it's kinda like wouldn't anyplace be pretty much just the same as this. . . . Yeah. . . . I know, you're right, Amy."

Amy From the Phone had started calling the house sometime during Jan Term. One would answer the phone and a voice both pixielike and threatening—threatening in the manner of child ghosts in horror films—would say, "Hi," and then not another word. The unnerving silence had inspired many of us to begin babbling and then actually conversing with her, although on her end she only spoke the words *yes, no,* and *okay.*

It was not clear how we knew that her name was Amy. The only hard fact we knew for certain was that she had been calling the house of the local band Dinosaur Jr. for a few months prior; it was thought that someone there had given her the number of Mod 21, referring her to us, as it were. Theories about her identity abounded—an inmate at the nearby Northampton State Mental Hospital, an agent for the school administration, a groupie, even that she was a secret alter-ego of Dinosaur Jr.'s laconic front man, J Mascis. There was, however, not a shred of evidence to back any one of these theories and nothing was known concretely beyond the sound of her voice and her four-word vocabulary.

Something, however, about the lulling/maddening way she deployed her four words inspired trust in more than a few in the house. Jon, most of all, could be found in long conversations with her (all the more surprising because he seldom had long conversations with anyone), confiding secrets and inner pains.

Only Susie failed to be won over by Amy and would become livid every time she picked up the phone and heard her "Hi," cursing her within an inch of her life.

When I walked in that night, Jon was telling Amy about the stream of warnings falling upon the heads of every member of the house. In the first week of spring semester, Mod 21 had officially been placed on housing probation. Faith, the Greenwich House master, had dropped by and delivered a list of "conditions necessary to continue your housing eligibility," meaning if we didn't fulfill each of the terms, 21 would be broken up and we would all

potentially be banned from student housing, forced to find lodg-
ings off-campus. The list included: "No noise complaints. All trash
must be cleared of surrounding area. Damage to walls and structure must be repaired. Three consecutive cleanliness inspections."

Susie read the list aloud to the living room and was met with
a gloomy silence. Ox finally broke the hush. "That doesn't sound
too hard. . . ." Groans poured down on him from every corner of
the room.

Within the following days it seemed every member of the extended 21 family was placed on academic probation; at least those
were who were actually Hampshire students (which seemed to be
about a third of the house). Susie met her announcement in char-
acteristically grandiose fashion. Having been summoned to meet
Milton, her advisor, a writing teacher whose office she dropped by
once a year or so, she declared her impending departure for the
meeting several days in advance, giving us a countdown to the
final moments as she fussed over what outfit to wear, perfumes,
gifts to bring (although it was agreed this was hardly necessary; it
was well established he was in love with her already).

When the afternoon arrived, she descended the stairs adorned
in her customary black shirt and black leggings with a fluttering
skirt, aflow in scarves and tresses. We all rose and saw her to the
door. "Don't worry." Susie batted her heavily lined lashes at us.
"I've got charm enough for ten Miltons."

The trouble was, I learned after she left, that Susie had never
actually finished a class in her three years at Hampshire. As far as
anyone knew, she'd never actually been to a class—although some
said it was possible that in her first semester—her first couple
weeks of her first semester—she may have gone to a class then.
Certainly, everyone agreed, she'd never done a paper, a project,
completed a Div I, or filed her Div II. Even by Supreme Dicks
standards, this was an impressive record. Between the photo and
music classes available, most of 21 had at one time or another

stumbled into a class so undemanding that it was easier to finish it than to flunk it. Some of the room had even made major dents in their graduation requirements before the dawn of the Dicks. Ox was supposedly working on his Div III on Derrida. Jon didn't actually go to classes but was the prodigy of the film department. Even Arthur had found shop classes.

The tension in the living room grew thick as we awaited Susie's return.

"They couldn't really expel her, could they?" I asked Ox.

"Ohhhh, I don't know. Probably not. But the school's being pretty crazy."

The door opened and Steve Shavel flew in. "Lars from the Greenhouse Mod overheard the president talking at Central Records. She told him her motto this year is Just Say No to Supreme Dicks on campus."

"Dick persecution rears its head once again."

Steve nodded. "It's Hampshire's only socially acceptable form of discrimination."

We sat glumly. "What will Susie do if they kick her out?" I whispered to Ox.

"Oh, what do you mean, what will she do?"

"Um, well, will she have to go someplace . . ."

"Yeah, maybe. I guess she could stay at Joel and Chris's place in Northampton."

Three, then four hours passed without her return. Our discussion of her fate had evolved into an argument about avant-garde film, with Steve Shavel making an impassioned defense of Godard, *Pierrot le Fou* in particular, while Jon insisted that Godard was no different than Steven Spielberg and that *Week End* looked exactly the same as *E.T.* to him.

Sometime after ten, Susie threw open the door and paused dramatically in the doorway, a sackful of books in her arms and a gust of frigid air filling the room. She took two steps forward and collapsed onto the couch.

"How did it go?" everyone asked.

"It was horrible. *Je suis fatiguée.* Do we have any wine?" she asked, insanely.

"What happened?" I pleaded.

"Milton"—she paused for dramatic effect—"wants to leave his wife."

"What?" everyone screamed, confused. "For you?" Ox asked.

"Probably, but I told him he wasn't allowed to talk about that. He told me he hasn't loved her for years and that she mocks his poetry."

"Wow." We took this news in. Milton's wife was, it was known, an art librarian at Smith famed for her stern, dramatic, but very sexy older-lady bearing. Why she was with the schlumpy, whining Milton was a source of frequent speculation, the answers usually descending into elaborate S-and-M fantasies.

"His poetry is pretty bad." Jon yawned.

"That's not the point," Susie snapped. "He's a loving husband and he deserves better." We all looked at each other. No one seemed to agree that he deserved better, but with Susie worked up, we conceded the point.

"So I guess he didn't kick you out?" Ox asked.

"Kick me out? Of course not! The poor man, though. Yvonne"— the dean of faculty—"is giving all our advisors so much trouble. He really is having a hard time keeping them out of my hair. I just feel terrible."

"So did they give you any . . . punishment?" asked Marilyn.

"Don't be ridiculous, darling. We came up with a contract. I told him that if it will get him out of trouble, I would love to do a Div One this semester."

"A whole Div One!?" Ox blurted.

"Yes, idiot. I can do it. It's only one little paper. I'm going to write about Zelda Fitzgerald!" She beamed with pride. "Milton took me into town to buy some books on her. You know, I've always said Zelda was the genius of the pair. Just look, everything decent Scott ever wrote he stole from her."

Susie rattled on about Zelda, radiating excitement. Everyone else glanced at each other with undisguised skepticism.

"What's wrong?" I whispered to Ox.

"A whole Div One! That's pretty major for Susie."

"How long does it have to be?"

"I don't know. . . . At least eight pages . . ."

"Double-spaced?"

"Maybe ten double-spaced."

"You don't think Susie can pull that off?"

Ox shook his head. "I just don't know. . . ."

My own warning came a few days later, heralded by what I now dreaded as the surest harbinger of doom—opening my mail slot and finding a pale beige envelope with my name and box number typed on the front, the red Hampshire College logo in the upper left mocking me like a jackal. Since the last few times I had been summoned, I always braced myself for one of these envelopes waiting in my mailbox like a time bomb; nothing good could arrive in an envelope bearing the college insignia. On any average day I was secretly cowering in fear over being caught for at least three things I had recently done. These trips to the mailroom had become games of Russian roulette, leading up to the agonizing moment of suspense as I opened my box and peeked inside to see if I was being expelled. I generally avoided checking for weeks at a time; the more I had to fear, the longer I stayed away.

But knowing that, one by one, we were all being called in, I was slightly prepared for the stationery of doom and merely sighed with world-weariness when I saw it waiting for me. Inside, the note from Leo was brutally to the point.

We should talk. Please stop by this week.

The note was dated two weeks before. Back at 21, I showed it to Steve Shavel and asked for advice. He studied it thoughtfully.

"This is just the first note?"

I nodded.

"Then that's not a problem. It's not until the third or fourth summons that you have to take it seriously."

"You don't think I should go hear what he wants?" I asked.

"Do you want to hear what he wants? Is there a chance he wants to give you a merit badge for outstanding campus citizenship?"

"But if I don't show up, can't he just expel me?"

"He can't expel you if he can't find you."

Sensing my unease with simply sweeping the matter under the rug, Steve laid out an alternate plan. The next day I sent back a note reading,

> Leo,
> Thank you for the recommendations. I can't wait to check those out.
>   See you soon,
>   Richard

A week later, fortifying myself from the flask-sized bottle of Jack Daniel's in my overcoat pocket, I returned to my box. The expected envelope was there, and after taking a deep swig from the bottle, I cavalierly snatched it out of my mailbox and tore it open with the dashing aplomb of a buccaneer. It read:

> Richard,
> I must have made a mistake in my last letter. Please come see me right away. We need to talk. But I'm glad you liked the books.

On Steve's instructions I wrote back:

Are you sure you didn't get that information about the
financial instructions? I am really certain I sent it a
week ago.

Two weeks and four notes later, as Leo's temperature rose and the notes began to allude to higher authorities, Steve finally conceded, "It might be time for you to see him."

The meeting when it came was mercifully brief. After apologizing about the mix-up with the notes, he asked me what classes I was taking that semester. I was able to tell him truthfully that I had enrolled in three, although I didn't mention that it had been weeks since I had poked my head into any. Leo nodded sternly, stroking his beard, and said he thought it might be a good idea to place me on academic probation. The terms, he said, required me once again to finish two classes this semester.

I nodded grimly and we glanced at each other in quiet resignation, like a couple finally expressing out loud what they had each privately feared—that their faithful old Labrador who hadn't moved from his spot by the fire in almost a month was, in fact, dead. Leo stared at me with a look of self-pity mixed with anger at my having put him in this position. Feeling sorry, I attempted to console him, suggesting, "I guess even alternative education has to have rules."

He exploded. "My teaching has never been about rules. You know, I'm the one who stood up when they tried to bring in grades in '79! I fought for the pet policy! And now look, you and your friends are making me act like—like I'm one of the pigs, for crying out loud."

I rose and smiled as benignly as I could. "I'm sorry this happened to you."

His white beard flapping, he asked me to leave his office immediately.

It was the first day since winter began that the frost had given way to just a hint of warmth, the thermometer climbing into the low thirties. Steve Shavel and Ox sat perched on a low wall outside the Social Sciences Building, waiting for me. We walked into the dorms quad, where for the first time in months, people were lingering slightly in the outdoors—if not plopping down on the muddy, iceberg-dotted lawns, then at least pausing for a moment or two before they returned to shelter again.

I told Steve and Ox what had happened. "Two classes?!" Ox looked alarmed.

Steve, on the other hand, grew reflective. "The great experiment is over."

"What's that?"

"Hampshire College." He waved grandly around us. "The greatest experiment in educational innovation mankind ever created has ended. Once they start telling us how *many* classes we should take, they may as well be telling us what classes we should take, and what we should learn from them. No, no, it's over, the idea that you can regulate intellectual growth is against everything that we stand for here."

"How many years do you think intellectual growth should take?" Ox asked, poking at Steve's decade-plus tenure at Hampshire.

"Asking how long it should take is like asking what color your thoughts should be. There's no answer to that. For some, enlightenment could happen five minutes after they get their dorm room key. For others, it's an evolution that will take the rest of their lives."

"Oh, really, well, I hope you don't tell your parents that," Ox cracked.

"So do you think I should protest?" I nervously asked.

Steve shook his head. "You should, but the die is cast. They have decided to do away with us all."

I shuddered. As much as I enjoyed the drama of all this, the thought had been growing on me that I could actually be expelled. And as much as I wanted to imitate my housemates and not care one way or the other, the forbidden thought of "What would I do then?" kept picking the locks of my skull and pushing into my brain.

As if reading my thoughts, Steve burst in. "But they've made a critical mistake with you, Richard. I think two classes is very manageable. We can get you through this."

"Really? How?"

"Don't worry. I can handle this. I'm going to make sure that even though they may bring down the rest of us, while you're here the Supreme Dicks legacy will live on. Ox, what do you think?"

"*Shades of Gray*. Minneapolis. Nineteen seventy-seven," Ox replied, staring up at an open window on the top floor of Merrill House.

"Excuse me?"

"He's having a flashback," Steve said, and pointed out the sounds of drumming coming from an open window. "Someone's playing a bootleg." Although Daniel Oxenberg had long since shed the hippie trappings of his freshman year, certain stimuli could spark flashbacks and draw him back to his native state. As we trudged back to the Greenwich woods, Ox thumped out every beat to the remaining twenty-five minutes of the drum solo, drumming along on his stomach.

It occurred to me to ask something. "How come they haven't put you on any probations?"

"Ah, yes. Well, they tried, actually."

"What happened?"

"I told them that I'm not enrolled. They can't put me on probation if I'm not a student."

Ox and I nodded. "Brilliant," he murmured, and Steve seemed to agree.

As the rain of probation notices drizzled down on Mod 21, Jon seemed completely uninterested. "I mean, I guess there's not really much reason to stay here much longer." As a film student, Jon lived in a world still isolated from the turmoil we confronted in the other branches of Hampshire academia. The Hampshire film department was in the hands of devotees of avant-garde filmmaking who reared their pupils on the experiments of Stan Brakhage and Maya Deren. In my early days at Mod 21, I had salted my conversation with frequent references to Godard, Fellini, Antonioni, and Fassbinder, whose names and titles I had learned to drop during my high school years spent in L.A.'s revival houses. From Jon and the others, however, I learned that these supposed icons of intellectual cool were in fact as stodgy a handful of references as if I'd thrown around the names of Steve Lawrence and Eydie Gormé. "I guess I just have a hard time buying that any amount of narrative isn't a total cop-out," Meg, also a film student, said to me.

Around the mod, much whispering surrounded Jon's own films—brief three-minute experiments that had been declared "brilliant" and "the best student films in Hampshire history" by the film program overlords. However, few of Jon's films had ever been seen outside of his professor's office, as Jon generally declared his work "pretty bad" and refused to show it to his friends. One film, featuring Jon as a hunchback and Susie as his wife, allegedly based on a W. B. Yeats poem, had been screened for his peers, and moments from it were still being picked over and dissected a year later like nuggets of Kabbalistic wisdom.

In any event, Jon would occasionally slip out of the house, a Bolex camera under his arm, allegedly to the room of a fourth-year in Prescott named Michelle to shoot pieces of his coming Div

III opus, which he refused to discuss with anyone, waving away inquiries with "It's going to be really bad."

But it was unclear whether Jon's ambivalence about the growing likelihood that we were all about to be thrown out was owing to his secret confidence in the film and a certainty that he would be graduating in May; or because he so dreaded finishing the film that he would happily welcome expulsion as a way out of it; or because, as he claimed, he just didn't particularly care one way or the other if he went to or graduated from Hampshire. Some even thought that he had been so disillusioned and shattered over what had happened to the Dicks that, like Colonel Kurtz at the end of *Apocalypse Now*, he just wanted it to end. Whatever his motivation, whenever the topic of the falling arm of the law was broached, Jon would dismiss it with a shrug, asking, "Why do you guys want to be here so bad?" And my unspoken answers, "I'd get in big trouble if I got expelled" and "I don't know what I'd do after that," filled me with shame.

But as the warnings stacked up, my efforts to maintain nonchalance became more and more strained. One night, with as much bravado as I could command, I asked Steve Shavel what he thought my chances were of getting thrown out. He looked thoughtful.

"Well, traditionally, it's close to impossible to get expelled from Hampshire."

I tried not to look relieved.

"However," he continued, "times are clearly changing. At least for us. Now, if you had made the Triple Crown, I'd say you were doomed."

"The Triple Crown?"

"The Triple Crown of probations—academic, behavioral, and housing. In Hampshire history, no one has ever earned the Triple Crown and survived to the next semester. The last person who had it, pre-Dicks, was Brian Elgar in '81, and I believe that was the last time a non-Dick was expelled. Most of the Dicks have now made the Triple Crown. But"—he stroked his chin and polished his glasses—"you haven't been given behavioral probation yet, have you?"

"No."

"Just as I thought, somehow they let that slip through the cracks. So with only two probations, I'd put your chances of surviving at roughly forty-eight percent."

I nodded solemnly, unsure whether to feel reassured by the statistic or to cry out in panic. "That sounds reasonable," I said. "Not that I want to stay here or anything."

"Richard," Steve said, "forget what these fools say. You should stay here as long as you possibly can."

Coming from a man entering his second decade as a Hampshire student, these words carried some weight. "I've visited the world out there, and it's a terrible place." He shook his head in sadness. "Never graduate from college, believe me."

But my worries about the looming specter of expulsion had to compete against what for a time became an even greater obsession—round-the-clock thoughts of Elizabeth. For a couple weeks, our drug run/slumber parties settled into a cozy pattern. After our first kiss that night, the experiment was repeated on subsequent nights, generally with the same results; that is, the same results and nothing more. We'd come to a quiet moment when, the drugs failing, our chatter gave out and with "Hong Kong Garden" or Alex Chilton playing in the background, I'd kiss her and on most nights, she would kiss me back. Then, a few minutes later, she would pull away, roll over, say, "Good night," and drift off, leaving my nerves shattered between coming down from the drugs and the excitement of the kiss. I'd lie awake beside her for the rest of the night, gazing down at her and wondering about how she could possibly look so peaceful.

The next evening, when I showed up at her room in the Merrill House dorm, I found Lucy sitting with her. The three of us divided up the cocaine and sat together on Elizabeth's floor, talking. Or rather the two of them talked and I twitched uncomfortably, counting the seconds until Lucy left. Exhausted from the sleepless night before, and even more rattled from the drugs, as the hours went by I listened to Elizabeth and Lucy share inside jokes largely made in a private language of squeaks and growls, and wondered if I would collapse. But grimly I dug in, determined to wait Lucy out in a battle of endurance.

Finally around four A.M., lost in a stupor, I barely noticed as Lucy stood up and without a sound walked to the door and left. Elizabeth, watching her, sighed and stretched out on her bed. I got up and joined her, moving my face in close to Elizabeth's.

"How you doing?" I asked.

"Frustrated. Why don't we have any more coke?"

"We could go up to Prescott. . . ."

"It's too cold."

I moved in for a kiss. Elizabeth pulled away and emitted a guttural squeal. "Unnnnhhh. Why are you doing that?"

"Because . . . I dunno. I guess it's fun."

"Lucy thinks you're going to murder me."

"What?" I sat up.

"She thinks you're a killer. She's got a lot of psychic energy, you know?"

"I don't think I'm going to kill you."

"Wouldn't it be weird if you did?"

As I thought about it, Elizabeth rolled over and faded to sleep.

The next night, Elizabeth again repulsed my attempt to kiss her. The night after that, she kissed me again, more deeply than the first time. The following night, she said it was weird that I kept wanting to do that. We debated why I would want to. I thought of telling her, *Because I really like you, because all I do every day is count how many more minutes I have left until I can come see you.* But something inside, something in her sneer, something in the looks my housemates gave me as I shuffled muttering out the front door, told me that if I said those things, I would turn to stone then and there. So instead, when she asked why I wanted to kiss her, I answered, "It's just what I feel like doing right now?" or better still, "There's nothing else to do."

Finally the inevitable night came when I could not manage to sneak away to drop by her room. On the Saturday night following our first kiss, Zach and I had to be at the Amherst radio station at four A.M., for our show. Since the buses stopped running at midnight, however, we had to take the last one into town and sit up in the station's foyer until our show started.

In our fourth week on WAMH, it somehow at last dawned on Zach and I that we had been played for prize fools by taking on the overnight shift. Like all college DJs, we spent a good portion of our shows begging for calls or requests. But quickly we realized that our pleas were falling on perhaps not just deaf but nonexistent ears when not a single call came in during our first two weeks. On our third week, someone named Don called and demanded that we play a Huey Lewis song. The moment it was done, the phone rang again and Don this time demanded two songs by Art of Noise and Ratt. As we rushed to get them on the air, we began to address the show entirely to him ("Don, we have a public service announcement for you. This week the Pioneer Valley Historical Society celebrates its seventy-seventh . . . "). At first we giggled through these addresses to Don, joking to each other about how weird it would seem to others tuning in to hear the mystery listener's name constantly invoked, assuming that someone would soon call and demand we stop it, and cut off Don's abysmal selections. However, as the hours dragged on, and no one called, we realized we were, in fact, performing the entire show for Don alone, and our steps became leaden as we raced to find the right Boston album.

The sun was just weakly rising as Zach and I stepped off the bus onto the sleeping campus. "Great show," he told me, nodding.

"Best yet. I think Don really liked it."

Zach started walking toward the dorms and I walked with him. "You're not going back to Twenty-one?"

I shook my head. "I've gotta, sorta, you know, like deal with something first."

"You're not going to visit that Elizabeth girl?"

"I'm celibate!"

"Yeah, we all are." (Zach and Nathan had signed on to Supreme Dick orthodoxy as well.) "So why are you visiting Elizabeth?"

"I left something there I need to pick up."

"On another celibate visit?"

"Exactly."

We walked in silence a moment. "You can make a mockery of our philosophy if you want, but that girl is weird," Zach said.

The hall door slammed behind me and I thundered down her still, silent floor, not a soul alive on a Sunday morning. I tiptoed to her room and, as gently as I could manage, knocked on her door. There was no answer. I knocked again, slightly louder, calling her name. I wondered where the hell she could be and realized I was inches away from falling asleep and passing out. Was she with Lucy? Not possible. Lucy always threw her out of her room when she went to sleep. Where had she gone last night? There was supposed to have been a party in Prescott. Who would have been there? Could anyone still be going at this hour? Was it even remotely possible that she was waiting for me in 21?

I snapped out of my reverie and looked at my hand, which was now hammering on the door without restraint, the knocks filling the hall. I also noticed I was calling out, "Elizabeth! Elizabeth!" near the top of my lungs. And then I noticed that, dressed in robes, boxer shorts, and with towels wrapped around them, her hallmates had somehow emerged and were packing around me.

"She's not here, man," one said.

"She has to be. Lucy would've—"

"Then I guess she doesn't want to get it on with you, dude," he shot back.

"I'm celibate, actually," I stammered.

I was propelled by the shoulders through the hall and down the stairs, and soon stood outside at the foot of the dorm, shaking my head and trying to make sense of what had happened through an increasingly unraveled brain. The thought entered my head, *Does Elizabeth even know my name? Has she ever used it?*

I spent most of the next few days trying to think of ways not to think of Elizabeth. I had no idea how I was supposed to address what had happened. Had she been in the room listening to me? Or had she skipped our regular meeting-up time? Did we have a regular time? Did she know what it was? On what grounds did I have any right to care where she was? In the confusion, I steered clear of the dining hall, snack bar, and any other place I might run into her, but I considered it an Olympic-medal triumph every time I could get through ten straight minutes without thinking of her.

One night, Ox invited me to follow him into Amherst to visit some friends. It was much whispered that Ox had been spotted with an Amherst High School girl named Christie, a member of the local punk scene. Christie, it was said, had an older sister whose name was invoked only in hushed reverence. Ramona had been described to me as some kind of dark Valkyrie, the "Death Rock Queen of Amherst," a cold beauty of such power that she had in her time, allegedly, lured both Robert Smith of the Cure and Ian McCullough of Echo and the Bunnymen into her clutches. J Mascis, lead singer of the local postpunk band Dinosaur Jr., was said to have been driven mad by his relationship with Ramona and composed the entire first Dinosaur album about her.

The ties between the Supreme Dicks and the local punks of Amherst and Northampton were strong, the punks often dropping by 21 to pay their respects when they visited Hampshire campus for a concert or to buy drugs. Since moving in, I'd gotten to know most at least by sight and kept abreast of their gossip, which centered largely on Dinosaur Jr.'s internal politics and, more cautiously, whispered tales of Ramona. But although the Dinosaur members drifted through the coffeehouses, I had never laid eyes on Ramona or even her little sister Christie, so when Ox suggested a trip into town "to visit friends," a reference pregnant with the hint that Christie might be among these friends, I leapt from the couch and scampered after him.

On the bus into Amherst, I asked Ox directly, "Are we going to see Christie?"

"Oh, Christie? I don't know. I just thought we'd stop in at Clase Café" (the Amherst diner that was the local punk hangout).

"So I don't suppose she'll be there?"

Ox became coy in response to the implied violation of celibacy. "Wow, maybe. Yeah, I guess she might. Yeah, probably. I think you're right."

As it turned out, Christie was there. A petite punkette with blond hair streaked with black tied back under a bandana, she sat at a table in the center of the smoke-clogged diner with five others of her tribe, most of whom I recognized from their visits to Hampshire. Ox walked up behind her chair and stood quietly coughing to get her attention, while Christie talked about the Sonic Youth concert coming up in Boston the next weekend.

"Oh, wow, Christie. Oh, right. You're here," Ox finally broke in.

Christie turned around and looked at him and smiled shyly, as though they shared some scandalous secret. We sat down and joined the table, where the conversation inevitably soon turned to Dinosaur Jr. gossip (there was said to be strife within the band). I studied Christie for signs of royalty and determined that she did indeed have regal, princesslike qualities about her. Where the rest of the table seemed hyped up, boisterous, shouting, jittery from too much caffeine and God knows what else, Christie was poised, unflappable, and almost supernaturally confident and secure. When she spoke in her soft, girlish voice, the rest of the table quieted and leaned in attentively. I also noticed that despite her leather jacket and shredded jeans, Christie projected something clean and almost farm-girlish.

More surprising, though, was the reaction Ox provoked. Whenever Ox mumbled a half-comprehensible observation, I noticed with envy how Christie touched his arm and laughed at every witticism. I, meanwhile, struggled for the attention of Christie's friend, a stringy girl with ironed-out dirty-blond hair named Tasha, badgering her with questions about Amherst High School, which she barely dignified with answers. Around 21, it was a common joke to refer to Ox as the Supreme Dicks' teen heartthrob, but this was the first time I had witnessed the phenomenon and it was fairly breathtaking.

After the table had finished off five successive plates of Clase's famed grease-ridden, overcooked French fries and I had swallowed two chocolate malted frappes, Josh, one of the punks, suggested we return to his house. His neighbors, he said, had thrown a party the night before and their keg was sitting on the back porch at most half-finished. We walked through the dark streets of the picture-postcard Amherst neighborhood. The cold had let up to the point where we could, in our overcoats and gloves, almost linger outside without risking frostbite.

On the way, I asked Ox about Christie.

"So were you, like, hanging out with her?"

"Rich!"

"I mean, have you helped her problematize her celibacy?"

"Oh, right. Well, maybe sometimes I've been able to help her with that."

I asked about Tasha, but Ox only knew that she had just moved to town. "She talks a lot about London."

Three hours later, the beer keg abducted, we lay sprawled in various corners of Josh's unfurnished living room. The glow of a single white bulb sitting atop a shadeless lamp provided the sole illumination, a Butthole Surfers album blasted from a turntable, and a broken window let in the cold as we sat wrapped in our jackets. Josh held the center of the room, doing an extensive and brilliant imitation of Amy From the Phone. He was fairly certain, he explained, that she was an inmate at the Hampshire County Mental Hospital in Northampton. A friend of his who had been admitted there a few weeks before said he talked to a girl on his ward who had been locked away after an extravagant series of suicide attempts. The friend, Josh claimed, was 90 percent certain that this girl spoke with the voice of Amy, although she feigned ignorance when confronted. She also, apparently, had a Dinosaur Jr. sticker on her backpack and supposedly—although this claim seemed more tenuous—had been overheard telling another inmate that she had friends named the Dicks.

In one corner of the room, Christie and Ox sat in deep conversation. In the opposite corner, I sprawled against a moldy rolled-up blanket with Tasha. I intensely watched her as she intensely watched Christie and Ox talking. Finally, she looked back at me.

"What are you looking at?" she asked.

"Oh, nothing. I mean, I wasn't looking, I was just, like, somewhere else and not using my eyes."

She nodded. "Have you ever been to London?"

I noticed I was very drunk. "No. I mean, yeah, when I was really little."

"I'm going to go there."

"Wow. That's cool."

"There's this amazing market by the canals. You can get leather boots for ten dollars."

"That's rad."

"Rad?"

"Oh, right. Sorry. I'm from California." We talked more about London. I offered to go with her fifteen or twenty times but she managed not to acknowledge my offers. I looked across the room, which, after a dozen cups of stale beer and half the Jack Daniel's from my overcoat pocket, teetered back and forth like a carnival ride. I wondered how Josh remained standing so straight. He had begun playing a guitar along with the album, when I noticed, out of the corner of my eye, the front door open and a dark figure walk in. Tall, thin, with long black hair, ghostly pale, dressed entirely in black, she stepped in and paused at the doorway, surveying the wreckage of the room, like an avenging demon standing coldly atop the rubble of the apocalypse.

"Oh, my God," I said a bit too loud.

Josh, hearing me, dropped his guitar and turned around. "Ramona!" he said. "When did you get back?"

"I thought Amherst might be less depressing than Boston for a day or two," she murmured. "Of course, I was wrong."

"You want a beer?"

"I just need Christie. Mom sent me to find you."

Christie stood up and I noticed I was standing myself, as though at attention. Mouth agape, I stumbled forward before I could stop myself. "It's a pleasure to meet you. I'm a big fan." I stuck my hand out.

Ramona furrowed her brow, looked me up and down, and

turned her back to me. "Josh, if you're coming to Sonic Youth, you can't bring Charlie. He's not allowed in my house."

"Yeah, totally. Charlie's got a job anyway."

Christie pulled herself together to leave and to my disappointment I saw Tasha get up to go with her. She walked over to me. "So I guess, cool hanging out with you."

"Yeah, it was. I mean, yeah."

"Are you going to Sonic Youth?"

"Yes." I nodded. "Yes, I am."

As she left, it occurred to me that I hadn't thought about Elizabeth in nearly an hour.

In the next breath, I tapped Ox on the shoulder. "We better get back to campus," I said. "I need to check on somebody."

CHAPTER TEN

The End of the End

As the semester crept along, there was never much doubt in the big sense how the story would end for Mod 21, just uncertainty about when and how heavily the hammer would fall. But by the atmosphere around the house you would never have known you were watching the death throes of a golden age. Although we were too cynical and too committed to our sense of persecution to be consoled by false hope, no group of friends was more skilled at burying their heads and avoiding a subject. The procession of probations, warnings, inspections, and administration conferences trooped by, and it became unmistakable that we were being led to our doom. But just as the alarm mounted to a defeating pitch, all went quiet; the seriousness of our dilemma made it seem ridiculous to talk about—or at least to talk about with anything other than casual disdain for the prospect of expulsion. And so we marched toward crucifixion with sneers on our faces, strolling along like we were headed to a family picnic.

I, however, was having a harder and harder time suppress-

ing my mounting panic, and I often fled the disintegrating situation, taking comfort among the punks of Amherst, or even
occasionally dropping in on Elizabeth and hiding out with her,
although each time I did this, her aloofness, no matter what
transpired between us, made me vow never to come near her
again.

After my conference with Leo, I made a brief stab at knuck-
ling down and taking my classes seriously, but I found that focus-
ing on schoolwork only reminded me of the hopelessness of our
situation and made me panic all the more. Much more effective
for my mental heath, I found, was to maintain my wall of denial
by pushing away anything that might remind me of Hampshire
officialdom, starting with classes.

I finally reached my I-just-need-to-not-think-about-this-now
moment during a lecture in my World Food Crisis class. The professor was earnestly leading us through a dissection of American
corporate farming techniques, explaining how big farming tied
agriculture to the world-dominating interests of the corporate
state, which had a vested interest in keeping the rest of the planet
hungry and dependent. As he explained how millions were dying
because of government strategies, all I could hear were the words
in my head, *Where will I live next semester?* The impending catastrophe of being expelled from college or even just losing my campus housing drowned out his chatter about starving millions. I
looked over at Zach, who had fallen asleep, and felt the fear rise in
my throat. While Zach slumbered, I gathered up my books and
stumbled out.

One afternoon sometime later, sprawled on the floor at 21,
cutting out pictures from Susie's old *Interview* magazines to decorate tape covers, I realized that it had been well over a month
since I had been inside a classroom. At that same moment, the
revelation came to me that by checking out of class entirely I had
in all likelihood guaranteed that I would be expelled. I looked at

the clock and realized that my Tolstoy class started in twenty minutes. I jumped to my feet and looked at my copy of *Childhood, Boyhood, and Youth,* which had lain on the living room floor for weeks. I picked up the phone on the wall and dialed Tasha, asking her if she wanted to meet me at Amherst's punk hangout Clase Café.

"Yeah, that's where I'm going."

"Cool, then I'll see you there." I raced to the bus stop and into town.

I spent much of the following weeks in Amherst hanging with the local punks and waiting to see Tasha. My entrée to the Clasé society had been paved by the surprising endorsement I'd received from Ramona herself. A week after meeting her, I had tagged along with Josh to the Sonic Youth show in Boston and had crashed at her house. Throughout the weekend, she had barely noticed me despite my desperation to get her attention, not wanting to squander these precious moments in her royal presence. Pondering how to honor my generation's muse, I decided to compose a poem. While the house slept that night, I crouched at her kitchen table over a stack of white notebook paper. I started and abandoned a dozen or so stabs at a homage worthy of her. Finally I stopped and asked myself, *What kind of poem am I trying to write here?* One of the few poems I knew by heart, Byron's "She Walks in Beauty," came into my head. Something like that would do, I realized. I started scribbling.

> *She walks in beauty, like the night*
> *Of cloudless climes and starry skies;*
> *And all that's best of dark and bright*
> *Meet in her aspect and her eyes:*
> *Thus mellow'd to that tender light*
> *Which heaven to gaudy day denies.*

The next morning, as Ramona made coffee in her kitchen, I handed it to her.

"This is for you."

She squinted at the page. "You wrote this?"

I nodded. "I just put the words on to the paper. You were the one who created them." She scrutinized the words for a few minutes, then folded it up and put it into the pocket of her robe. She nodded at me and said, "Thanks," without inflection, but I detected, I was almost certain, the merest hint of a smile at one corner of her mouth and my heart leapt.

Whatever the effect of the poem, and whatever her private conversations had been with the girls, on the ride back from the concert Tasha actually seemed to notice that I was sitting next to her, crushed in the back of Josh's car. On the way to Boston, she chatted with Christie and nothing would have indicated she was aware that she was shoved up against another human being in the crowded backseat, that her elbow was digging into a human stomach and not mere nylon seat lining. On the ride back, however, she went so far as to share a cigarette with me and to my amazement, Christie asked me several questions about whether I liked Hampshire.

In the following weeks, I spent every afternoon at the Clase waiting for Tasha to get out of school. When I saw Elizabeth on campus I was able to wave at her from afar, at least 50 percent of the time, I calculated triumphantly, free of desperation. It occurred to me in the next breath that I was replaying with Tasha the exact pattern that had tormented me with Elizabeth, and I wondered how one was supposed to break this cycle of wanting more without ever being able to express that it was more you wanted.

At the beginning of April I asked if anyone at 21 was going anywhere for Spring Break, a question met with predictable blank stares. The campus soon emptied and we roamed the thawing lawns oblivious that all the other students had decamped. With the sun meekly shining through after months in hibernation, we sprawled for hours in front of the closed library. For once, with Hampshire's paths empty, its brick-and-cinder-block buildings rising around us peacefully, we experienced a taste of the pastoral ideal promised in the admissions brochures.

Around this time talk focused on the looming question of whether we would be allowed to play at Spring Jam. The Dicks' performance at the previous year's Jam, coming just in the wake of Billy's death, had been the traumatizing event that had sealed the group's status as Campus Enemy numbers 1, 2, 3, and 5 through 158. (Oliver North held the number-four slot.) Given the current climate there might have been little reason to suspect that we would be allowed to play, except there still remained a mild queasiness about repressing free speech on campus, at least with Luntz and the leather-jacket-wearing guys who ran the school's music events.

Relations between Luntz and the Dicks were among the more complicated in our universe. An aficionado of bands like Sonic Youth, Soundgarden, and the Butthole Surfers—all of whom he had brought to play on campus during my first year—Luntz should naturally have been aligned with the Dicks' anarchic nature. But whether it was that musically, he felt the Dicks turned anarchy into mockery or the infuriating passive-aggressive way that Jon, Ox, and Steve had of refusing to get to the point with everyone who tried to talk with them, or his lingering sense that somehow they were making fun of his music—whichever of these elements pushed Luntz over the edge, the hatred in his eyes when he saw the Dicks was unrivaled by that of any Women's Center petitioner or Housing Office apparatchik. Nonetheless we remained more or less on the same side of the fence, each loosely bound to the school's punk caucus. And so it was thought that given these bonds, the shame of caving in to the administration and outright banning us from the Jam would be more than Luntz could bear, hate us though he might.

Which left the question of *what* we would perform. After last year's debacle, could the Dicks just get up and play songs? The legend of the previous Spring Jam had inflated until it was retold as Hampshire's crash of the *Hindenburg;* when the Dicks took the stage, the entire school would be braced for a world-class outrage. How could we possibly meet those expectations? How could we ignore them? In long afternoons at the Clase and late nights at the Red Lion Diner, everything was put on the table—human sacrifice, child abduction, satanic incantations, bestiality. But it also seemed that for most of the group after five to ten years on campus, the possibilities for shock had been thoroughly exhausted.

Jon seemed to think the whole thing was "silly" and serially mocked each scheme that was proposed. During this period he spent most of his time locked away in an editing bay, cutting his mystery Div III film, about which he refused to speak. The group endlessly speculated the film was based on a relationship Jon was secretly having with a girl in Pennsylvania, whom people claimed he would visit during his unexplained disappearances from campus. Others, however, disagreed. "I don't think Jon would make a film about anything as conventional as a relationship," Meg said.

I visited Susie in her room, where she had been closeted with her Zelda Fitzgerald for weeks, and asked what she thought might happen.

"Oh, I'm sure they are going to do something idiotic and everyone will get upset and there will be a big fuss."

"Will we all get thrown out?"

"I don't know. I think we all need to get away from this place, frankly."

I gulped, then looked around the room at the sprawling books strewn everywhere.

"How's the paper coming?"

"Oh, Zelda, Zelda, Zelda. So *impossible*. But I would say, at last, that it's almost done."

"You've written it?"

"I'm up to the point where I've done just about everything except write it."

In the meantime, the empty campus gave us an opportunity to pursue one of the Dicks' most precious goals, a Holy Grail upon which we had sat up many nights dreaming; a mission the Dicks had trained for, planned, and debated for years, but somehow had never gotten around to actually executing. This mission had become such a cornerstone of Dick lore that fulfilling it had taken on impossible dimensions—akin to restoring the Ark of the Covenant to a rebuilt Solomon's temple in Jerusalem. One day while we were lounging outside the library, Steve Shavel announced that it was time we stole back the orgone accumulator from the Cole Science Center.

Reich had conceived of the accumulator, one of the great scientist's cornerstone inventions, as an artificial means to stimulate orgone flow. He had, in his writings, specified a number of possible designs; Steve Shavel and a few others had built one of them for their joint Natural Sciences Div I that was roughly the size of a small outhouse—a wooden box on the outside, encasing "alternating layers of organic and inorganic materials"; in this case a layer of steel wool lined a space between the wooden outer and inner walls. Inside was a small bench, barely large enough for one person to sit on.

I had asked Steve how it felt to sit inside the accumulator. "Invigorating," he insisted, although others said it didn't feel like anything at all except sitting in a wooden sweatbox. The accumulator had already claimed one victim, however. Steve recounted how after building it he had moved it to the Art Barn so he could decorate the exterior. One night, still up working at three in the morning, he had decided he could use a little orgone boost and had taken a seat inside. Minutes later, he saw through the crack between the top of the accumulator's door and its roof Hampshire's art professor, the celebrated sculptor Geoffrey Robbins, walk into the barn and start inspecting his students' works in progress, bottle of whiskey in hand. As Steve watched through the open slat, Robbins looked at one painting and suddenly unleashed a tirade of hate, waving his hands while spewing profanities at the work as though he were attempting to subdue a runaway crocodile. When his rage was spent, he moved on to the next piece, a wire mobile. Robbins stopped, cocked one eye at the piece, and erupted again, pummeling it with odium. Steve became increasingly terrified for his safety and tried to quiet his breathing as Robbins worked his way closer to the accumulator. Finally, the moment came and he stood directly in front of the box. Quaking with fear, through the crack Steve saw Robbins raise an eyebrow, look at the accumulator, and then mutter, "Well, this isn't bad." He moved out of Steve's range of vision to inspect it on all sides, murmuring, "I rather like *this*," until he came back to the front and, his face pressed close, peered right inside through the open slat and made eye contact with Steve.

Steve claimed that at that moment he wanted to say something reassuring, but no appropriate words came to him. Robbins froze, eyes wide as dirigibles, as Steve stared back. He fell backward, knocking into the mobile, and, letting out a shriek of horror, he ran from the building. According to Steve, he didn't return to teaching until the next semester.

Whatever its decorative merits, the professors who reviewed the project were less than overwhelmed by the accumulator's scientific strengths. As often seemed to happen when Steve was involved, the dispute grew heated; he accused the professors of being part of a science establishment cabal to cover up the truth about orgone energy, which, if it were known, would put all of them out of business. By the end of the discussion, the accumulator had been impounded by the School of Natural Sciences and shoved away in a back corner of the third-floor lab, and Steve was forbidden to remove it.

"It wouldn't be such a crime," Steve explained, "but they keep it under fluorescent lights," which apparently poisoned an accumulator's effectiveness.

When night came, the plan to reclaim the accumulator rallied the extended family of 21, carrying everyone back to the glory days of the bell theft two years before. It didn't occur to any of us gathered for the great heist that this was the absolute wrong time for us to be doing something like this. Around three A.M. we crept out of 21, giggling through the woods and around the back way to the side door of the Cole Science Center.

Unfortunately, inevitably, everything immediately went wrong. The twenty of us scampering through the dead quiet night were about as discreet as the UMASS marching band might have been if they suddenly decided to hold tryouts on the main lawn. (Why our plan required twenty people instead of say, two, was a tactical flaw no one addressed.) The noise of our mass shuffling and guffawing drew the attention of two security guards walking in front of the library. As they yelled out, "Hey!" and raced over, most of us fled careening in every direction. Only Steve and two others ducked inside and raced up the stairwell they knew would be open. Getting to the top floor, they found the accumulator and lifted it and lugged it to the stairwell. They managed to get it down half a flight, but when they heard the door on the ground floor open, they dropped the box and it tumbled down some stairs while they raced back to the top floor and hid out in various supply closets, where they crouched until morning, when they quietly slipped out of the building.

While they sat in hiding, however, Meg, Angela, and I were

creeping back across campus toward 21. Just as we passed beneath the library bridge, a security officer stepped out and shone a flashlight in our faces.

"Mind telling me where you're going?" he asked.

"Home," I stammered. "Twenty-one."

"Yeah, I know that. So how about telling me what you lot were up to over there?"

"I don't know what you're talking about. We're coming from the tavern."

"The one that closed two hours ago?"

"We took the long way."

"So what's so big going on in Cole? You trying to get at the dean's records?"

"Honestly . . ."

"Well, it won't do you any good. Everyone knows it's all over for you kids."

"Ummm . . . so you want to copy down our ID info?"

"That's fine. We don't need that anymore."

We walked back to the mod in silence. I realized he hadn't even asked our names. Back at the house, alternate plans to liberate the accumulator were immediately offered. Four years later, when I finally left Hampshire, it still sat tucked away in the back corner of a classroom on the third floor of the Cole Science Center, stacks of books heaped on its meticulously decorated roof.

In the final days before Spring Jam, the question of the Dicks' performance became the consuming obsession, and the more it was debated, the more hopeless it seemed that we would find a solution that was both adequately grandiose and dismissive of the entire Spring Jam enterprise. After Spring Break, Jon checked out of the conversation entirely. "I don't even think I'll play," he said. "You guys just do whatever you want."

I bounced the dilemma off Tasha one afternoon at Clase. "I've heard that concert is pretty cool," she said. "Dinosaur might do a set this year."

I stammered a bit. "It's not cool. It's like, you know, the fascist hierarchy."

She stared blankly at me.

"They are trying to destroy the real power of liberation, Dick music, beneath this—this veneer of rebellion. Orgone energy, it's like, a million times more powerful than a bunch of guys in leather jackets flailing at guitars."

She looked at me for an agonizing moment more. "Why don't you guys just do a show?"

I sputtered. "Because it would be just upholding the deadly-orgone-radiation paradigm."

Ramona, visiting from Boston, rolled her eyes and said, dangling a solitary French fry between two fingers, "What is it about your school that makes everyone so boring?"

I sank into my seat. A few minutes later, Tasha got up to leave.

"So do you want to talk on the phone later?" I asked her.

"Yeah, maybe, no. I'm going to be out until later."

"Oh, really. Out?" I looked over to Christie, to my knowledge the only person she would be out with. Christie gave no reaction to Tasha's statement.

"Oh, okay," I said. "Probably me too."

Sensing my gloom, Ramona leaned a little toward me and murmured, "Don't worry. Someday soon this kinda stuff will happen and you won't feel anything at all."

The day of Spring Jam everyone was miraculously awake by noon, even though we were not scheduled to go on until six. Nothing had been resolved about the show; it hadn't even been definitively decided that we would play, although Luntz had grudgingly sent word through his girlfriend that the Dicks would indeed be allowed to go on.

As the hubbub built in the living room, Jon sat picking at an unplugged electric guitar. The debate over what we should play gathered steam and grew into a roar before petering out for lack of any consensus. As usual, the room turned to Jon for instruction.

"I dunno," he said, not looking up. "Do you guys really want to play this show?"

We groaned.

"I guess we could do the vegetable song. What's the big deal?"

The show that year would long be remembered as the apex of Spring Jams. The bands included swinging sixties pop collective the Malarians, the country/western Jersey Slim and the Prescott Playboys, a punk group the Lonely Moans, girl rockers the Five Dumb Broads, funksters known as Jambone, and underground sensation the Loneliest Christmas Tree—each of whom drew a huge following on campus and in the area. The long winter was finally behind us—the day was perfect New England spring and a crowd of a thousand or so sprawled on the vast lawn, eating tempeh burgers from the snack bar, hacky-sacking, and enjoying the assemblage of musical giants that Hampshire had produced.

I found Tasha sitting with Susie and some of the other Amherst punks. "So what are you guys gonna do?" she asked.

"I dunno. I guess just play."

The little group looked at me, incredulous. They believed that a historic disaster had been promised.

"That's cool," Tasha said, turning back to the group.

I looked across the vast lawn and surveyed the scene. For the first time since I had been at Hampshire, the hippies, punks, hardcore feminists, art scenesters, NYC nightclubbers, Preppy Deadheads, and machine shoppers had all come together in one happy, contented day at the park. It looked like a finale scene of contentment and celebration from some postapocalyptic underground film, the ending of *8½* cast with the extras from *The Road Warrior*.

And then it was our turn to go on.

As the Dicks climbed onstage, one could feel the peaceful idyll become tense and jittery. A few rose to leave. Scattered boos were heard. The show started uneventfully enough, just as the sun was setting. For this show, some ten guitarists stepped forward to join the group, along with Steve Shavel on slide guitar and Mark on drums. As usual, the set started with no clear delineation between tuning the instruments and actual music, no clear indication that the set proper had begun and we were now actually in a song.

At some point the random chords resolved themselves into something resembling a steady drone, driven on by something approximating rhythm. At some point Steve Shavel took a microphone and, in a deep sonorous voice, began what sounded like a medieval monk's chant. The audience sat mildly annoyed for a few minutes but as ten and then fifteen minutes passed of the same, more boos were heard, barely, over the drone. The boos grew louder and louder and soon were equal in volume with the music itself. I looked around the lawn, and half of the people were on their feet yelling. The other half seemed to be leaving. I saw campus security look for guidance to Luntz, who shrugged and yelled something at the stage.

Jon and Tim moved toward each other and began playing their guitars directly in each other's faces, in fumbling mockery of two arena rock band members sharing a jam, except instead of the gleeful expressions one might find on Jon Bon Jovi and Richie Sambora's faces at such a moment, Jon and Tim were blank and emotionless, absorbed in their own drone. Then, with a sudden burst of aggression, Jon shoved his guitar at Tim, who, showing no surprise at all, violently shoved back. The necks of their guitars met, and in what looked like a sword fight with their instruments, the meeting of the twain created such a god-awful noise that most of the crowd at once covered their ears. As the howls of protest from the crowd grew louder, Jon and Tim's fight looked intensely real; Jon's normally goofy expression seemed twisted in a determined and hate-filled grin. Security moved toward the stage.

Just as the fight seemed at a stalemate, their guitars locked together, splinters flew out of the instruments, and a huge one shot directly into Jon's forehead. Within moments his face was covered with blood. The others continued playing as though nothing had happened. The boos of revulsion from the crowd became overwhelming. Luntz moved to turn off the sound and security rushed onto the stage.

It was at this point that I looked back toward the mixing table and saw Dennis, Luntz's first-year protégé, a laughably self-serious punk-nerd whom Zach, Nathan, and I had routinely mocked—kissing Tasha. I gasped for air as the mysteries of the past month unraveled in an instant. Onstage, the ten Dicks outnumbered the six security officers chasing them around the platform. The officers would shove one off the stage and go after another and the one shoved off would jump back on. I looked to Liz and Marilyn, who stood beside me. We shrugged our shoulders and jumped onstage, too, joining in the standing sit-in. For the next half hour, security played Whac-a-Mole with us until we all tired out and the lawn completely emptied. With Spring Jam over, we called it a day.

The first announcement informed us that 21 was officially disbanded. A little note, sealed in the dreaded Hampshire stationery, was delivered to each of our boxes, saying that we had each lost our residential privileges for Greenwich and Enfield Houses for the following year and that Mod 21 would be reassigned to incoming students in the fall. This meant, it occurred to me, that should I be allowed to return the following year, I would be banned from three of Hampshire's five houses. I asked Steve Shavel whether this was a record for a first-year. He suspected that it was a first in the eighties, but he recalled hearing stories that a decade before there had been a hippie girl who, during a four-month acid trip, had been thrown out of all five houses in her first semester. But still, he consoled me, it was a considerable achievement.

Returning to 21, eviction notice in hand, I expected to find a sullen room of defeated faces, but to all appearances, no one was taking any notice. A tape blared while Arthur and Tim played their guitars. A few more quarreled in a corner. A bunch of people were getting ready to go to the quad, where one of the NYC club crowd had summoned the whole campus to lie on the ground in the shape of a peace sign. She had rented a helicopter and was going to fly overhead and film the spectacle for her Div III—a music video.

Meg read a music magazine in the middle of the floor. Half-eaten sandwiches lay stuffed between cushions on the couch just like every other day, as though nothing in the world had happened. The cockroaches—whose population had exploded since spring began—strode up and down the walls with unusual energy and swagger in their step. For a moment I wondered if the news had made it back; then I saw a copy of the same note I'd received tacked to the wall between the illuminated portrait of the Apollo 11 astronauts and a Bob Weiner for Congress poster.

"So I guess it's over," I said, to no one in particular.

"Yeah, sucks," Meg said without looking up.

"Oh, wow. Where do you think you're going to live, Rich?" Ox asked, concerned.

"I guess I still don't know if I'll be back."

Ox nodded. "That's true."

Upstairs, Susie was trying on a springy dress she'd bought at a thrift store in Northampton. ("Isn't it weird that all our clothes come from dead people?" Ox had asked on the trip.) I noticed her Zelda Fitzgerald library had disappeared from her room.

"Did you finish?" I asked.

Susie made a face. "Ach, no. Milton is being ridiculous. I don't think he understands Zelda at all. I really don't feel like dealing with him anymore."

"So you're not upset about the mod, then?"

"It's really not healthy, all of us being cooped up here all the time. I've got to tell you, I'm getting sick of these people. They're just lazy."

"So what will you do?"

"Go to New York, I suppose. Be beautiful. Become a star." She turned to inspect her dress from another angle in the mirror. "What do you think I should do?"

"I would get out of here, too, if I were you. Really, Hampshire has gone completely downhill. If it had been like this three years ago, I never would've come."

In desperation, I decided to go to class. I recalled that my Tolstoy class started in ten minutes. On the brief walk over, I wondered if it wouldn't be awkward to show up to a class after a two-month absence, but none of the twenty or so other students or the professor seemed to notice or care that I hadn't been there before or that I was there now.

The professor was actually one of Hampshire's most exciting, and seeing her gave me pangs of regret that I hadn't come to class more often. Ninotchka was a dead ringer for Morticia Addams, down to the long, slinky dresses she wore in black, gray, or red. She sat down and apologized to the class that she might have to cut things short today, since she was suffering from walking pneumonia.

Since I hadn't read *Anna Karenina,* the lecture and discussion were fairly obscure, but Ninotchka's musings on Anna's suicide were absolutely captivating. At the end of the class, Ninotchka reminded everyone that final papers were due the following week. In a whisper I asked the guy sitting next to me how many papers they had written so far. He shot me a dirty look and said, "This is the first."

After class, walking nearly on tiptoes, I approached Ninotchka and asked her for another copy of the assignment, saying I'd lost mine. She handed me the page, giving no hint that she realized I had not been in class all semester. I asked her, "Do you really think Anna needed to kill herself?"

"Oh, yes. . . ," she drawled, looking up at me from her desk.

"But how come she couldn't go back to whatshisname?"

"To Karenin?"

"Right, him."

"She's been with Vronsky now. Once you've lived your romantic ideal you can't very well return to the mundane, can you?"

"No. You really can't."

"I'm glad you see that." She smiled and it occurred to me that I should become a student of Russian literature.

After the disappearance of Tasha from my life, I once again sought out Elizabeth, and once again found myself confused and frustrated by every encounter with her, and by my own inability to explain, even to myself, what I would have wanted from her.

One night we were hanging out in her room, sharing a bottle of bourbon I had, along with some Darvon she had been given at the Health Services for headaches. Feeling exceptionally at ease, I asked her, "Do you think we should go to that show Saturday night?" (referring to a concert at SAGA by the band Half Japanese).

"Why wouldn't we go?"

I nodded. "Yeah, of course."

"You mean like together?"

"I dunno. Maybe. Whatever."

"Do you want us to go together?" She looked me dead in the eyes. I turned away.

"Probably, you know. Since we're hanging out a lot." I paused for a moment and thought. "But I guess I should check what's going on at Twenty-one first. . . ."

She laughed. "Okay . . . ," she said, and chased a handful of the remaining pills with a swig from the bottle.

The following night Zach and I had our radio show at Amherst. I still had a hangover from the night before, which had lingered on to well past noon. In the end, Elizabeth had declined to come back to 21 with me but, still miraculously wide awake, had left me in front of the library and wandered off in the direction of Prescott, where, I couldn't help but think, there lived an acid dealer named Neal whom I'd noticed her chatting with in the past.

As Zach and I settled into the booth, I fumed, thinking of Elizabeth hanging out with Neal, tripping, the two of them perhaps even brazenly listening to my show. I reached for Hüsker Dü's *Zen Arcade* album. "Happy morning, Pioneer Valley," I said into the mike. "To start things off, here's a smash hit from those lovable mop-tops from Liverpool, Hüsker Dü, which goes out to a special someone, who maybe at this moment is hanging out in Prescott House. I hope you're listening." I started up the song "Never Talking to You Again" and sat down to soak it in.

When the song ended, Zach was still fumbling for another album, so I picked up the needle and started it over from the top. When I did that a second time Zach asked, "Are you trying to send someone a message?"

"Maybe."

"But is there any chance in hell that they are listening?"

I thought about that for a second. "No. I guess there isn't."

Zach nodded. "Nice work, then."

"Thanks," I said, starting the song over once again.

Three plays of the song later, Zach said, "I know sending this message to all zero of our listeners means a lot to you, but I'm getting sick of it. Can we play something fun?"

"Fun?!? Like what?"

He grabbed Dexy's Midnight Runners off the shelf and started "Come On Eileen" on the turntable. "Like this."

I started to object but then stopped and listened, and soon found myself nodding along. "I have to say, this speaks to me."

"See? Life is a big bowl of happiness. Toora Loora Toora Loo-Rye-Aye."

I took this in. "Let's listen again." I started the record over. And then again, and again.

At six A.M. Todd the station manager walked in wearing pajama pants and a baggy Police *Synchronicity* tour T-shirt, his head askew with tousled bed hair. "Hey, guys." He glanced at us nervously. "Great song."

We nodded. "It is. It really is." He smiled, clearing his throat. Dexy sang, "These people round here wear beaten down eyes/ Sunk in smoke dried faces, they're resigned to what their fate is."

"It's beautiful," I whispered softly.

"Yeah, well, hey. I don't want to tell you how to run your show."

"Good," Zach said.

"Huh-huh. Yeah, but—"

"Here it comes."

"I've been getting some complaints."

"Complaints?" we said in unison, eyes wide. We looked at each other. "You mean someone is listening?"

"Some people are."

"*Some* people are. . . . There's more than one person listening?"

"Well, I've gotten a bunch of calls. I mean, people, especially the Amherst campus, sorta depend on this station to provide them with some basic atmosphere."

"But, Todd," Zach cut in again, "don't you understand what this means? We're a hit!"

"I wouldn't say that exactly."

"We have several listeners!" Zach and I whooped, high-fived, and raced around the studio for a few minutes in a victory dance, pausing to restart the song.

"Okay, guys. Before you get too excited, it's finals week. Everyone is doing all-nighters getting ready."

"Oh." We stopped in our tracks. Todd's invocation of tests and their relationship to sleeping habits introduced such a foreign element, we had to pause and take it in. If Todd had told us that they were listening to the show because they calibrated the radio waves and used them to cook their breakfasts in order to have energy to telekinetically reassemble their home planets, it would have been only slightly less startling. But whatever he meant, the bubble of excitement about our explosive audience-growth patterns was duly popped.

"So I'm not telling you what to play—"

"You said that before and I said good."

"Heh, right. It's just, maybe you might mix in some other songs here and there?"

"So you *are* telling us what to play?"

"No, no, no. Play anything you want. Just try maybe another song during your slot."

"Fascist," Zach spat.

"Guys . . ."

"You never told us censorship was part of the deal."

"Come on. . . . I'm not censoring. . . ."

Zach planted himself directly in front of Todd. "I think you need to leave."

Twenty minutes later we were on the bus back to Hampshire. "I don't care what he says," Zach said as I dozed off to sleep in the next seat. "I love that song."

The shoes fell and fell. Ox met with his Div III committee. He had turned in, by his accounts, a still very rough, unfinished draft of his Div III thesis entitled "Beyond Logocentrism: The Postmodern Philosophies of Derrida, Nietzsche, and Foucault." I wondered to myself when he had found the time to even come up with that title, let alone flesh out any part of a paper. He returned stoically from his meeting. "Yeah, I think maybe it's time for the Dicks to play on a bigger stage."

"So you're not going to finish it next year?" I asked. Ox was at this point at the end of his sixth year.

"Oh, well. Probably not. I mean, the world needs us, don't you think?"

Arthur announced he was moving back to Iowa. Others were summarily granted diplomas, some against their will. "If they've done any work since they got here, it's easier for the school to graduate them than expel them," Steve mused.

"Graduating people against their will," Ox reflected. "That sounds like a human rights violation."

For myself, just as I had tumbled into the abyss of despair, a ray of hope shone onto me. One afternoon I confided to Steve Shavel that all was lost, that I had no chance of fulfilling the terms of my academic probation; that I was going to have to go back to California, where, separated from the others, I'd meet a fate so ghastly I dared not contemplate it. Steve asked to see the academic contract Leo had drawn up, and my Tolstoy assignment. He put on his glasses and studied the papers carefully. "I think we can do this."

"What do you mean? How can I finish two classes?"

"Ah, but, you see, it doesn't just say two classes. It says two, *or* one class plus a Div One."

"That's even worse. I'm not going to be able to do some monster project in the next four days. I wouldn't even be able to get a professor to work with me on one."

Steve took off his glasses, blew on the lenses, and polished them off. "In my day, yes, you would've been doomed. But two years ago the school instituted a little travesty of alternative education known as the two-course option."

"I see. . . ."

"Which gave students a choice for each of their Div Ones: Instead of doing a project, you can take two classes in that field, and you can count those two classes as a Div One. Didn't you say you finished the Nietzsche class first semester?"

"Yes . . ."

"So if you finish the Tolstoy class, that's two in Arts and Humanities. You've got a Div One."

"But don't I need that class to count toward the finishing one class on my contract?"

"There's nothing that says it can't count for both."

I paused to think. "So one Tolstoy paper can be parlayed to fulfill all the requirements of my probation?"

Steve nodded. "Now, mind you, Supreme Dick scriptures do not approve of the two-course option. But I can see where we might grant wartime emergency exemptions."

"But there's one problem: How am I going to read *Anna Karenina* in four days? It's like eight hundred pages."

"Again you're not reading the fine print. Ninotchka says the paper should be on Anna or any work covered in this class."

"And . . ."

"I took that class my third year—"

"What was that?"

"Never mind. But I just happen to know the first book that class reads is *Master and Man*. Which is under a hundred pages."

I gazed upon Steve as though I were looking at one of the great thinkers of human history, a Socrates or Isaac Newton walking among us. "That's amazing," I murmured.

Four days later, after two consecutive all-nighters, I sat down and typed, "The repression of man's nature and subversion of his will and instinct toward the servitude of other men comprise the motivating force behind Tolstoy's *Master and Man*." Four pages later I wrote, "Lying on top of Nikita, while the storm is closing in around him, Vasilii Andreich realizes himself through this liberation of his sexuality. His petty societal protections far away from him, he is finally able to liberate his sexuality, and merge with the universe."

I tore the last page out of the typewriter and raced over to Ninotchka's office, handing her the paper just as she was about to leave for the weekend.

Jon screened his top-secret film for his committee and passed his Div III. Meg reported that the word around the film/photo building was that his professors had told him it was the best student film they had ever seen and demanded he enter it in festivals. In response, Jon said he would probably "throw it out." We all went to the final film showing, sat through hours of abstract color experiments and, ultimately, the much-awaited music video featuring half the school lying on the ground in the shape of a peace sign shot from a helicopter. Jon's name was listed on the program, but when his turn arrived, they skipped ahead to the next film. In the end, none of us ever saw the fabled work and the rumor spread that Jon had burned it.

On graduation day, Zach, Nathan, and I stood at the back of the lawn, watching from a distance, as Jon, Tim, and a handful of the others accepted their diplomas.

"Do you think that someday, seven, eight years from now, that will be us up there?" I asked.

"No," Zach firmly replied.

"I'll try one more semester," Nathan said.

A group from 21 gathered around Jon to look at his diploma.

"Can you even imagine what these guys are going to do now?" Meg asked me.

"What do you think they'll do?"

"I don't know. Something major," she said. "But a year from now, this school is going to really regret it treated them this way."

A lazy heat covered the school, the first grips of summer's mugginess. I sat by myself on the wall outside the library and watched the crowds wander off from the central lawn while crews loaded the chairs and platforms onto a flatbed truck. The warmth and light sun made everyone walk in slow motion and made the campus look relaxed, pleasant, and happy, and I wondered for a moment what we'd all been so worked up about. Down by the road, cars crammed with luggage honked a final salute as they carried people away, the campus breaking up, many, including my friends, I thought, never to return. I sighed and lit a cigarette, thinking back on all that had happened since I'd walked up that lawn, duffel bag on my back, eight months before.

Someone sat down next to me and from my peripheral vision, a glimpse of long red hair made me gasp.

"Elizabeth!" I managed to say. "You're still here."

"Where've you been?"

"Oh, you know. Pretty much around."

"Lucy misses you."

I nodded. "You know, I mean, this semester. It was, like, you know. We had fun, I think."

Elizabeth smiled benignly as I babbled, watching as every trace of cool I had struggled so hard to assemble was shredded into tatters with each word out of my mouth. I kept going. "I think maybe next year, do you think we should, I dunno. I mean, what were you—"

She finally took pity and whispered, "Shhhhh," and put her index finger over my mouth and then her lips. We kissed in the open for the first time in the warm summer day.

"Can I write to you this summer?" I said when she pulled

away. She smiled and wrote an address down on a graduation program that was lying on the ground.

"I'll be staying with my friend in San Francisco. You can write me here."

"I will." I nodded. We kissed again and then I watched her walk away. I lit another cigarette and soaked in the campus. What was all that fuss about indeed. I smiled to no one and looked down at the address, written in Elizabeth's hand. Were zip codes only four numbers long? For a second I panicked and, seeing her walk down the path toward the dorms, thought about running after her but brought myself to order. Maybe in San Francisco they are, I told myself. Maybe they are.

Later that day, everyone gathered at Joel Joel's house in Northampton to observe one of the Dicks' most hallowed traditions, the *Blonde on Blonde* Dickel. According to Steve Shavel, every nine months the Supreme Dick extended family must assemble to listen to Bob Dylan's *Blonde on Blonde* album and drink Dickel whiskey, because "that was what Tennessee Williams drank himself to death on," he said, I later learned erroneously. According to tradition, the day would also be marked by Steve Shavel jumping off a roof. At the last BBD he had leapt from the top of 21 and gotten stuck in a tree. This time around, we assembled on Joel Joel's balcony, which hung a good twenty-five feet above a concrete sidewalk. I looked down dubiously as Jon and Ox described Steve's leaping history. "Somehow Dickel makes him a little weird," Jon said. On cue, with a roar, Steve leapt through the window and out onto the balcony. Racing toward the precipice, he lunged for the edge, stopped only at the last moment by Arthur, who grabbed him by his skinny tie.

While Arthur and some others bound Steve's hands and feet with extension cords, Jon, Ox, and I talked about their plans. "What are you guys going to do now?" I asked.

They looked at each other as though this were a subject they hadn't really discussed before. Ox's head bobbed in nods. "I guess I might go to New York. Maybe to the East Village."

"To do what?"

They both looked astonished at the question. "I suppose get an apartment. Oh, why, is there something going on?" Ox said.

I looked at Jon. "Are you going to New York?"

"Yeah, maybe. I don't know. I guess I have to think about it. I mean, what's really the point in picking something or someplace when you're probably going to change your mind once you get there, you know?"

Yeah, I nodded. I looked around the balcony at the thirty or so people who had become my friends, who, as far as I was concerned, had saved my life at Hampshire. Many were bellowing along, loudly, badly out of tune, off-rhythm, with "Visions of Johanna," Steve, lying tied up on the floor, singing the loudest. I remembered how desperate I'd been when I found them and wondered if that was the life I'd return to in the fall. I wondered if this group would ever get together again. And I wondered, not having been told that I was being expelled, if that was that, the coast was clear, and now that the Dicks were gone, I was free to return.

As if hearing my thoughts, Ox said to me, "Maybe we should see if people want to go to Denny's tonight. . . ."

A week later I lay on my bed in Mod 21 listening to the quiet. The others had moved out—Susie went back to New York, Jon was living with Joel in Northampton, Arthur had loaded up his car and driven to Iowa. In fact, the entire campus was empty, the school having shut down after graduation. I had planned to drive back to L.A. with my high school friend Will, but as Vassar didn't get out for another week, I had time to kill. Whenever I looked at my room, the thought of packing depressed me so much that I had to open a detective novel to chase the feeling away.

I spent my ghostly days in Northampton, sitting with Jon and Steve at the sidewalk tables of Bonducci's Café enjoying the now warm weather with an endless chain of cigarettes and espresso shots. At night I slunk through the empty, deserted campus, jumping into the woods when I saw a security van approach in the distance and slipping back into 21, lights out to avoid drawing attention, to sleep there alone. On the final morning I lay in bed for hours, listening to the silence. I realized I was having some issues with letting go of 21 and I wondered if I should do something about it.

The silence broke and I sat up straight in bed as I heard the front door spring open and a pair of gruff voices stomp inside. "Holy crap, look at this place!" I heard one of them say.

"It would be easier just to torch it."

I heard the steps draw closer. They opened the door of the room next to mine. "PU!"

And then the door to my room flung open. Two workmen in overalls stood in the doorway looking at me lying in bed, reading a comic book. I looked up and smiled. "I was just leaving," I said.

CHAPTER ELEVEN

What's Left Behind

In September I was assigned to a room in Merrill House, one of the two remaining dorms where I was still allowed to live. Along with Dakin, Merrill House formed the other half of the brick-and-concrete dorm quad surrounding the cafeteria. While Dakin took in the dregs of Hampshire housing—the Ellis Island of incoming freshmen—Merrill had a somewhat more selective, urbane reputation. About 10 percent of each incoming class was sent directly to Merrill, forgoing their Dakin initiation. It was widely believed that the school selected the worldly sophisticates of each class to go straight into Merrill's social big leagues. It was never clear how the housing offices would have determined their selections when they barely knew our names, let alone how well we might mix at parties. Nevertheless, it was undeniable that an outsized percentage of incoming students from New York City were sent directly to Merrill.

Built in three wings of four floors, Merrill House was also home to Hampshire's famed clothing-optional hall. The house's older students were an odd grab bag. While possessing the social skills necessary to mingle in Merrill's swift currents, they were missing one or another DNA particle that would have guided them through the communal demands of mod life. Typical among these was Dirk Cahill aka Duke. In his fifth or so year at Hampshire, Duke was a paramilitary enthusiast who often threatened those who rubbed him the wrong way with complex revenge plots featuring exotic imported weaponry. Every night Duke and an oddly assorted gang of Merrill's older students sat in the dining hall at a corner table adorned with candles, where they ostentatiously served each other from bottles of red wine.

I limped back to campus and carried my duffel bag to the dorms with a sense of doom, remembering the trials of the last year and still not quite believing that my friends were gone; my home in 21 was no more. I was set a bit at ease, however, when I found my new hallmates on A-1 were considerably more welcoming than those who had greeted me on J-3 a year before. Among my new neighbors were Ike, a freshman from a Pennsylvania Quaker school who spent long hours strumming REM on his acoustic guitar; Sarah, a perpetually cheery Preppy Deadhead girl from Westport; Sally, a slightly sullen, borderline hippie social science student from Vermont who, I was delighted to find, had a small collection of Sinatra albums; and Frank, a working-class rocker who soon became one of my closest friends.

While I had been hiding away in the Greenwich woods the previous year, Frank and a few other first-years had formed a post-punk band named the Butt Buddies, which had alternately become the terrors of the dorm and the gravitational center for the discontented fringe of the class. When I told Frank that I had been a member of the Supreme Dicks, he was at first disbelieving; having heard the Dicks legends, he'd thought it an ancient clan long extinguished. "No, we were very real," I told him.

Real as they may have been in my time, the void left by the

disappearance of Jon, Ox, Steve, Arthur, Tim, and all the others from campus was constantly in my mind. I knew that Jon and Steve, at least, were probably in Northampton, but I wasn't sure how to get in touch with them. Since May, I hadn't received any letters with their new phone numbers or contact info. I thought to go into Northampton and ask at Bonducci's, but in the first weeks of the semester, there had not yet been time. Steve was still, I believed, an enrolled student at Hampshire, or at least, since he hadn't been expelled or forcibly graduated the year before, he was eligible to become a student again, so I assumed he would appear on campus eventually.

I soon learned that one of the responsibilities of living in hall A-1 was greeting a constant parade of visitors to the Hampshire campus. Several times a day, I walked out of my room and found a stranger, or several strangers, standing in the hallway, seemingly looking for someone. If I greeted them, they would reply without hesitation, "Could I buy some pot from you?" To the entire East Coast liberal arts community and to a good percentage of the surrounding counties at the time, Hampshire College was legendary as a land where drugs grew from every tree, where dorm rooms were wallpapered in LSD, where Quaaludes were passed out at the beginning of each lecture. Throngs of drug seekers wandered onto campus every day in search of this magical kingdom of drugs and honey. When they came to campus, they generally wandered toward the dorms. And when they got to the dorms, they walked into the first door they saw, which took them to Hall A-1. Amazingly, none of the campus dealers had thought to take advantage of this walk-in trade and set up shop on our hall, but my hallmates knew where to refer the visitors and cheerily sent them on their way, later visiting the dealers they had pointed the way to and asking for a referrers' discount.

More disturbing than random drug seekers were the signs of a terrifying new trend in the incoming class. One afternoon in the dining hall, Zach and I met a trio of long-haired, flannel-shirted metalhead first-years, who told us they were starting a band called Power Slave. The hyperactive lads gave us a little demo of their sound, air-guitaring and drumming one of their songs on the table. But our jaws dropped when, to our horror, they began bragging about the number of classes they were taking—five apiece. They went on to explain how they planned to finish all their Div I's in their first year.

"I'm not sure you guys understand how this place works . . . ," I said. "First year is supposed to be about getting to know yourself. Understanding what, you know, like, motivates you."

"Fuck that," one of them bellowed. "What motivates me is to get into a decent grad school as quick as I can." Zach and I looked at each other and wondered what sort of world we were suddenly living in.

Another element that perversely seemed to act in our favor was that the previous year's steady trickle of demonstrations against the injustice of the week had now exploded into a flood. Almost every night at SAGA, dinner was interrupted by some earnest group announcing an urgent community action, an all-campus demonstration against sexual orientation discrimination, or gender bias, or racism or classism or harassment. The announcements often droned on for as long as twenty minutes, ruining many a dinner, but they had the ironic effect of taking the attention off those who remained from the Supreme Dick ranks. With the campus constantly running off to one or another teach-in or sensitivity training session, mobilizing against the great isms of our times, everyone seemed to have forgotten their loyal adversaries of yesteryear, the Supreme Dicks. Those few who bothered to remember seemed to have forgotten that Zach, Nathan, and I had once been members of the campus's most hated social club. And so we slid back into the general population unnoticed, back into lives of tranquillity and dissolution.

By the end of September, life at Merrill House felt if not idyllic, then at least manageably annoying. The fog of marijuana smoke was persistently irritating, but I had managed to bond with enough of my hallmates that I did not live in dread of coming home every night. Frank and the Butt Buddies gathered on most nights for some sort of impromptu party. I even took steps to sign up for classes, although I realized as I did it that this was a pointless, if noble, step. What's more, my advisor was so flummoxed with the way I had weaseled through last semester's probation, he hadn't bothered to renew it.

I was even inspired to decorate. One night in the laundry room, my eye was caught by the stunning array of colors of the lint sheets removed from the dryers. I gathered up an armful, gently carried them up to the hall, and stapled them to the wall. I spent the rest of the night visiting the other laundry rooms around campus to complete my Wall of Lint. Frank and Ike seemed impressed, but Sarah and Sally shrieked and demanded I tear it down. I refused, accusing them of wanting to stifle my artistic expression. Sally settled the dispute by summoning the House Office, who declared my installation a fire hazard and demanded I remove it at once. I complied but found myself muttering, "Narc," under my breath every time Sally walked past for the next few days.

Since my first moment back on campus, I had both prayed for and lived in fear of my reunion with Elizabeth. During the summer, in one of my lowest moments of melancholy thinking back to the lost friends of Hampshire, I poured all of my thoughts and regrets—all of them—into a letter to Elizabeth and sent it to the address she had given me. Two weeks later it came back— apparently a zip code needed more than four digits, even in San Francisco. But somehow, despite the fact that she had never received my gushings, the fact that I had set them down on paper, the fact that I myself was aware of them, put me in terror of running into her again.

For the first few weeks our paths never crossed. I heard Frank talking about her one day and learned that she had moved into a mod in Enfield with some friends and that things had gotten "really intense out there. Those guys never go out." At the tail end of a few drunken nights I had come close to wandering across campus and knocking on her door, but always held myself back.

Finally, halfway through September, at a party in Prescott, I saw her. I was walking up a stairwell. The steps were wet with spilled beer. I slipped and grasped the metal handrail for balance, only to discover it was gluelike, sticky beer. Prying my hand loose, I looked up. Elizabeth was standing at the top of the stairwell, Lucy by her side, glaring down at me. I looked around to see if there was still room to run, but finding myself trapped, the crowd pushing up behind me, I pulled myself together and stumbled to the top.

"Oh, hi, Elizabeth. Hi, Lucy," I muttered.

"Those stairs don't like you," Elizabeth said. I noticed, through my own drunken haze, that the glassy distance in her eyes was even more pronounced than it had been last spring.

"No, they don't," I said. "I guess this school doesn't like me. You know, they broke up Twenty-one."

They nodded. "Our mod is like . . ." Elizabeth looked at Lucy to finish the thought.

"A magical harem." They both burst into giggles.

"That sounds great," I said. "Elizabeth, I've . . ." I tried to find my thought. Elizabeth smiled open-eyed, while little Lucy at her side glared up at me skeptically. "I guess I wondered when I'd see you."

Elizabeth smiled. "When you'd see me see you seeing me." They broke down in giggles again.

"Well, maybe I'll stop by," I said, slinking away while they continued laughing.

Three hours, a dozen drinks, and a couple pills Frank had prescribed later, I stumbled across campus to Enfield House. Her mod was lit in the dull violet light from a batik-covered floor lamp. Elizabeth lay on a couch, staring at her hand. "Hello," she said, not bothering to move.

Over the following months, I found myself stopping by her mod late at night on a regularly irregular basis, each time producing the same thrill of being reunited with Elizabeth and, the following day, the same confusion of not knowing what we were, or even whether Elizabeth, who barely left her mod, had any sense that this visit was not the last one and thus that there was any cumulative weight to our time together. But as many times as I swore never to return, driven by my frustration with my own inability just to "be cool" about the feelings whirling inside, I kept finding myself at every party I went to scanning the room for Elizabeth, and over and over again, late at night, wandering back to Enfield, hoping to catch her alone.

Manageable though Merrill life seemed, quickly enough, a note of chaos found its way into my world. One evening, as I sat in the back room of the dining hall with Zach, Frank, Nathan, Sarah, and some others, we looked over at Duke's table. One of the group's traditions was that when one of them went for a beverage, he or she brought some back for everyone. As we looked over, a curly-haired boy in a black blazer pinned with minibuttons was carrying a tray of coffee cups back to the table, and he passed them out to his friends.

"This has to stop," Zach muttered.

"I think it's sweet," Sarah cooed.

"Zach, I think you got a point." Frank nodded. "That's no kinda behavior for a respectable dining facility."

The next evening ten of us lined up at the front door before SAGA opened. We raced inside and took seats at Duke's table, settling in for a siege. Within minutes, trouble started. The mod guy and a red-haired girl walked into the back room, saw us, and stopped dead in their tracks. The mod guy's jaw fell. He whispered something to the red-haired girl, then ran back down the hall. A couple minutes later, Duke and five others of his group strode in and marched over to us, a bloodthirsty look in their eyes.

Duke leaned on the table, palms pressed down hard, and stared us in the eyes one by one, nodding at each of us to send the message that he was committing our faces to memory for his files. Finally he spoke. "Very. Fucking. Funny. Guys. Very. Fucking. Funny."

We sheepishly smiled up at him.

"Okay, I can deal with your little stunt. But lemme tell you, if this ever happens again, every person at this table is a dead man. A. Dead. Man."

"That sounds fair." Zach nodded.

"Shut the hell up, freak," Duke barked. He gathered his men together and carried over a neighboring table, which they positioned so that one of its corners touched one corner of our table, preserving, technically at least, the continuity of his unbroken sitting-at-the-same-table string probably dating back to the mid-seventies. We ate uncomfortably next to each other for the entire two-and-a-half-hour SAGA dinnertime. When at last Duke got up to go, he repeated his routine of looking each of us in the eyes and reminding us, "Never again. Not if you want to live."

With that threat on the table, the decision had been taken out of our hands; we had no choice but to line up the following night at SAGA and occupy the table once more.

"So the rest of the dining hall won't actually let him kill us, will they?" I asked the others.

"No way," Frank said. "This place has just been waiting for someone to start the revolution. Believe you me, these folks have got our backs." Looking around the room, however, I saw a great many people laughing and pointing and, if I wasn't wrong, shaking with glee at the thought that we were about to be mass-murdered before their eyes.

When Duke arrived, on cue his face turned red and the smoke poured from his nostrils. The time for gentle warnings had passed. He stood at the head of the table and raged at the top of his lungs, detailing the ways he was going to massacre us, collectively and individually. Pots of boiling hydrochloric acid were mentioned; Green Beret units parachuting onto the Merrill roof were invoked. He picked up the table and knocked our trays of lasagna and SAGA's famed "Calico Skillet" to the floor. He grabbed Zach by the shoulders and shook him. But through it all, we held our ground. I wondered how at this peace-loving school, at this peace-*studying* school, people could just watch idly, even contentedly, while violence and tyranny exploded in their midst. But somehow they found the resources within themselves to do just that.

Eventually, Duke and his friends finished venting and moved on, constructing the adjoining table once again. Each time they passed behind they made sure to knock their trays against our heads. When finally they left, we let up a little cheer of victory, which the rest of the hall did not join.

The next day, three separate people told me that Duke had outlined to them the ways in which I would soon meet my doom. To one, he explained he had miniature tear gas cartridges that were small enough to slide under my door and time-fused to explode moments later. To another, he promised that he wouldn't actually kill us but that through his connections in the FBI and CIA he would make our names disappear from all records, erasing us as though we had never existed, making life impossible—at least if ever we wanted to get credit cards. Frank and I warned the rest of our hall that someone might come in to bomb us with tear gas. Most seemed vaguely concerned and promised to keep a lookout, although I noticed the tiniest hint of a smile sneak across Sally's face.

In the following issue of the Merrill House newsletter, a photocopied samizdat produced by the House Office and distributed to every bathroom stall in the dorm, Duke had authored an article entitled "20 Ways to Kill Dickheads," which outlined the various assassination methods one could use against us. The Merrill House staff handed out copies to whoever came into the office, including to Frank and me. I marveled that September wasn't even over and already I felt completely uncomfortable in yet another dorm.

Again, I made initial stabs at getting some academic momentum rolling. I signed up for a Tolstoy class taught by Ninotchka, and also tried out "Ways of Un-Being: Perspectives on Madness in Modern Literature," despite an ominously dense class description in the course catalog. On the first day, the professor assigned a reading from Michel Foucault's *The Archaeology of Knowledge*—"just to get us all on the same page, linguistically," she said.

That night I started reading, tearing through the pages at a breakneck pace. *This is easy,* I thought as I reached page ten. Then I realized I had no idea what I had just read. My eyes had walked over the pages. I had taken in the sentences but they passed over me like a mild breeze, leaving nothing behind and no memory of the experience. I tried again and after another ten pages, I shook myself off. It was as though I had gone into some kind of trance. I had no clue what it was I had just read. I resolved to focus and looked down, going very slowly over each word. I read:

Moreover, the unity of the discourses on madness would be the interplay of the rules that define the transformations of these different objects, their nonidentity through time, the break produced in them, the internal discontinuity that suspends their permanence. Paradoxically, to define a group of statements in terms of its individuality would be to define the dispersion of these objects, to grasp all the interstices that separate them, to measure the distances that reign between them—in other words, to formulate their law of division.

The book fell from my hands and I gaped slack-jawed, betrayed and wounded as though Foucault had just lulled me into trusting him and then reached out and punched me in the nose. Could that have just happened? Cautiously, I picked the book up off the floor, opened it, and reread those sentences. What could this possibly mean? The professor wouldn't have assigned this to an undergraduate literature class if it was written in a foreign tongue, I assumed, so why couldn't I make out what the hell was going on here? The next day I ran into a girl from my class.

"I love Foucault," she gushed. "For me, that's my airplane reading."

"But did you understand it? I mean, the writing . . . ?"

"That's the best thing about him. His beautiful language. It's just fun! Not like Barthes—just between us, although I totally respect everything he has to say."

I had better luck on a class in Global Farming Issues, taught by a professor who, Zach had tipped me off, was Hampshire's version of Crocodile Dundee—the head of the Farm Center and New England's champion dogsled racer. Hal, indeed, did not disappoint on my first visit. Dressed in a plaid flannel jacket and matching cap, he gave us a slide show that depicted his trip across Haiti in the company of "one of the best monkey hunters in the whole Caribbean." In a later class he gave us a slide tour of his farm, where he was experimenting with new mulching methods. It became increasingly obvious, as Hal began to slur his words and shout dramatically, that he might well be deeply drunk. I looked around for any sign of a bottle, hoping Zach and I might be able to grab it while Hal was lecturing.

When he came to the end of the show, he slumped into his chair. "So that's my farm. That's how I've been trying to save the world. My kids, they don't want any part of it. They want to go off to school and become artists. The commies and the hippies, they all say, 'Hal, that's so great what you're doing!' but when I say, 'You want to come help out?' they say, 'You got ten bucks an hour?' So when I'm gone, what's going to happen to it all? Who's going to care?" The class was dead silent as he buried his head in his hands. "Somebody get the lights!" Hal sobbed as we all filed out.

I turned to Zach. "Finally, a decent class at this place!"

Eventually I tracked down Jon and Steve in Northampton, where they were both living—Jon renting an apartment and Steve crashing on the couch. In his years after Hampshire, Steve would spend much of his life in residence on various couches, and he explained that this was his way of restoring civilization to a decadent age. "In ancient Greece," he said, "hospitality was the principle on which society was built. By law, any Greek citizen was entitled to demand hospitality of any other Greek citizen for two days and three nights. I am a lone knight for civilization, forcing people to live up to these ancient standards."

"But two days and three nights?" I asked. "You've been on Jon's couch for over two months."

"There's been a great deal of inflation since Greek times, if you haven't noticed."

In Northampton, Jon and Steve's existence rotated each day between Bonducci's Café, the venerable browsing room of the Smith College library—where Steve napped on deep couches and pored over his Wittgenstein—and late nights at the Red Lion Diner.

Northampton during this era teetered between two worlds. The small town built around a four-block Main Street appeared from a distance like a miniature version of a classic northeastern industrial town with cigar stores, a Woolworth five-and-ten, an ancient cemetery, churches, and an opera house. But another element had begun to encroach like some fatal tree fungus that would eventually spell old Northampton's doom—between the old-timey bait-and-tackle shops, every third window featured a display of wind chimes, handcrafted candles, or a poster lauding the nutritional benefits of wheatgrass juice.

Another element colored the idyllic New England experience— in those days Northampton was home to the richest collection of insane people I had ever encountered. At some point in the early 1980s, cutbacks had supposedly forced the Northampton State Mental Hospital to deinstitutionalize wagonloads of patients at a time, releasing them into the community. The result was that walking down Main Street one darted between old men arguing with invisible friends and others lying on the sidewalk guffawing and pointing up the skirts of passing girls.

Every night they all came to the Red Lion Diner, as did Jon and Steve. The little eatery occupied a refurbished red train car that sat just below the tracks of the Northampton Train Depot; strong waves of terror rocked me every time I met Jon and Steve here. On a typical evening at the Red Lion at least one patron lost his marbles and exploded in a screaming fury at the manager or at anyone close at hand. Each time I stepped inside and saw a row of God's forgotten men spitting and muttering to themselves along the counter, I thought to myself, *I have pushed my luck too far; this will be the night I will die for my scrambled eggs and wheat toast.*

And remarkably, even in this company, Jon had managed to make himself despised.

The manager of the Red Lion was a bullet-headed ex-Marine

named Mike, who walked the floor with a seven-inch hunting knife on his belt, sneering back at the lunatics and grumbling gargoyles. Every night we watched Mike absorb waves of abuse from his guests, saw him poised, hand on knife, and wondered if we would be here when he plunged it into some patron's throat. But his demeanor of general contempt for all humanity was somehow pushed to the breaking point every time Jon walked in the door.

One night Jon had mentioned that "Mike hates me," but I found that hard to believe, saying, "Mike hates everyone."

"No, but he really hates Jon," Steve confirmed.

Sure enough, the moment we walked in the door, Mike threw his notepad down on the counter and bellowed, "Ruin my fucking night!"

As we ordered, Jon shook his head. "He's going to do it." When our food arrived, Mike brought Jon's bowl of cereal with exactly two cornflakes sitting alone at the bottom of the bowl. "I can't believe he did it again!" Jon tried to flag Mike down to bring the matter to his attention, but Mike refused to look our way for the rest of the night.

The week before, Jon and Steve told me, it had been even worse. A gruff woman named Jesse—either Mike's wife or mother, we weren't sure—had been on duty. It was Jon's habit to put as many as ten or fifteen spoonfuls of sugar in his coffee. As Jesse cleared the table, she had glanced inside Jon's cup, noticed the residue and, apparently, cracked. "Now I have to wash the fucking cup!" she screamed, and then, deciding this was too much for a person to bear, threw the mug with all her might at the wall above Jon's head, where it shattered, showering Jon and Steve with shards of ceramic.

It was in this atmosphere that we met at night to plot the next stage of the Dicks movement. "The Hampshire era had to end," Steve said. "Once they added the two-course option, they turned their back on experimental education and then it was only a matter of time before we were eradicated."

I nodded, thinking of the God knows how many years I still had left there. I told them about the guys who wanted to do their Div I's in their first year. Their jaws dropped with dismay. "We got out just in time."

"Dick music is the future," Jon said. "Hampshire College is the past."

Back at Merrill House, sensing that our lives had stabilized to a manageable threat level, Duke's bluster aside, Zach, Frank, and I decided it was time to do probably the single dumbest thing one could do at Hampshire College—we decided to start a fraternity. As it turned out, we already had in hand the critical cornerstone for such an institution—the hat. The previous summer, while driving across country, my high school friend Will and I had stopped at the gift store of Slippery Rock State College, where on a whim I had bought a purple corduroy baseball cap that read "Sigma Pi." The thought behind starting a fraternity was not actually to infuriate the entire school—that was a fringe benefit—but to serve a larger good by getting money from the student activities fund to buy alcohol with.

The activities fund was one of Hampshire's more celebrated boondoggles. For a school too perpetually short on cash to light its hallways properly, it nonetheless always nursed an endless slush fund disbursed to any person or group of people who could with a straight face describe themselves as organizing a community activity. Some of these beneficiaries received gargantuan piles of booty—the campus Women's Center had a full-time staff and an office off the Airport Lounge. Others, such as the Alternative Music Collective, threw concerts, and still many others just sponsored parties at the dining hall, which was our intention.

Zach, Frank, and I consecrated ourselves the fraternity officers (treasurer, sergeant-at-arms, and president, respectively) and filled out and submitted the forms to the elected student council (known as the Community Council), which handed out the dough. A week later, we were duly notified that our application had been rejected.

"Where do these people get off rejecting us?" said Frank, who was new to pariah status.

"Are they allowed to reject people?" Zach wondered, listing some of the more ridiculous groups that had been funded (Frisbee fellowships, transgender dramatic societies, et cetera).

We decided that this could not be the last word on the subject, that a project as noble as our planned fraternity could not be allowed to suffocate in its cradle, its cries never heard. That night we stood outside the Tavern and browbeat every person who exited to sign a petition demanding Community Council support for Sigma Pi. (We only asked the departing people, figuring they would be too drunk to know what they were signing.) By the end of the night we had gathered four hundred signatures, nearly a third of the school. A week later, bowing to the public outcry, Community Council allocated five hundred dollars to Sigma Pi Fraternity.

Calling Sigma Pi to order, our first task was to print our Christmas card. It was only October, but we figured if the fraternity was going to make a splash we needed to get our message of goodwill out to the masses. Marilyn took a picture of the three chapter officers lined up, serious stolid expressions on our faces, purple corduroy cap on my head. We printed it postcard-size in grainy black-and-white, the backs reading, in block letters, MERRY CHRISTMAS FROM SIGMA FRATERNITY.

In retrospect, it is impressive, even to me, to look back upon how many idiotic moves we made that semester. Anyone taking a cursory glance at the Hampshire situation of the day could have told us that this was not the time for such shenanigans; knowing my history and near-death situation with the Dicks, knowing how dry was any reservoir of goodwill we might once have had, seeing the rise of political correctness, as around this time this phrase was first used nonironically by our campus activists to describe their program. Someone might have warned us that it was not the time for people with our ironic tendencies to be launching *anything* at Hampshire College; and if we must, the last thing to be launched was a fraternity, even as a joke; and if we must start a fraternity, to stay as far away from school funds as possible; and if we must take them, for God's sake, what the hell were we thinking putting our pictures on the front of a postcard and letting everyone know who we were?

But no one told us any of those things. So start a fraternity we did, getting school funding and sending out postcards emblazoned with our faces to the entire campus.

At about noon on the day the postcards went out, I started noticing funny looks as I walked around the school. Even scattered boos and hisses. Frank noticed it, too, but brushed it aside. "They're just jealous," he spat.

With $460 left, we got to work planning the party.

In the spirit of the season of demonstrations, we decided a cause-oriented event would match the mood of the day. We booked the SAGA back room for what we called a Safe Sex Concert, promoting the message, central to Supreme Dick philosophy, that the only Safe Sex is no sex at all. As headliners we booked Frank's band, the Butt Buddies.

One would hardly suppose that people could get so riled up about an abstinence awareness concert, but somehow in the logic of the times, the tamer our words, the more they seemed to provoke the campus into a fury. For the following two weeks until the show, we spent our time around the clock fending off attempts to cancel our event. From the moment it was scheduled, the Women's Center and the Safe Sex Education Coalition went into overdrive, pressuring the administration to cancel the show, claiming it undermined *their* safe sex message.

In a climactic final meeting with the dean of students, our suggestion that the above groups didn't own the term *safe sex* was met with an icy silence. "I'm very disturbed that the sensitivities of the community mean so little to you."

We nodded. "They mean everything to me," Zach said.

The dean probed for a hole in our plan. Trying to prove that we were up to no good, he asked what our feelings were about safe sex, about AIDS in general, about why we had started a fraternity and what we were going to tell the national office of Sigma Pi, and about what was on the program at the show. Finally he turned to me. "And my file says you are one of the Supreme Dicks."

I shivered. "There are no Supreme Dicks at Hampshire. They've been eradicated."

"But are you saying you're not one of them?"

"I've never been much of a joiner," I stuttered.

"Hmmmm . . . and what about this band, the Butt Buddies?"

"They're fantastic," Frank declared.

"I'm sure. But—but tell me, just between us, what's their real name . . . ?"

The three of us looked at each other. "Their real name . . . ?"

"Come on, you guys know what I'm talking about."

We shook our heads.

"What do you guys really call that band?"

Another half hour back and forth on this theme and the dean broke down. "My sources tell me the real name of that band is . . . the Butt . . . Fuckers."

We broke into laughter, which we were unable to suppress until we were shown the door.

On a Saturday night the Safe Sex show went on. In the run-up to it, however, we had been so focused on getting beer to campus and fighting back attempts to cancel the concert, we hadn't had time to think about the program; we all assumed that something scandalous would occur. There was no way, it was clear, this event could go off without a giant ruckus. But as it happened, nothing scandalous did occur. The bands played. Free beer was distributed to the smallish crowd that showed up. In all the commotion about keeping the event from being canceled, we had gone ahead and set a place at the table for debacle, without checking to see if debacle had RSVP'd. As the night ended, we polished off the final keg of beer, a strange aftertaste filling our mouths.

The next day we realized we had forty dollars left in the Sigma Pi account—enough for one keg of cheap beer. The following week, our friend Dave was coming back from a trip home to L.A., and so we decided to throw him a welcome-home party at the mod he and Zach shared. "We really need to get this guy laid," Frank proclaimed.

A week later, I was sitting in the Airport Lounge when Sarah rushed in. "Where are Frank and Zach?" she asked.

"I dunno. Why?"

"You guys are in so much trouble. The Community Council just voted unanimously that the three of you should be expelled."

CHAPTER TWELVE

Wet T-Shirt Night

Within forty-eight hours I discovered I possessed magical powers. I could make the entire Airport Lounge fall silent when I walked in. In class, seats on either side of me miraculously stayed empty, even as people crouched on the floor for want of chairs. In the dining hall, food flew at my head from mysterious unseen corners. My hallmates, amazingly, didn't recognize me when I encountered them in public.

In my Supreme Dick youth of the previous year, I thought I knew what it was to be a pariah. But in truth, I had been merely the most junior and obscure member of the hated group, my name not known to any but our most committed enemies. Now I was front and center, my picture in every mailbox. When in the midst of the fuss Zach and I looked back, we realized how gentle and collegial the protests against the Dicks had been compared with the fury of a mobilized campus.

It took a few days to sort out what had happened. After scheduling Dave's welcome-home bash, Frank, disappointed with the fairly tepid turnout for the Safe Sex Concert, had decided to turn this into the party of the year. With his working-class, "man of the road" elocution, Frank was a natural salesman and a gifted story-teller, spinning yarns that grew with each telling. Frank had gone to SAGA and wandered from table to table, inviting people to the greatest party Hampshire had ever seen. By the time he reached one large table of girls, which included our hallmate Sally, the party had grown to epic dimensions. He envisioned a grand soirée that would feature a battle of the bands, Jell-O wrestling, and, most pertinent, "a kiddie pool filled with beer," which, he added fatefully, would serve as the stage for a wet T-shirt contest.

It is interesting to ponder how different history might have been had Frank just excluded that last phrase from his pitch, had the words *wet* and *T-shirt* never left his mouth. But oblivious as we were to the political turmoil around us, we never even noticed the blasting powder piling on the campus sidewalks and never thought how small a spark it would take to blow the entire place to smithereens.

Moments after Frank left the table, Sally sprang from her seat and made a beeline to the Women's Center, which called an emer-gency meeting of its membership that very night. Of the feelings of hurt and outrage that were expressed at that meeting, I am told, the greatest was the pain caused by the knowledge that *Hampshire women* had agreed to drench their shirts in beer and parade themselves for the amusement of patriarchal tools like Frank, Zach, and myself.

The next day at the weekly Community Council meeting, an angry delegation from the Women's Center stormed in, demand-ing that something be done about this out-of-control fraternity. Excessive arm-twisting was not needed. The council members competed with each other to express their outrage that such a thing as a fraternity could exist on Hampshire's hallowed grounds ("I came here to feel safe from things like that") and that the school had allowed itself to slip so deep into sexism and prejudice that Frank, Zach, and I felt comfortable using official funds to lure Hampshire women ("taking advantage of underprivileged financial aid students") into a contest for our sexual, misogynistic amusement.

There was some discussion about whether it would be adequate punishment merely to ban the party, outlaw Sigma Pi, take away our housing privileges, and make us publicly apologize to the community; but in the end it was decided that, no, all these measures failed to rise to the occasion. Sexism and patriarchal enslavement were on the rise, one might say they were running amok across Hampshire, and this was the Council's one last desperate chance to "fight for progress before it is too late." If we were allowed to remain on campus, it would be a sign to sexists that they were safe to practice oppression willy-nilly wherever they liked. When it came time to vote on the motion that the gentlemen of Sigma Pi fraternity be expelled forthwith and any trace of their presence be erased from the scrolls of Hampshire history, the resolution was carried by unanimous consent.

The Community Council, however, had no power to actually expel, and voting on student disciplinary matters had never, as far as anyone could remember, been in their line of duty. "In my day, the only students who tried to get other students in trouble lived very lonely lives," Steve reflected. "And even the narcs could be reasoned with." But like the Pharisees, the Community Council referred our case over to the person who could impose a death penalty, the dean of students. With a recommendation that the highest penalties be imposed, the Council sent us on to the administration, where our fate would be decided.

Before meeting with the dean I had a showdown with Sally on our hall. "You can't blame me for telling. What you guys were planning made me feel unsafe in my own home."

"You have to know," I pleaded, "that there is no way we were going to actually have a wet T-shirt contest at Hampshire. Even if we wanted to, how could we have pulled that off?"

She shrugged. "That's what Frank told me you were doing."

"But it never occurred to you that he was just babbling. You live with him, you know he says all kinds of things."

Her eyes narrowed. "There are some things you don't joke about."

"Like wet T-shirt contests?"

"Everyone agrees. Everyone. People are going to have to start being a lot more careful what they say around here." She turned and stormed off.

On the second day of the crisis every student received a letter from the Women's Center in their mailbox; a warning to all Hampshire women to beware of predators on campus, naming Frank, Zach, and me as the school's reigning masters of exploitation. Our friends noticeably began to squirm when we spoke to them in public. "Everyone asks me how I can be friends with you," Marilyn said.

"Do you say it's because we didn't do anything wrong?"

"No one wants to hear that."

A candlelight vigil was held outside Zach's mod, a public mourning at the site of oppression, or of planned oppression.

Amid this furor, we were called into the dean of students's office. We sat at his round conference table and he stared hard into our eyes, a sneer of hate across his lips.

"How could you guys have done this? Do you know how many people have been in my office demanding your heads?"

"How many?" I asked.

"The whole damn campus!"

"That must be tough." I nodded. "But the thing is, we haven't actually done anything. . . ."

"So this is just trouble following you around again? Everywhere you go, trouble just comes chasing after you. Have you ever stopped to think that maybe the trouble is *you?*" Frank, Zach, and I looked at each other. That hadn't occurred to any of us. But now that he'd mentioned it, the dean might have a point. . . .

"We," Zach finally broke in, "we are innocent men." We explained to him how the commotion had started, with Frank's comments in the dining hall, mere bravado, we explained. The dean listened impatiently and finally broke in,

"Innocent!? You call that innocent!? Do the standards of this community have any meaning to you?"

"We're all for the standards," Frank said.

"We love the standards," I agreed.

"Because of you, a lot of people feel very uncomfortable here."

"But we—"

"Don't tell me again that you didn't do anything. If you guys weren't at Hampshire, there wouldn't be this trouble, would there?" We couldn't argue with that.

"But still," I insisted, "you can't actually expel us if we haven't done anything. There'll be"—I paused before whispering the word I knew could stop a charging college administrator cold in his tracks—"there'll be lawsuits."

The dean let out a blast of harrumph and glared as though he were willing me to never have been born. After a few minutes of silent stare-down, he said quietly, barely audible, "Get out of my office."

"I mean, we'll own the school if you do that," Zach prodded.

"Get. Out. But don't think you're getting away with this."

Outside his office a cluster of activists waited and vigorously booed as we left.

Later, we learned that the demonstrators had been so incensed that we had walked away unexpelled that they had begun taking steps to occupy the Gold Coast (as the hallway of the Cole Science Center that housed the administration offices was known). Just before the ramparts went up and the occupation pizza orders were placed, however, the dean persuaded them that though Hampshire's wheels of justice moved slowly, once they began moving no force on earth could stop them; justice would be served in due course. That seemed to satisfy the activists only very briefly. By nightfall, as we camped out in the living room of Zach's mod, friends brought news that the word was sweeping the campus: The administration hadn't really failed to move against us but had revealed their true colors—shown themselves to be in league with our wealthy parents and the sexist, classist, racist cabal that held the school in its iron grip and would never allow its own to be punished. If we were expelled from Hampshire, the theory went, our inexorable rise to the heights of society would be halted. The zillion-dollar-a-year corporate jobs overseeing Burmese slave labor camps we had been promised from birth would be withheld from us if we were expelled. Thus we would not go on to join and contribute to the ruling class and we would not be able to write the annual seven-figure checks we'd otherwise give Hampshire. Thus, as the administration had proved by failing to lop off our heads at the first hint of a wet T-shirt contest, the patriarchy was firmly in the driver's seat at Hampshire College and only a mass mobilization could bring it down.

"I don't have any rich parents like you dopes!" Frank exclaimed in outrage. "I wash dishes in SAGA, for Chrissakes."

"That makes you worse," Zach said. "You're a class traitor."

Outside, the planning continued as the activists now saw this was about much, much more than expelling three wayward oppressors; this was a battle for the soul of education.

The next day the campus simmered while the dean sat across the table from the student leaders. Somewhere amid the deadlocked discussions, a burst of inspiration ignited the room. Even more ef-

fective than expelling us would be to force us to prostrate ourselves before the college, issue an apology for our insensitive
behavior, for violating community norms, and for the scope of
our entire lives, which we would acknowledge had been dedicated
to oppression, imperialism on a global and personal level, and to
objectification of "the other" in all its forms. It was suggested that
expelling us would in fact be doing the community a disservice
because once we were gone, they wouldn't be able to punish us
anymore (and—the thought flashed through their heads—no new
oppressor might present himself for years). After we had completed a seminar taught by heads of the Women's Center and rep-
resentatives of any other groups whom our behavior had offended,
we would make a public declaration of fealty to principles of inclu-
sion and progress. And then, the dean told us, smiling, "and then
I think the community might be willing to put this behind us."

The dean and the two other administrators who flanked him
on either side smirked at us. "I really think we've found a great solution here."

"So you're not expelling us?" Frank asked.

"Once you've completed the course we've prescribed, I think
we'll be able to take that off the table."

"So let's talk about your apology," the woman on the dean's
left said. "We were thinking we could call a gathering in the gym
where you apologize—"

"Apologize? For what?" I said.

The dean and his cohorts threw up their hands. "We're trying to
work with you. Please tell me you're not going to start that again."

"Damn right we're starting that!" Frank fumed.

"Besides," Zach said, "even if we were planning what they
said we were, I don't see anything in the student handbook about
not throwing a wet T-shirt contest in a kiddie pool full of beer."

The three smirks vanished and were replaced by grim looks of
concern.

"Look," said the dean, "if you don't understand why you need to apologize for making people feel unsafe at their school, I really question whether you belong at this institution. We are offering you a way out of this mess you've created."

Zach suddenly stood up. "The only way out I see is the door. Good day, gentlemen."

That night, at the Red Lion, Steve Shavel confirmed the wisdom of our actions. "If they could expel you, they would've done it. They know they can't get away with that."

"So we just tough it out?"

"I think that's your only plan."

"But they can make life miserable for us."

"The road of a Supreme Dick is long and dark," Steve consoled. Still nominally a student—although again not enrolled this semester—Steve was embroiled in his own battle. For his past seven or eight years as an undergraduate, Steve had taken all his classes from one professor—an esoteric philosophy professor, a specialist in the works of Ludwig Wittgenstein, who taught, fortunately for Steve, only at night. This professor's classes were attended by a small but fanatical legion of followers who sat in for marathon debates winging late into the night. These classes were a sort of quiet alternative to the critical theory workshops that dominated the Hampshire literature curriculum, in which Roland Barthes, Jacques Derrida, and Michel Foucault competed to define the postmodern ironies of our civilization—as well as to make the classes completely incomprehensible to anyone who dared join them. In contrast, Steve's professor offered what resembled an old-fashioned, almost ancient, philosophy lecture and dialogue, drawing little from "recent texts" or "critical rethinkings" and offering an intense but traditional approach to modern philosophy.

This professor not only sent Steve down his all-consuming road of Wittgenstein studies, but he served as Steve's advisor, and thus the person who had kept him in good academic standing for a full decade. When, a couple of years before, he had been forced by the administration to put Steve on an academic contract, the two wrote out and filed the following plan: "Whatever Steve accomplishes this year will be exactly what we have agreed upon."

A Hampshire professor could get away with having a minuscule following and enrollment in his classes. He could also get away with teaching at odd hours and lackadaisical attention to administrative duties. A professor could even get away with thumbing his nose at the Hampshire establishment. But in this time of campus upheaval, he could not get away with all that while teaching an uncritical study of dead white male philosophers. Steve's professor had been informed by the reappointment committee of the School of Humanities and Arts that his contract would not be renewed the following year. For the professor, who had spent almost his entire teaching career closeted away at Hampshire, this was a career catastrophe. For Steve, without the professor's protection, there was little likelihood he'd be able to draw his Hampshire career far into a second decade. Along with Nathan, who had also become an acolyte of this professor, Steve began planning the fight to save him, but the hopelessness of their position was quickly becoming apparent and Steve was sinking into a depression.

"Hampshire College has mortgaged its soul to a bunch of carnival hucksters," Steve mourned into his tomato juice. At the counter, one of the crazies was screaming at the top of his lungs, calling Mike a "toy fucking soldier" and threatening to murder everyone in the diner.

Steve sighed. "You used to be able to get this kind of atmosphere in any Hampshire dorm hall. Now the Red Lion is the last refuge for intellectual stimulation."

The next day I was told that the faculty had joined the Community Council in voting unanimously to recommend that Zach,

Frank, and I be expelled. Sitting in Ninotchka's Gogol, Turgenev, Chekhov class, empty seats on either side of me, I wondered whether *unanimously* had included Natasha. Had this woman who had spoken so seductively about *Dead Souls* really voted my presence so offensive that the only hope for peace in our time was that I be removed headfirst? I studied her for signs of disgust when she glanced my way, but then realized that she probably didn't even know my name and had no clue that I was the person whose fate she had cast her vote on. For that matter, Ninotchka didn't look like the type who spent a lot of time hanging around faculty meetings. At least, I managed to convince myself of that.

The pressure to publicly apologize mounted. One night in my dorm I received a secret delegation from the activists. Janet, an acquaintance loosely connected with the Butt Buddies who also did a weekly shift in the Women's Center, stopped by A-1 to talk with me and Frank.

"They're good people," she explained of her comrades. "People are just scared. They are scared of what can happen to them here."

"I don't care if they're scared of the Loch Ness monster. I don't see how that adds up to us apologizing for a party we never even got a chance to throw," Frank shouted, "and that would've been amazing," he added, still not quite able to accept that the bash would never occur.

"Can't you just appreciate what they're going through? Why can't you guys think about someone besides yourselves? They are willing to forgive you—"

"Forgive!"

"But you've got to give them something."

The drumbeat for our apology grew louder and louder and then, as Thanksgiving approached, began to subside. Having made us pariahs, having demonstrated, protested, and raged against us, they could do little in the face of our unwillingness to be cast out. The dean, after a few more rounds of browbeating, had apparently consulted with the school's lawyers and decided, much as it pained him, that while we continued stonewalling, expulsion was not in the cards. Other punishments would have to be found down the road. By the time he finally announced our sentences, a month after the kerfuffle began, the campus's attention had moved on. The dean told us that we were all three being placed on behavioral and housing probation, that Zach, who lived in the mod where the party was to have occurred, was to move out and was banned from living on campus, and that Frank and I had to vacate Merrill House. I realized that in a mere year and a half I had been banned from four of the five houses at Hampshire. *This* really had to be a record, I planned to challenge Steve.

The dean dismissed us with stern warnings about this being "the last time" and not wanting to ever see us in his office again. Outside, the cold was returning and people rushed from building to building, the passersby barely pausing to cast looks of scorn our way.

"I don't know if I can ever look this place in the eyeball again," Frank declared. It would be a while before we would return to semblances of "normal lives" at Hampshire. And then, far worse was yet to come.

CHAPTER THIRTEEN

The Writing on the Wall

The furor over wet T-shirtgate had died down. As December arrived, the campus took cover from the cold, like frontline troops digging in for winter, keeping their ammunition dry and ready to recommence hostilities with the first spring thaw. Winter break came, then Jan term, and eventually I stopped even noticing the leers as I wandered campus.

But while the campus had gotten past wet T-shirtgate, little did we realize that it had only been a prelude to greater adventures for the ongoing PC uprising. The lion had been awakened, had tasted flesh, and its appetite would not be sated until it bathed in blood.

Once again I was hunting for a new place to live. Things being what they were, I wasn't terribly heartbroken about saying goodbye to Merrill House; the accumulated bad vibes had long since poisoned what domestic bliss I had found in its cinder-block halls. My days on A-1 were capped by the fun of living with Sally, the person who began this party. We showered in neighboring stalls in icy silence.

The only house left on campus where I was still allowed to live was Prescott—traditionally known as the party house, where the New York types and the punk-affiliated lived, as opposed to Preppy Deadhead–centric Enfield and hard-core hippie Greenwich. Throughout the eighties, Prescott's tin village of towering ski chalets had been the scene of Hampshire's most notable debaucheries; it was through its narrow alleys that one would search for a party on any Friday or Saturday night (or Monday or Tuesday night, for that matter). Prescott House was also the location of the campus Tavern, which, to the disgust of many, had begun carding for beer, another sign, it was said, that Hampshire had sold its soul. Although, by process of elimination and banishment, I had no choice in the matter of where I lived, it seemed that in Prescott I might find a home at last.

I was lucky just at this moment to find a friend in Prescott with an empty room. It was a campus axiom that there were no weirder people at Hampshire than the ones who looked really normal, and Tyler was one of the leading examples. From Nebraska, of all places (Nebraska!), Tyler (whom we called Tollah, short for Ayatollah, short for the Ayatollah of Rock 'n' Rollah) had short brown hair and he typically roamed campus in white cotton oxfords, blue jeans, and blazers. Often mistaken because of his appearance and midwestern background for the president and sole member of the campus Republican Club, he was in fact the school's most subversive wit.

With two rooms open, both Nathan and I moved into mod number 89, dominated by one of the school's more Warholesque trios. Deidre, a platinum-blond Edie Sedgwick look-alike from Philadelphia's Main Line, was a burgeoning performance artist and, with her low, barely audible voice, one of the school's deadliest terrors. Roger, who resembled a blond David Byrne, was an abstract painter; Danielle was a Preppy Deadhead and an insanely wealthy heiress from New York City, who, thanks to some unseen deviant streak, had fallen in with the pair. I had seen the three of them lurking in the corners of various parties, scowling at the rest of the crowd, but I had been too intimidated to approach. Whenever the rest of a room became infuriated with the Supreme Dicks, the trio merely rolled their eyes at antics they had given up five years ago. On my first night in 89, Deidre started to tell my fortune with tarot cards but, after looking at the spread, refused to speak, saying, "Oh, I'm sure it won't be *that* bad."

With Prescott to roll home to, and a gathering somewhere within forty feet or so every night, I managed to get through January Term and well into the new semester without ever setting foot in a classroom. And somehow, while the rest of the school was getting all uptight and angry, in Prescott one could still hold his head up high while sleeping until three, and then going straight to the liquor store and loafing around the Tavern playing Galaga until dinner. I found the Prescott lifestyle suited me. Had I at last come home?

Amid the party in Prescott House, the upheaval spreading over the rest of the campus seemed a distant memory from a faraway land. One night in February, a girl in the Tavern told me about a demonstration she had gone to that day, apparently set off by some offensive graffiti that had been found.

"What did it say?" I asked.

"We don't know exactly. Thank God the person who found it erased it before it could really do some damage."

"Well, what were you protesting about?"

"The woman who found it said the content was sexist, homophobic, racist, and imperialist."

"All of those?"

The girl nodded grimly. I smiled in sympathy, very happy to be safe in another land.

The next morning, I rolled out of bed around noon and found Tollah sitting in the living room with Deidre, Danielle, Roger, and Nathan gathered around. "Danielle," I bellowed, rubbing my eyes, "you need to drive us to the liquor store."

No one replied. They all sat looking glumly at the floor. "What the hell? Who died?"

"Tyler is having a little problem," Deidre said calmly. I sat down and they told me the story. Two nights prior, Tollah had been out wandering the campus with two other Supreme Dicks refugees—Edward, an Asian-American second-year who had transferred from University of Vermont, and Janet, a motorcycle-jacket-wearing belligerent lesbian. Drifting around, they had run into Henry.

"Who is Henry?" I asked.

"You know," Tollah said. "Henry. From Northampton."

I nodded in unison with him. "Riiiight . . ."

With Henry in tow they had wandered campus until well after three A.M. At one point, Tollah explained, Henry had left them and disappeared, only to return to their sides a few minutes later.

The following morning, the graffiti was discovered, setting off the most furious manhunt since Steve Shavel stole the bell. By that very evening, the case was cracked. One young woman had recognized Edward walking in the vicinity of where the graffiti was found and had called security. By nine P.M., he had been hauled into the dean's office. Hearing that he was about to be charged for the crime, Janet came forward to the dean to say that she had been with Edward and he hadn't committed the vandalism. But to her dismay, the administration seemed to hear the part about "I was with Edward" while missing the part about "He didn't do anything" and were on the verge of charging her with the crime as well. Wanting to support her, and make clear that, no, we hadn't done anything, Tyler then came forward and admitted that he, too, had been with Edward and Janet, and, yes, he could confirm that no one had written any graffiti. The administration's takeaway from this was—we have our three suspects!

Sitting in the dean's office, Tyler, Janet, and Edward suddenly thought they were about to be strip-searched and told to place their orders for their last meal. The dean charged out from behind his desk and asked them point-blank whether they had written the graffiti. The trio denied it vehemently. Pressed, however, about whether they knew who might have done it, they paused and said, it was possible that this guy Henry, when he had parted from them, just might have done something like that, they couldn't be sure, because if he had, he had done it when he was not with them.

They were interrogated about Henry, who, they explained, was an acquaintance from the Northampton scene. No, they didn't know his last name, or his phone number, or how to get in touch with him, he was just someone they ran into at parties now and then. For the hours that followed, late, late into the evening, Tollah, Edward, and Janet were relentlessly drilled about this Henry character. But to the dean's disgust, the three stuck to their stories. They were warned, however, as they were released into the cold after-midnight campus, that there was much more to come.

The campus uproar that ensued made the noise over wet T-shirtgate seem like a child blowing on a kazoo next to the University of Michigan marching band. When word got out that the school had identified the suspects but had not yet disciplined them, rage boiled over and the campus was soon awash in a sea of protest. The protestors, this time led by the minority students group SOURCe (Students of Underrepresented Cultures), appeared everywhere—grabbing the podium at the start of classes, speaking in front of the library, stopping the music at the Tavern—to demand that at last justice be done for their people. Round-the-clock meetings were held to decide how to deal with this ultimate threat. Even the peaceful remove of Prescott was shattered as the voices of protest spoke up everywhere and began to make clear that anyone who didn't join this movement was, in effect, in league with the perpetrators of this foul crime.

The question of whether the suspects—names still unrevealed—should be expelled was so basic, it seemed not even to merit discussion. Of course they needed to be removed from campus at once, and every minute they were allowed to live in our midst was a minute the administration tolerated, nay, encouraged racism as the dominant means of social discourse. This was so obvious to all that it barely needed to be stated. The protestors wanted an answer to the question of how the administration would use this moment, when racism held the campus in a grip of steel, to send a message to the world that intolerance was going to be wiped out. With an iron fist, they demanded at last that the forces of "social change" should be given not just a seat at the table, but the table itself.

Tollah, Janet, and Edward cowered in fear that their names would be revealed as the causes of this commotion. Sequestered in round-the-clock interrogation sessions with the dean and half the administration, the trio quickly forced the negotiations into a stalemate by refusing to back down from their story. Much as the administration wanted to hand their heads to the mob on a platter, all they had to work with was one girl who had seen them walking around that night, and their admission that they had been in the company of Henry, who had been out of their sight. As seen in wet T-shirtgate, by the rules of due process that applied even to the administration of a private college, this was not enough to go on. However, the rules were about to change.

With so many administrators involved in the case, and so many of them in deep sympathy with the demonstrators, the suspects' names inevitably got out. They leaked initially through the rumor mill but then spread across the campus in minutes. It is heartening to look back today and see how effective word-of-mouth was in the days before the Internet, delivering this information to every last person on campus in a matter of seconds. When the names were unveiled, and it was revealed that Tollah was the white male oppressor among them, a massive "Aha!" shook the campus. This was followed by a tiny pause, and a noticeable campuswide scratching of heads when they learned the remaining two perpetrators were an Asian and a lesbian. But this only lasted a second. The movement was on the march and not to be delayed by such contradictions. Oppressors had always bribed lackeys and Uncle Toms into doing their dirty work. As the clamor against them built, Tollah spent most of his days darting from interrogation sessions to hide out in our living room, not even daring to go to class.

The fuse had been lit and the bomb went off in short order. One afternoon, word raced through the school that an African-American first-year girl living in Dakin had been attacked while entering her dorm room.

"Attacked?" I incredulously asked the hippie girl who brought this news to our table at SAGA.

The girl nodded. "Her room was booby-trapped."

"What does that mean?" From neighboring tables shouts of horror sounded, speeches erupted, crying for justice.

"Someone put a pin in her door so she'd stab herself. It could've been poisoned!"

"Was it poisoned?" I asked.

"No. But it easily could've been. She was stabbed!"

"I don't understand," Zach asked. "How do you put a pin in a door so someone will stab themselves?"

"Maybe in the keyhole," the hippie said, growing flustered by our questions.

"They stuck a pin in the keyhole?!"

"I don't know!" the girl suddenly shouted. "Why are you

guys hung up on these details when racism is raging out of control and people are being attacked? This is what happens when intolerance is allowed to go unpunished, and don't think we don't know you're friends with them!"

The neighboring tables stopped what they were doing and turned to glower at us. Zach, Nathan, and I sank down in our seats. "A pin in the keyhole . . . ," Zach muttered.

The following morning the campus awoke to find that the Dakin house master's living room was under occupation by protestors demanding social justice.

The bells of freedom sounded across the campus while one question sat in every throat. "What the hell is the Dakin house master's living room?" And so the first duty of the provisional government of the Dakin House Master's Living Room was to explain that the staff supervisor of Dakin House, known as the house master, actually lived in the little building attached to the Dakin House office and that the living room was, well, her living room. They went on to explain that without this critical piece of real estate in the administration's command-and-control structure, the campus would shriek to its long-promised standstill. It came out later that the living room had actually been selected because the house master suggested to some kibbitzing protestors that they would be comfortable there, what with couches, recliners, television, plenty of floor space for sleeping bags, and easy access to the kitchen in the next room. Which would raise the question, to almost no one, if the person whose space was being taken over had offered up the space as a convenient and comfortable place for a takeover, and helped the demonstrators move in, how taken over were they really? Was a slumber party the same as a takeover?

Students poured into the Dakin Quad to cheer on the occupation force. Classes were canceled and people walked around grinning with a sense of exhilaration, smiling and laughing like Parisians after the liberation. Since Hampshire's founding, at some point in the semester in every class, the professor would clear his throat and gently intone, "When I was in Chicago in '68 . . ." For my friends, this was the cherished signal that it was time to begin our naps. However, for another slice of the campus our faculty's tales of the 1960s antiwar movement were glimpses into the great epic of our time; they clung to and repeated these stories as though a figure out of Homer had stepped up to the lectern and said, "Lemme tell you what was going on with Achilles that day. . . ."

At last *our* time had come. And everyone needed to stand together, *everyone*. Banners were draped across the administration buildings; speeches were heard day and night in the Dakin Quad. The names of the living-room occupiers—the SOURCE leadership—were intoned as mythical titans standing bravely before an impossibly invincible adversary. So impressed were the faculty by the nobility of this movement that even before the occupiers had issued their demands they agreed (unanimously, of course) that they should be excused from any schoolwork they were forced to miss during the occupation.

After the initial hoopla, the uncomfortable question loomed, what exactly *were* the occupiers' demands? That the school end racism, of course. (And sexism, and imperialism, et cetera.) And, needless to say, rid the campus of racists (and sexists and imperialists). But beyond that, details remained murky. The occupiers dug in to sort through the hard business of what exactly they wanted while volunteers shuttled in food and treats from the dining hall, forming a human shield out front to repel any SWAT team raids or commando assaults.

For the Ayatollah, Janet, and Edward, in the midst of seemingly permanent interrogation, the uprising proved to the administration that their suspects had beyond a doubt "disturbed the

community." If the community was upset, it followed that someone must have upset them. The fact that the occupiers would be
missing class and jeopardizing their education was laid at the trio's
feet. Added to their list of crimes was creating an environment
that had directly led to the assault on an innocent first-year; in the
eyes of the demonstrators, Tollah might as well have personally
put that pin in her doorjamb, or her doorknob, or wherever. (It
would be rumored months later that the first-year had admitted
to the administration that she had put the pin in the door herself
as a ploy to get her parents to let her leave school and come home.
But that would be revealed far too late to do Tollah much good.
And when that news did leak out, people would still make the case
that if she hadn't been in a community where she felt unsafe, she
wouldn't have been forced to do that.)

Tollah, Edward, and Janet's conversations with the administration went more or less along the same lines as my discussions
had gone during wet T-shirtgate, albeit with an even more acri-
monious tone; the fact that the three were not delivering themselves to justice drove the administration to rage. The circular
dialogue went roughly:

—Aren't you sorry about what you've started?

—But we didn't do anything.

—If you didn't do anything, then why is the entire school in
an uproar?

—Because they're crazy?

—They're crazy for wanting to feel safe in their own
community?

—They're crazy for thinking it's our fault that they don't,
when we didn't do anything.

—I think you just proved right there how insensitive you are
to what people of color go through at this school.

—(Edward) But I *am* people of color.

—Then you should understand.

Through it all, they stuck to their story about the mysterious Henry who had appeared and might possibly, for all they knew, have committed the heinous crime when he was out of their sight.

Soon conversations about the trauma the graffiti had wrought became even more pained. Those who supported the occupiers (i.e., everyone) upbraided me and any of the trio's circle who appeared in public, hollering in our faces about how the graffiti had unleashed a tidal wave of hate across the campus, making three-quarters of the campus cower in their beds each night for fear of the intolerance running wild. If I dared bring up, "But no one even knows what the graffiti said," of course I was only proving my insensitivity and inability to empathize with the underrepresented experience.

At Prescott House, which I had thought immune from political ferment, the war finally came home. A small portion of the Prescott residents got actively involved in the movement and between them managed to put a damper on the entire house. On the weekends, parties no longer spilled out on the staircase. The Tavern became the scene of solemn discussions of how best to support the movement. The mood of the house was begrudging support; yes, the campus had a real problem, and, yes, we, too, would do our part to fight it. Those who didn't agree found it best to keep their yaps shut.

Even Elizabeth, in near permanent drug-addled lockdown with her group of friends, took notice. One quiet night in the middle of the hoopla, I made my first trip in six weeks to her mod. I found her sitting with five other girls on the floor of her room, listening to a Bad Brains album and smoking hash, the bunch of them looking to all appearances like a witches' coven gnawing on the bones of their latest victim. She looked up and said, "Hiiiii," with enough enthusiasm in her voice that I wondered if she was mistaking me for someone else. "What have you been up to, man?" she asked.

I told her about Tyler and the demonstrations. Some of her friends nodded, indicating they had heard about this, although I wondered how, because the lot of them looked like they hadn't left this room in months.

"Yeah, I guess racism has gotten really bad," Elizabeth said.

"Do you really think so?" I asked, confused.

Elizabeth looked back at the rest of the girls. "I don't know," she said to them. "Do we really think so?" They exploded in giggles. With nowhere else to go that night, I determined to wait out the group and sat in a corner leafing through Elizabeth's copy of *Story of the Eye* while they babbled to each other in a tongue I did not possess. After giving me a dirty look when I declined to inhale from the hash coil, the girls ignored me sitting in their corner. As I looked up from the book to watch them, it occurred to me that I hadn't laid eyes on Elizabeth and Lucy for weeks and since our last meeting, they had taken on a rather alarming appearance. While they always had looked fairly sinister, they now seemed to have cultivated that demeanor in a very coherent, even organized, way, with layered clothing, dramatic makeup, and the like. Now, there was a wildness to their look—Elizabeth's long hair knotted and unwashed, her long skirts torn and dotted with strange substances. In their eyes, too, there was something beyond the standard disdain for humanity; no longer did they seem to be choosing to ignore the world about them. Their furtive glances had an absent quality—as though Elizabeth and Lucy had retreated far inside themselves and could not be reached through the normal channels. I had heard talk that there had been tumultuous times in their group—an overdose or two, perhaps a breakdown. I knew one of their circle had recently left them, after which they had all been driven almost completely underground. I saw now that, as intense as what I'd been experiencing seemed to me, Elizabeth had become alienated from the school on a whole other level.

Sometime after three, the girls around the circle began to stand up and drift away or pass out where they were. Finally, Elizabeth climbed onto her bed and clonked down. I climbed in beside her and hovered above, watching her sleep for a moment, her face still as beautiful to me as it ever had been. I shook her and she opened her eyes.

"Oh, hi."

"What's going on?" I asked.

"Mmmmm . . . Are you coming to sleep? I'm tired."

"Elizabeth," I said, "I think we should get out of here."

"I'm sooooo tired."

"I mean, like leave school or something. Go away. I think if we stay here, terrible things will happen."

Elizabeth smiled, eyes half-closed. "You want me to ride away on a horse with you. . . ." She reached her hand up, tousled my hair for a moment, and then passed out asleep. I lay beside her for an hour or so, not sleeping, and then got up as the sun was rising and walked back across campus in the painful dawn light.

During this time, Zach and I did, however, manage to achieve a real victory of our own—one we had long dreamed of but whose fruit proved surprisingly bitter: We fought our way to the end of Double Dragon. Since our first year, we had been regulars at the Tuesday Night Special at the neighboring Dead Mall video arcade, so called because the mall was empty of all stores except the arcade and a movie theater. Legend had it that years before, the mall had been a thriving hot spot, but that suddenly all the pets in the pet store had died of unexplained causes, leading the tenants to stampede away to the newer mall across the road.

Each Tuesday night, the arcade management filled each game

with unlimited credits and for a four-dollar flat fee, one could play for three straight hours. Since the beginning of our second year, we had worked on Double Dragon, but had yet to make a significant dent in it. Finally in February, we felt ready to conquer the Dragon. Our skills and patience had developed; we had acquired formidable punching and kicking games both, as well functional knowledge of the array of jump/kick, jump/punch, elbow/punch moves available. With the Hampshire campus in flames around us, it was time to find what glory could still be had in this world.

Our first Dragon run was a miserable failure; after an hour our hands ached and we collapsed, walking away from the machine somewhere in the middle of the factory stage.

Two weeks later, we returned rested and prepared. Side by side for three full hours, we battled minotaurs, defeated each of the four underlings, and fought our way over conveyor belts and collapsed bridges. For three hours we bucked each other up when our strength flagged, covered for the other, battling alone when the other needed to massage the cramps out of his hand, carving our way ever onward with our fists, elbows, and boots. After three long hours of battling death, as the arcade prepared to close, we were deep in the hideout of the Black Warriors and at last encountered Willy, the Boss. After a grueling showdown, we took him down. We were informed that we had won the game.

However, we barely had a moment to celebrate when, to our horror, we looked at the screen and saw the words *Now Fight Each Other*. After three hours of camaraderie sown under fire, we were forced to battle each other to the death. Zach destroyed me easily. At the end of the journey, our victory had torn us apart as the fight itself never could have.

We walked silently out into the frigid night, our hands and eyes aching. "That was like a metaphor," I said.

"It certainly was." Zach nodded.

———

The Ayatollah was by now a virtual shut-in in our mod. But even in the squalid tranquillity of our linoleum-tiled home, the campus's fury seeped in. Luke, our quietest modmate, had always been a reserved but welcome presence, loafing around the living room or occasionally party-hopping with us. An upsettingly studious preppy, Luke hailed from a different tribe than the rest of the house, but his low-key affability had made him a welcome presence nonetheless. However, Luke had a girlfriend, Suzanne, a Preppy Deadhead who became very visible in the front lines around the occupation. As the uprising continued, Luke spent less and less time at 89, eventually only appearing long enough to race into his room, fill up a duffel bag, and race out again. One day we stopped him as he charged past and demanded to know, "Are you avoiding us?" He wouldn't look us in the eyes, only shaking his head and muttering, "I'm sorry, guys," as he bolted out.

In due time, the occupiers presented their complete set of demands. The list was the standard stuff (more multicultural professors and staff, funding for a multicultural center). A massive rally at SAGA was planned—a night when "everyone" had to come together to support the movement. Once again, a good cop was sent our way. Zach, Frank, and I received a surprise visit from an ambassador from the movement. Kathie had been a friendly and pleasant RA in Merrill when I lived there, and whatever her leanings were among the RAs she didn't seem to despise the earth for creating me. I had stayed on good terms with her despite the tension between myself and the rest of Merrill House. As the preparations mounted for the rally, she stopped Frank, Zach, and me outside SAGA, saying she needed to speak with us.

We went into her room in Merrill and sat on the throw pillows. There was silence for a moment as Kathie beamed at us. "So, you guys, I think I have something you're going to be really excited about."

We waited.

"I think I could have the chance for you to get yourselves back in good graces with the school."

We waited some more.

"I talked to the committee. Listen. I'm sure you understand there's a lot of hostility toward you guys." She waited for us to agree. We said nothing.

"Well, anyway, time has passed. I made the case that you're not evil people, and that after all you've been through, I'm sure you've grown from learning how much people are suffering here. Soooo . . . the Council has said they would be willing to give you time at the rally to stand up and offer your support of the movement."

We looked at each other. "Excuse me?" I asked.

"This is your chance to show that you share our values. To re-join the community. It's such an opportunity they're giving you. You don't even know how people are fighting to get speaking spots."

"But what," Zach asked, "what if we don't support the movement?"

Kathie sat up straight and made a face like she had just inhaled an onion. "Why wouldn't you support it?"

"Well," I said, "these demands. I mean, I don't know if I want any of this stuff."

"But, you guys have to see that conditions here, they have to change."

"Well, I dunno. . . ."

"Don't you understand what people are going through here? The fear people feel being at a place like this. I would've thought, after all you guys heard when you were in the spotlight, that there was no way you'd still be blind to what's happening."

I nodded. "I'm not sure we see eye to eye on this one."

Kathie shook her head. "I'm just really shocked."

Frank stood up. "Well, we're just fulla surprises, ain't we?

Let's go, boys." We left, knowing that our refusal to speak at the rally would be seen as the moral equivalent of burning a cross on the campus lawn. If there was any room left on our coffins to hammer more nails, we had just added another fistful.

And with that bridge burned, we made a decision that was stupid on such an epic scale that, decades later, it is still difficult to understand what the hell we were thinking. With the campus increasingly hostile, with Elizabeth lost in her drugged stupor, with the Ayatollah's fate hanging in the balance, we fled campus and headed for Spring Break in Daytona Beach, Florida.

CHAPTER FOURTEEN

The Last Spring Break

n early April, five of us squished into the Ayatollah's 1967 Volvo and drove from western Massachusetts to Daytona Beach, the Spring Break capital of the world. For the passengers in that Volvo, the consequences of that vacation would echo down the corridors of history for the rest of our lives.

Before that trip, I had stumbled and snoozed through my education, blithely oblivious to any expectations of the school, my parents, or society, and indifferent to the gazillions being squandered on bettering me. I had survived three semesters with only the most token nods toward schoolwork. And through the haze of it all, through all the probations, the demonstrations, the meetings with the administration, the expulsions, the housing bans, nothing seemed more far-fetched than a suggestion that there could be consequences to my behavior; that my choices and actions would have any lasting effect on me or anyone else. As depressing as it had gotten, somehow it was still only Hampshire.

I think back to one night when, emerging from Clase Café,

Zach and I stumbled into an Amherst party. The soirée was at one of the school's vestigial fraternities, and we were quickly accosted by the icy wind of condescension the fine students of Amherst cast out whenever they met their brethren from down the road, "Hippie Harvard," though we may have considered ourselves. After several minutes spent absorbing their snide comments, the sight of the house's fire alarm was too tempting to ignore and we dutifully pulled it, racing out into the freezing rain with half the house on our tail.

Eluding our pursuers, we found ourselves in the town commons, dripping wet, shuddering with chills, and stung by a sudden awareness that we had missed the last bus back to campus. We hid by the side of the road in an ankle-deep slush puddle, and tried to hitch a ride from the very rare passing cars. Just as we were a breath away from hypothermia and wondering which of our limbs would be amputated first, a pickup truck hauling a load of sod took pity and swerved to a muddy stop. The driver offered us swigs from the bottle of Jack Daniel's he was chugging, which we accepted gladly. He sped down the iced-over two-lane road through the country, visions of death by frostbite alternating with images of dismemberment as we skidded through each turn—the skids causing our driver to whoop with delight and speed faster. Finally, at the gate of our campus, he slammed the brakes, sending the truck sliding off the road and spinning out in a series of 360s before coming to rest in a ditch. The driver high-fived us and we shuddered our way back to the dorms, bursting with excitement to tell our friends about the night. It was perhaps the greatest night we'd ever had at Hampshire. And if there had been any doubt beforehand that we were indestructible and that life's pageant would always lead us safe and warm back to our dorm room, it was erased. Until Florida.

Of the many half-baked ideas behind the trip, perhaps none was more glaring than the notion at its very core, that we five postpunk antisocial misfits should go to Florida for Spring Break. But in the spring of 1988, as the movement had taken over the campus, the only sensible place for us to strike back against it seemed to be the massive weeklong wet T-shirt contest in Daytona Beach, Florida. We may have been banned from throwing a wet T-shirt contest at Hampshire (even if we didn't actually want to throw one), but we were going to attend the biggest wet T-shirt contest on the planet and all the power of every protestor and every administration official couldn't stop us.

Somehow, as April rolled in, we shook ourselves off and realized we had survived the inquisitions, the probations, the demonstrations. The campus had hit us with its best shot and we were in many ways bloodied and broken men, but we were still standing. For now.

The Ayatollah was the only one of our circle with a car, and insanely, he volunteered to drive. His badly rusting late-sixties Volvo sedan looked as though it might disintegrate in a moderate breeze, but of course, the dilapidated state only added to the romance of this grand adventure. We discussed whether we should have the car looked at before the long trip, but we all agreed that if we kept the gas tank filled and we didn't drive it into a wall, the car would run just fine. The Volvo's age only reassured us. It had been running longer than we'd been alive, and nothing bad had happened to us in all this time. So what could happen to it now?

Joining Frank, Zach, Tolla, and me was Carmella, better known to us as our Strange but Interesting Friend from Italy, or "Italian." Carmella had come from Milan to study animals at Hampshire's Farm Center. To the rest of us, the idea that anyone would travel so far to come to Hampshire to *study* defied every known law of nature. Thanks, however, to Carmella's indecipherable dialect, we could make out little about what it was she actually did in her long hours at the school's on-campus farm. One of the few stories that she successfully communicated through pantomime involved her sticking her arm inside living cows to inspect their uteruses, at least that's what we thought she said. Equally incomprehensible was what she was doing, or what she thought she was doing, hanging around with us. In Italian, we wondered, did Zach, Frank, the Ayatollah, and I translate into something glamorous and interesting? It also was not at all clear that Carmella had any understanding about what a Spring Break was or why we were going to Florida. But whatever her translation, she seemed to enjoy hanging around with us and was more excited than any of us to drive to Florida. "Spring Break, it's the season of the salty dogs" was the mantra she repeated with barely contained excitement.

And so one fateful blustery New England morning, we climbed into Tolla's Volvo and pointed it south, sneering farewell to the campus as we puttered out the front entrance onto the highway. We licked our chops with excitement at how enraged our enemies would be by our tales from Florida when they learned we had survived their attempts to have us burned at the stake and lived to "party" once more.

Our first stop was Frank's house in mid-Connecticut. Frank had gone home a few days before to take care of some family business and we promised to swing by and pick him up. We all prepared our polite responses to what we pictured would be Frank's trailer-park family home. In our group of overindulged, spoiled indigents, Frank was the only one from a working-class background, a fact he reminded us of hourly. Alone in our clan, Frank held a campus job, and the most unglamorous job imaginable, no less—in the cafeteria's dishwashing room. Given his dirt-under-the-fingernails credentials, Frank fashioned himself a working-class poet, writing songs of urban wastes. His favorite, "Life on the Road," had been much invoked as we prepared for the trip:

Life on the road,
No cup of tea.
Life on the road,
It's home for me.

When the rest of us would sing it back to him, mockingly, Frank would shake his head in rage. "You guys don't understand how it is."

So it was with no small amount of I'll-be-durned head-scratching that we drove up to Frank's family's house, or rather drove onto the grounds of his estate. We stared at the stables, the guesthouse, and the perfectly coiffed hedgerows. One thing immediately became clear: how ridiculously hokey his Man of the Road routine was and what suckers we'd been to buy it.

"You gotta be kidding me," I said to Frank as he greeted us.

"Don't you start," he warned back, clearly prepared for our feedback.

"I've gotta hand it to you, Frank. You've had it bad," Zach said, glancing around.

"You guys." He shook his head. "It's not about that."

"I can't believe you didn't tell me I could breed with your horses here," Carmella shouted with indignation.

We barged inside and gave ourselves a tour of the three-story colonial manse, Frank nipping at our heels saying, "You don't wanna see this shit. Let's get out of this joint." Before we left, I realized in a sudden panic that I hadn't brought anything to read and grabbed a paperback off Frank's sister's shelf, *California Dreamin': The True Story of the Mamas and the Papas* by "Mama" Michelle Phillips.

By the time we reached New Jersey around nightfall, Frank was so furious with the nonstop ribbing that he sat silent, arms crossed, staring out the window, red-faced and humming to himself, trying to shut us out. We stopped at our first motel that night, somewhere in suburban Maryland, and he grumbled with extra vigor about the phoniness of the in-room movie selection, the individually wrapped soaps, the patterned bedcovers. "How can you people just live around this crap? It's like being in a prison."

"Prison doesn't sound so bad about now." The Ayatollah moaned and collapsed on a bed, exhausted from driving all day, the final hour of which we'd spent cruising around looking for a cheaper place to sleep than the twenty-nine-dollar-a-night offer we'd gotten from a Red Roof Inn. The extra hour of driving finally paid off when we found, a couple miles back off the highway, a motel that would give us a room with two beds for twenty-six dollars, a savings of sixty cents each.

"This room is beautiful," Carmella cooed. "My cousin's is just like this in Milan and I was always so jealous of her." She pointed at a painting on the wall of two cats fighting for a ball of twine. "I love this!"

Frank harrumphed and went outside to play his guitar in the stairwell. Dividing up two to a bed, the Ayatollah, Zach, and Carmella passed out. I sat up reading about Michelle Phillips, and how she'd always just wanted a happy little home but somehow it always seemed to go very, very wrong.

The following day we made it as far as Savannah, Georgia. We had ventured into town, after being told by a gas station attendant that Savannah was "the *real* Spring Break capital of the world." Along the waterfront, scores of bars were bursting with young drunks, whooping at category-five force. We stumbled along the wharf, clinging to the railing opposite the bars as we listened to the belligerent shouts from behind the mass of neon beer signs. As we had shoved off from our tame little hippie school, we had bragged to the few who would listen that we were ready to party with the big boys. But now that the big boys were pounding Jäger shots not twenty feet away, it seemed apt to question whether the big boys were ready to party with us, or more to the point, whether the sight of us after several hundred beers would inspire them to beat us into bowls of turnip soup.

"Spring Break, my eyeball," Frank said.

The causes for our reluctance apparently did not translate into Italian, however, for before we could hold her back, Carmella broke away from our group, charging toward a bar that was about to explode from the reverberations of a Scorpions song. "I thought you guys want to party! Come on, let's get into fun!"

We glanced at each other and chuckled. I tried to explain. "Carmella, this isn't the real party. We shouldn't waste ourselves here."

"Don't be such a gay. I want some dancing!"

The Ayatollah pleaded. "We really need to get on the road if we're going to get to Florida tomorrow."

"You guys are ridiculous." In front of the bar, a cluster of young men in football jerseys were fighting, playfully or for real we couldn't tell, because the only time anyone ever shoved anyone at Hampshire was for demonstration purposes in harassment workshops. To the side of the fighting cluster, one of the combatants stopped for a breather. He teetered violently on the brink between falling over and throwing up. Just as he seemed to have settled on the former, however, he looked our way. Suddenly, he straightened and squinted through the darkness at us, as though the appearance of our little cluster across the wharf was some kind of apparition, possibly an unadvertised unpleasant side effect of his dollar-a-cup Miller Genuine Draft and Jägermeister. He looked to his friends, as if to see if anyone else saw us, but they were preoccupied with punching each other in the face. Undecided, he stared for a few moments more and we stood in our cluster and stared back at him. Then an inspiration struck. Smiling, he gathered himself together and, with all his might, threw his beer bottle at us. Considering his inebriation, his aim was remarkably good and the bottle shattered just inches from our feet.

"Hey!" Carmella yelled, and charged toward him. In balletic syncopation, the rest of us leapt gracefully forward, grabbed her by the shoulders, and hauled her back to the car, as she fumed and cursed that we'd let him get away with that.

Speeding out of town, haunted by the specter of the flying bottle, we tried to shake off the omen and its meaning for our trip.

"That's Savannah. No one goes there," Zach said. "Daytona Beach is going to *love* us."

"We were made for Daytona Beach, not that wharf bar crap," Tollah agreed.

Soon enough, we convinced ourselves that Savannah had been an aberration peopled with mere drop-in traffic. What we brought to the table could only be appreciated by the dedicated *full*-time party animals we'd find in Daytona.

Taking my turn behind the wheel, however, I noticed that the car, as if voicing our inner worries, was handling a little sluggishly. "Ayatollah," I asked, "how come I can't get this thing above fifty?"

"I think we're just too weighed down with stuff," he said. That answer made sense enough for me to brush away any sense of worry I felt.

That night, Frank angrily protested the waste of spending twenty-five dollars on a motel when real working people would just sleep out in the open. To prove his point, he unfurled his sleeping bag in some bushes along the driveway outside our room and spent the night there. In the morning, he proudly declined our invitation, delivered with some urgency, to come in and use the shower.

Within seconds of driving into Daytona Beach, the car was collectively transfixed by a riddle: What the hell did we think we were going to do here? We had thrown the word *partying* around a lot, mostly because it was anathema at Hampshire. But as we drove through the streets of Daytona, it struck each of us like a lightning bolt—we really had no idea what partying meant. Back at Hampshire, a "party" was what happened when students squeezed into a dank, mold-ridden, freezing-cold stairwell to wait on a line for flat beer while some sort of ancient funk music fried the speakers of a crummy old boom box and we shuffled around trying to keep warm, muttering, "This place sucks," to each other until the keg ran dry. In high school, all of us, except perhaps Carmella, had been for various reasons alienated from the social whirl and thus we didn't have three "ragers" to reminisce about between us. The Ayatollah, Zach, Frank, Carmella, and I had certainly had fun in our time at college, but that "fun" had usually been of a semi-solitary nature, like playing video games or making crank calls or driving to a distant diner, or cheering on an attempt to break the world's record for most hot dogs consumed in a minute, but none of these experiences gave us much sense of what it meant "to party," let alone to "par-tay."

But after years of ignorance, driving the first two blocks of downtown Daytona filled in many of the gaps in our education. We came into town high-fiving that we had made it; naysayers be damned, our day of partying was at hand. Zach threw the Stray Cats into the tape deck and we blasted "Rock This Town." Then we glanced around. Rows of shirtless boys lined every sidewalk in an endless row of deck chairs, bellowing at traffic and saluting the bikinied girls walking by. Our car crawled through the main drag and we were swallowed by a vast tide of drunken, loud people in bathing suits, any one of whom—we quickly did the math—could pummel the five of us into potato latkes before breakfast and still have strength left to rip the Volvo to shreds with his bare hands and eat it one piece at a time. As our car paused in front of each deck chair, a frat boy would gaze at the carful of geeks with hate in his eyes—although, in retrospect, they may have been squinting at the sun.

We parked and walked onto the beach, stepping into a gyrating field of thousands upon thousands of perfectly tanned, perfectly formed, undulating young bodies. We couldn't have felt more out of place if we'd enlisted as first-string sopranos in the Mormon Tabernacle Choir. We tiptoed our way between the blankets, even Frank taking extra care not to knock over any beer cups. Dressed in black jeans, high-top sneakers, wool sweaters, and hooded jackets, we looked like we had arrived to collect an unwanted corpse. Salt 'n' Pepa's "Push It" blasted the beach from giant speakers up at a hotel. By the pool, we could hear an announcer summoning the faithful to a belly flop competition.

When we found a free square of sand, we stopped and looked at each other.

"What's wrong you guys?" Carmella asked. "Don't you want to be swimming in the ocean?" Down the beach the ocean was packed with people throwing Frisbees, riding on each other's shoulders, making out in the waves.

"I didn't bring a bathing suit," I said.

"You come to Florida with no suit?" Carmella was incredulous.

"I don't have one."

"I guess I forgot to bring mine too," Zach said. Carmella looked disbelievingly at Tollah and Frank, who nodded—they, too, had neglected to bring swimming gear.

As Carmella berated us, it occurred to me that we could probably buy cheap swimming trunks at any of the fifteen thousand gift shops we'd passed in town, but I decided to keep that thought to myself.

Carmella continued her harangue, abusing us at the top of her lungs, her English, now that she was excited, completely indecipherable. People on nearby blankets turned to look at the strange woman cursing in gibberish at four young dorks fully dressed in black wool and standing in the middle of a beach. It took all of about eight seconds for the most muscle-bound pair in the city to intervene.

"Are these losers bothering you, baby?" the blond one asked.

"Want us to get rid of them?" the blonder one joined.

"Yes, please!" Carmella answered without hesitation.

We considered our options. Comparing notes later, we all agreed that our first and most attractive thought was to tell the Hercules twins, "Take our woman, please! Just let us live!" In fact, I did squeak, "You can have her!" Looking around at the hostile crowd, we fumbled for something else to say as Carmella explained her predicament to the blonds in an unintelligible tongue.

It was Frank who broke the tension with an inspiration. "How would you boys like to hear a song?" he asked.

"What?" They made as if to punch him.

He took out his guitar from the case and started strumming, beckoning in tune, "Gather around, everybody! The Men of the Road featuring the Italian are here!" He started playing a song, Roger Miller's "King of the Road," and nodded to us to sing along. Dutifully, and with no better ideas, Zach, the Ayatollah, and I joined in, braying like a pack of hounds, "Ain't got no cigarettes!" a heartfelt but ultimately incompetent version of the classic. The crowd listened, more puzzled than approving, and when we were done they regarded us with a wary silence. They seemed to be appraising whether the amount of meat to be gotten off our bones made it worth the trouble to kill us. One of the blonds broke the moment.

"Gimme that!" he said, grabbing Frank's guitar, which he handed over without a peep. He bent a knee, hunched over the instrument, and beat a blues chord out of it. For the next two hours we watched as various members of the crowd tried to pluck out B. B. King songs on Frank's guitar. Apparently, when frat boys get into the blues, they suddenly see the value of having weirdos around, giving them a chance to demonstrate their kinship with the wretched of the earth.

We drove to a Denny's a few blocks off the beach. The Volvo was handling even more sluggishly than it had on the highway, sort of drifting indecisively through intersections without ever quite picking up and lunging forward. We all conferred on the matter and decided that crowded city driving was an awkward change for the car after so many hours on the open highway.

Denny's was packed and we were the only people other than the ninety-year-old hostess not wearing swimsuits. At the neighboring table two couples were making out. We stared glumly at them, except for Carmella, who was trying to get the jukebox at our table to play "Push It," a song that had captured her imagination after her introduction to it at the beach.

"I've got an idea," Zach said. "How about we go home?"

"Just like that?" Tollah asked.

"Well, yeah. Maybe," I said.

"I can't believe you guys," Frank spat. "All your big talk and it turns out you're afraid of anyone who doesn't have a textbook in their hand."

"If you didn't notice," Zach said, "your good friends out there wanted us dead."

"All I know is I'm not leaving this town until I get laid at least twice."

"Oh, yeah, you were beating them off with a stick on the beach, Romeo." Tollah laughed.

"I've had it with you fools holding me back. Tonight, I'm on my own and you just watch."

As quickly as our illusions about Daytona had faded, none of us wanted to miss the spectacle of Frank trying to hit on girls.

And when it came down to it, none of us were willing to admit to ourselves, or to the jury we'd face back at school, that after all the bravado about partying in the majors we'd thrown around, we'd fled from the face of partying in less than twelve hours. At least, we weren't ready to admit that yet.

"LEMME HEAR YOU SAY, 'YEAH!'"

We huddled together in fright as a crowd of thousands hoisted their fists and bellowed back at the announcer a blood-curdling war cry of "YEAH!"

"LEMME HEAR YOU SAY, 'HELL YEAH!!!!!'"

The chorus thundered back. Even Carmella seemed alarmed. We pushed our way through the crowd at the poolside nightclub, threading through the shirtless tans as daintily as possible.

"LEMME HEAR YOU SAY, SPRING BREAK '88 KICKS ASS!"

"So when are you going to start getting laid?" Zach shouted to Frank.

Struggling to retain his composure before the thundering crowd, Frank remained unbowed. "Just get me to the front. I need some room to operate."

"YOU GUYS ARE AN-EE-MALLS!"

We found an air pocket to the side of the stage just as the wet T-shirt contest began, and we paused for a moment to savor the symbolic triumph. Months after nearly being expelled for joking about a wet T-shirt contest, we had lived to show them all. As Frank wandered off, Zach, the Ayatollah, and I smiled at each other, drinking in the satisfaction of victory.

Half a second later, it occurred to us that we were going to die.

Pressing in from all sides were nearly naked, very drunk young men, waving their fists at the women shaking it onstage. To urge them on? To threaten them? Was this the kickoff of a beer-based revolution? We were unsure, but Carmella, for once, showed signs of alarm. "I think maybe we should not be being here," she said.

"No one wants to party?" Zach asked.

Across the crowd, Frank chatted with a pair of bikinied girls. Actually, he looked like he was arguing with them more than chatting. Onstage the MC was berating the crowd to stop throwing ice at the wet T-shirt contestants. I looked back at Frank. The girls had been joined by a phalanx of about seven men who glowered down at Frank from Olympian heights above. He threw up his hands and marched away.

"So did you get any?" the Ayatollah asked.

"I wouldn't touch these girls if you paid me," Frank fumed.

I looked around at the thousands of girls in the crowd, any one of whom by conventional standards and symmetrical considerations would have made the best-looking girl at Hampshire. I tried to imagine a world where I might talk to girls like these, where I would just walk over and start chatting to them like the hordes of my collegiate peers surrounding me seemed to have no trouble doing. My fantasy conversations got no farther than me asking, "What's your major?" before they evaporated under the weight of their implausibility.

"Let's get out of here," Frank ordered. For once, no one paused to taunt him.

We spent that night at a campground just outside of Daytona. Frank was satisfied that we were living at least on the earth, if not off it, and graciously agreed to sleep in the tent with us. The campground, however, was not filled with quite as many soulful hobos as he would've chosen to bunk with; the patrons by and large being the spillover from the beachfront area. From tents clustered tightly across the patchy lawn, squeals and groans of lovemaking filled the night, while small fiestas formed around open car trunks and impromptu tapped pony kegs. Trying to plan our next move, we studied a map of Florida and realized we were not more than a three-hour drive from Disney World. Zach and I, who associated Disney with the comforts of our L.A. roots, suggested to the others that we should wake up and drive straight for Orlando. Carmella and the Ayatollah were game for any escape. Frank could only shake his head and mutter, "Figures."

When we had checked out our tent from the college Wilderness Office, Tollah and I had waved away the clerk's attempts to demonstrate how to set it up, telling him we were sure we'd have no problem, we were second-years after all. The instruction sheet he had forced into my hand had long since been swallowed by the mounting rubble on the Volvo's floor. We spread the tent parts out on the grass, Carmella beaming a flashlight onto them. Very quickly it became clear that there was no way we were going to be able to erect this thing. As I looked over the poles, it seemed impossible that they would fit together and hold up a tent tarp. Pieces that looked like carburetors and coffee urns suggested no clear usage.

"How is it possible that all of you together can be this stupid?" Carmella asked.

"It's our specialty," Zach shot back. "Why did you think we went to a joke school?"

Halfway through the night, by hanging strings from a tree branch and taping the ends to the top of the tent tarp, we managed to marginally make it stand. It looked like it would hold as long as no one moved inside. Which suggested another issue. Inspected inside, the tent looked like it was made to sleep a pair of campers, possibly three very skinny ones.

"Are you idiots sure this is a five-person tent?" Frank asked.

Tollah and I blinked at each other. "I'm pretty sure we said something about that."

I was too wound up from the day's struggle to fall asleep anyway. I sat up reading *California Dreamin'* by flashlight. Michelle

Phillips told of her pride when the title song was released and how many lives it changed in the sixties. She wrote about a lawyer in New York who, after hearing the song, left his wife and children to move out to L.A. and follow his dream.

The next morning, we drove southwest on a four-lane highway bisecting Florida's middle. The garish beach gift shops soon gave way to miles of swamp-lined tarmac. We stared, dazed, out the window as we charged deeper into the rain forest.

We weren't more than twenty minutes outside of Daytona before it was clear that something funny was happening with the Volvo; rasping, dry-heaving coughs echoed up from under the hood, and urging the car to even fifty miles per hour was becoming a chore. It lunged forward in mad bursts of energy before sinking into barely mobile torpor. The thought of what might be the problem, however, was so horrifying that we each privately vowed not to speak of it, as if we could vanquish the demon with our silent treatment—the strategy we'd each applied to our studies thus far at Hampshire to great effect.

None of us had slept much the night before in the cramped, suffocating tent, nor had we bathed that morning—the communal showers at the campground were too crowded for any of us to dare—and the quickie breakfast of three parts caffeine, one part grease had left us all a little aching and jittery. *Perhaps,* I thought, riding shotgun, *I'm just getting the nerves about nothing.* But very quickly it was clear that it wasn't nothing, and that ignoring the car's troubles wasn't going to make them go away. About an hour out of Daytona, Zach was the first to speak up.

"Ayatollah, is this really the fastest the car can go?"

Tollah, at the wheel, stared straight ahead at the road. "Yeah. It is."

"Does it have enough gas?" I asked.

"About two-thirds of a tank." We inched along the road, now

barely making thirty miles per hour. Traffic careened by, honking indignantly, a few giant trucks barely swerving away from a collision as they sped around us.

"Maybe we should drive on the shoulder?" Frank asked.

"Maybe you want to get this thing looked at," Zach said.

Tollah nodded. "Yeah, maybe."

At about eleven A.M., forty miles shy of Orlando, we pulled off the highway and into the first service station we saw. The man on duty took one look at our car chugging in and said, "You folks need a muffler!" We looked at each other and tried to nod in a knowing, just-as-I-thought agreement.

"Can you put one in?" Tollah asked.

"I think so. Don't work on these Europeans very often."

We told him we needed to get it fixed up quick, saying this in the most overbearing, intimidating voices we could muster to show him we weren't just a bunch of dumb nineteen-year-olds from an expensive but silly school in the hills of Massachusetts; we were seasoned motorists on intimate terms with our vehicle's private regions. The mechanic seemed duly impressed, nodded, and went back to the bay without speaking a word to us.

We spent the rest of the morning and afternoon in his waiting area, drinking from the Mr. Coffee and leafing through his collection of sports and mechanical journals. A six-month-old copy of *U.S. News and World Report* sustained each of us for a spell. I read from the previous December about the problems President Reagan was having with his Supreme Court nominee. "Does anyone know what happened with this Bork character?" I asked. "Sounds like a kook. Is he in charge of the courts now?" The others shrugged listlessly.

An hour passed and we saw no sign of the mechanic. Tedious as it was, we felt relief knowing that the shadow that had loomed over our trip now had a name, "Muffler," and a solution, and that in just a few minutes more, all would be righted and order restored to the heavens. Another hour passed, and another. In the midafternoon, Tollah and I crept over to the bay to see if he was still there. Indeed, he was digging deep inside the Volvo's innards and brusquely waved us away when we asked how it was going.

"Is a muffler under the hood?" Tollah asked.

I nodded. "I'm pretty sure it is."

As the sun was starting to set, and Carmella and Zach had passed out on the waiting area floor, the mechanic appeared. He was drenched from head to toe in grease and had a wild look in his eyes, as though he'd just emerged from battling a fearsome beast, barely escaping with his life.

"Well"—he panted—"the muffler is in."

"Good!" We cheered. "That's terrific!"

"But if you want to drive that car, you're going to need a new engine and a new transmission."

We gaped.

"How much?" I asked, abandoning all pretense of looking like I knew what I was talking about. "How much would that cost and how long would it take?"

The mechanic stared at us for a moment and then, with a deep hound-dog-like sorrow, shook his head and said, "I have no idea." He handed us a bill for four hundred dollars for the new muffler.

Despite the mechanic's advice that we leave the Volvo to die with dignity, we took the keys and drove it fifteen miles per hour down the service road along the highway, retracing our tracks to a Jellystone Park Campground Carmella had spotted earlier. We checked into the Yogi Bear–themed facility and rented a camping plot, a little triangle of lawn next to a parking space. About half the campground was devoted to semipermanent trailer-dwelling residents, the rest to a collection of itinerant campers, most of whom could be loosely classified as "bikers." On the plot across from ours a couple of shirtless, thin, rangy-looking fellows sat on the ground, leaning against the tires of their car, and snarled at us while we unpacked the car and spread our belongings across the lawn.

As darkness fell, we struggled to jury-rig our tent, erecting another dubious contraption of pulleys and misused stakes certain to collapse during the night. We glanced around for veteran campers who might advise us, but by this hour the neighboring plots showed no signs of life.

We dined by the light of a single yellowish bulb sticking out of the side wall of Jellystone's hot dog stand. Beneath it I noticed a peeling mural of Yogi and Boo Boo running off with a pic-a-nic basket. The campground by night seemed deserted except for the surly teenager manning the snack bar. It was only eight o'clock, far too early to sleep. I wondered how we would pass the evening. Silence prevailed as we nibbled on our dogs, each of us deep in his own thoughts.

"Is there a town we could go into?" Zach asked.

"I think it's about ten miles down the road," Tollah said.

"We probably shouldn't risk taking the car there. . . ."

"Probably not." Tollah frowned at his hot dog with skepticism. "Not tonight, anyway."

After a few more minutes of silence Frank suddenly got up, grabbed his guitar, and strode into the darkness. The Ayatollah looked around by the pool and found an old soggy deck of cards. He played Crazy Eights with Zach and Carmella, holding up their cards to the snack bar's yellow bulb to see. Off in the distance, we heard Frank's guitar strumming and his most sorrowful voice yodeling one of his songs. By the yellow bulb, Michelle Phillips explained how her affair with Denny of the Mamas and the Papas, Mama Cass's love, had been inevitable. There was some errant strand in her relationship with her husband, John, she wrote, that preordained that she would sleep with all of his friends.

The next day there was no discussion of doing anything, or at least we avoided taking any concrete steps toward putting our

Spring Break back on track. We avoided discussing where we would go next or how we might get back to school. The only clear plan anyone put forth was by Carmella, who around dinnertime suggested we walk the few miles back down the road to a Burger King we had passed. We laughed, brushing the idea aside as Italian foolishness. It would be a few days before it came to that.

We could've summoned a god of the credit card with a call home to our parents, which, after we absorbed a few hours or so of paternal bluster, would in all likelihood have yielded a wire transfer sufficient to get us bus tickets back to Massachusetts. But the humiliation of where we had ended up, combined with a growing grasp of the world-class imbecility that had gotten us here, kept us from making those calls. Instead, we waited it out, our bruised but still smoldering confidence telling us that a solution would yet present itself, somehow.

Our lives were soon stripped to their wilderness essentials, laid bare of all the basics of collegiate survival like the dining hall cereal bar, shopping mall video arcades, and the pill dispensary at the campus health services office—the raw elements on which we'd come to depend. With so few diversions to choose from, life at Jellystone calcified into a rigid framework. Mornings we awoke around five A.M., when the stench and heat of five people in the little tent functioned as a natural alarm clock, driving us forth into the day. We showered in the communal bathroom, relieved at least that the early rising meant we would not have to share the showers with our fellow campers. Frank, however, avoided the experience entirely, claiming our habit of daily showering was making us "soft." He stuck to this all the harder as the rest of us insisted his roadly stench had become downright apocalyptic. By day three in the campground, he wore his odor as a badge of honor.

After wandering in a daze for a few hours or sitting on a curb and staring into space, we breakfasted on egg sandwiches at the snack bar. Typically the day's activities included at least several hours spent trying to sleep in deck chairs by the tiny pool on whose surface floated candy wrappers and halves of old sandwiches, which fist-sized beetles used as rafts. Too much time by the pool, we soon found, raised troubling moral questions, as every hour or so one of the bikers would pummel a howling child into submission. Once the initial shock faded, we discovered how quickly we could entirely ignore the spectacle of unabashed child abuse. A two-hole putting green, with a couple little miniature turns, beckoned us for hours of tapping balls across gnarled Astroturf. We rented paddleboats on Jellystone's little pond. Carmella and I took one out but found we could only paddle about fifteen feet before we were hemmed in by the thick crust of moss on the water. We sat there afloat at the moss's edge, drifting while shooing away mosquitoes. I pulled a branch down off the tree and tried to carve my name in the moss, but it was too gooey to hold the etchings of complicated letters like *R*.

"This vacation," Carmella said, "it really sucks, don't you believe?"

I nodded yes, it did. I do believe. We paddled silently back to shore.

At five o'clock every day the children's clogging class was held (clogging is a form of dancing indistinguishable from tap to the untrained eye), taught by a mustachioed instructor named Eagle with curly hair and a floppy tie-dye shirt. Every evening we gathered to watch.

By the end of the first day, I had finished *California Dreamin'*. By the end of the fifth day, all the others had, too, and I started my second reading. We debated whether Mama Michelle really was doomed to sleep with her all her husband's friends. From where we sat, Tollah pointed out, it was easy to throw stones, but the pressure of being a super-hot sixties rock princess was something we couldn't understand.

Every other night there was a Bingo game in the Rec Room and some two hundred senior citizens flooded Jellystone. We were the only people under retirement age in the hall, a fact that we thought might endear us to the seniors, perhaps even leading to a dinner invitation or at least permission to come over and watch their TV for a couple hours. But instead our faithful attendance earned only shaken heads and looks of "You kids aren't supposed to be here." We had thought of Florida retirement communities as places where America stored the unwanted elderly, hiding them from the world of the living. But apparently, from the perspective of these seniors, they were here to hide from the young and they did not appreciate the intrusion. No one wanted to chat with us or know what we were studying back at our liberal arts college. We were the geeks of the seniors Bingo hall.

It was a Bingo custom to commemorate the moment when a number of personal significance was drawn with the sounding of noisemakers and festive whistles. For example, if your first child was born in 1921, when the number 21 was called, you blew a swallow-call whistle. After half a week in the campground, our badly frayed nerves were not prepared for the chorus of train toot-toots and silver bells that resounded after each number, throwing us badly off our game. In retrospect, this may have been the idea, because in a week and a half, despite the fact that we each began playing multiple cards, not one of us won a single game of Bingo. In a movie version of our trip, if you had cast a dwarf as the Bingo caller, it would be rightfully condemned as an over-the-top, hollow attempt at creating a macabre atmosphere. And yet Jellystone's Bingo caller was a dwarf, an insufferable dwarf who, when he pulled B-2, could not pass up a single opportunity to call out, "B-two. Two-B. Or not to be." I prayed he would let the joke slide just once, but a true showman, he knew this was his chance to roll out his best stuff and he never passed up his moment, not even once.

By day four, we had sunk our claws deep into each other's nerves. We spent most of our days, before clogging class, in solitary wandering around the perimeters of the campground, cursing each other and devising fantasies of abandoning the group and getting back to school. My fantasies generally involved meeting a northbound team of down-home truckers with hearts of gold who would encourage me to write the memoirs of my adventures. But, fantasies aside, the solution to the mess we were in was snubbing its cue badly, and the days drifted on with no means of escape materializing.

We needed a bridge over the river Kwai to build, an activity to draw us together. Every day we lay fallow on the fields of Jellystone we were playing Russian roulette with our remaining scraps of sanity. The Ayatollah suggested we revisit Carmella's idea and trudge down the highway to Burger King. No one thought the idea was a very good one, but as we had nothing better to suggest, we all signed up. We shrugged our shoulders and followed the Ayatollah out the Jellystone gates, marching apathetically down the dusty service road alongside the highway.

We pushed off after breakfast and made it to Burger King just before noon. After devouring consecutive trays of Whoppers and Double Whoppers, we sat outside in the parking lot and gazed around to see if there was any other activity in sight. There wasn't; only the highway streaming by, like the wide Missouri, warbling melodies of escape.

"You guys," Carmella said, "I'm thinking maybe we need to do something now."

"I could see heading back to school," Zach said. "I think we've made our point."

We listened to the sounds of traffic. I almost said, "At least we're not stuck in Daytona!" but then thought better of it and kept quiet, tossing pebbles at a bike rack

Back at Jellystone, a man dressed in a Yogi Bear costume was sitting on a deck chair by the pool chatting with the biker parents. In a desperate attempt to keep the meager esprit we'd conjured alive, we decided to play a round on the putting green. We listlessly tapped our balls along, no one bothering to keep score. Until, suddenly, out of nowhere, we were struck by a bolt of entertainment.

I stood in front of Carmella as she took her turn putting. But driven by some mysterious foreign instinct, rather than putting the ball toward the hole eighteen inches away, she decided to drive it, pulling her arm back and swinging with all her might. Her stroke missed the ball, but connected directly with my mouth. Before I could understand what had happened, my head was vibrating like a bell, and I looked over and saw first Carmella and then the others doubled over in laughter. As I spat up blood and bits of tooth, I joined in with them. Now, *that,* at last, was entertainment.

The notion gnawed at us all that somehow we still had to get to Disney World, which loomed just twenty miles away, an obsession that overshadowed questions about how to get back to school. Our potential options for returning to campus in five days remained: Plan A—wait for some magical solution to appear, or Plan B—have more faith in Plan A. So we fixated on getting to Disney World as the solution to our immediate spiritual needs. For Zach and me, native Angelenos who grew up with ritual quarterly trips to the Anaheim wonderland, stepping even for a few hours under the Disney umbrella would be a surefire balm for our scorched souls.

After a number of nonoutlandish travel options (bus, tour group, hitchhiking) collapsed under the weight of such road bumps as not being able to figure out how to find the bus schedule, we seized upon the nearest, and stupidest, solution at hand— to take the Ayatollah's Volvo for one last hurrah, rolling it down the highway at whatever speed it gave.

The night before we set off, tensions came to a tragic break in the tent. Once I had finished my second reading of *California Dreamin'*, the only luxury left in my life was a foam pillow I had brought from school. In a moment of inexplicable good sense while leaving, it occurred to me that the hard ground might take a toll on my delicate neck and I grabbed the pillow off my bed before rushing out the door. Through the long days at Jellystone, the thought that my pillow awaited me at day's end gave my life a faint taste of joy. That night, however, when I climbed into the tent, the breath flew from my chest as I looked down and saw Frank lying on my pillow, smiling up at me.

"Give me my pillow . . . ," I hissed.

"No." He smirked. "I want to use it tonight."

"You can't. It's mine."

"Hey, you gotta learn to rough it now and then. About time you saw what life is really like."

"What does a Man of the Road need with a pillow!?"

"I want it!" I lunged at him and we wrestled for it. Eventually, I won it back, pulling it away from him as the others stared on, more terrified that we would rip a hole in the tent than that we might hurt each other and no doubt, silently grateful for the excitement. The next day, throughout our visit to Disney, Frank and I avoided making eye contact or speaking to each other.

The Volvo drawled over the service road, shaking as though it were about to come undone as it pressed toward its limit of twenty miles per hour. Cars whizzed past and their drivers hurled obscenities unintelligible beneath the rumble of the dying beast's engine. We all stared at the RPM gauge, pushing deep into the red zone, and wondered how long it could go on like that.

"We probably could've rented horses that would get us there faster," Zach said. We all ignored him. Tollah stared at the road in front of the car as though it might disappear at any moment.

The service road ended after we'd traveled for about an hour and we were forced to get on the highway. Immediately, as cars raced toward us from behind and narrowly swerved away from catastrophe, it became clear that this wasn't going to work. The Ayatollah pulled onto the gravel shoulder, where we discovered that with the hazards on, we could rumble along at our own gait unmolested. We did so for the entire twenty miles to the park, arriving at around three in the afternoon.

Zach and I convinced the group to go first to Epcot Center; he and I had seen the Magic Kingdom's California equivalent so many times, but Epcot was still virgin soil for us. The ticket seller at the parking lot's entrance seemed unsure of whether to let our wheezing, quaking vehicle onto Disney property, but perhaps, moved by our desperate, pleading expressions, he raised the gate.

We drifted listlessly around Epcot's late-seventies vision of the future for several hours, none of us voicing much preference as to what rides we chose. We rode silently through a dinosaur panorama and flew across the World of Transportation. We ate lunch in the Italian pavilion of the park's World Showcase section. Carmella was unmoved by its resemblance to her homeland. We demanded to know if she took a gondola to school every day, but she waved us away. "This is like me asking if you have a hamburger for your mother and father every day."

Finally, as the sun set, we boarded the World of Imagination ride, on which a mystical sprite named Figment teaches visitors about the fun they can have just thinking things up. At some especially wondrous point, a camera secretly snaps a picture of each car; at the ride's end the photo is projected forty feet high onto a giant screen. As we approached the conclusion, we saw the pictures of our neighbors' cars displayed before us. Children clasped their hands together with delight, wide-mouthed adults pointed at the Wonders in amazement. And then our picture went up. The five of us sat as far from each other as we could get, each staring into an endless void, absorbed in a silent prayer for death to come quickly. We studied ourselves in the picture looking sadder and more lost than we had ever imagined we could feel, and we knew it was time to think about going home.

We were down to our last hundred or so dollars, enough to buy us another week at Jellystone, but no longer enough for bus tickets. School started in three days, and if we didn't head north right away, not only would we be late getting back for the new semester, we'd be making the journey without any money in our pockets. Remarkably, the more desperate our straits became, the more unthinkable it was to call home. Perhaps a week before, we still might have had the pluck to pour our hearts out to our parents and beg for help, but after ten days stuck at Jellystone, the humiliation was now too profound for any of us to imagine fessing up to it in a tearful call.

"If I try to explain this to my father he will pull me out from America and never let me come back," said Carmella.

Amazingly, it was the Italian herself who had the idea. Somewhere along the way, she suddenly recalled, Carmella had heard of something called drive-aways. "These people," she said, "who want the cars they have to go somewhere else, they give them to you to enjoy for your drive." It took us a few hours to sort out what she was getting at, but when we finally did, we raced to the snack bar and bought a local newspaper. Throwing open the classifieds we found, sure enough, a little section labeled "Drive Aways" where car owners advertised for people to drive their cars to distant locales, some of them even offering to pay the driver's gas and expenses. Our hearts raced as we scanned the listings, "Drivers needed to Alabama . . . Colorado . . . Texas . . . ," and sank when we saw not one of the damned listings was for a point north.

Over hot dog dinner, we faced up to the inevitable. It was Frank who put the idea on the table.

"First thing tomorrow, I'll be by the side of the highway with my thumb out. Just me and the road and I'll see you chumps later."

Instead of making fun of him, the rest of us sadly nodded. We had come to the point where Frank's crazy notions sounded like good sense. We were going to have to split up and hitch our ways back to school. Visions of gang dismemberment at the hands of speed-crazed truckers danced before us all, but we swallowed deeply and resigned ourselves to what we hoped would be fairly quick deaths, compared to the slow journey to the grave looming before us at Jellystone.

And then Frank threw out, "And I'm taking the Italian." His Man of the Road skills kicking in, he had beaten the rest of us to figuring what an advantage it would be to have Carmella when you were trying to flag down a truck. We spent the rest of the night bickering over who got her and who would have to carry the tent all the way home.

The next morning, we arose to face our doom. But before setting off, the Ayatollah and I went to take one last desperate look at the drive-away column in the paper. The snack bar was just opening. We flipped through the classified pages, very slowly this time—to postpone extinguishing the last flame of our hopes. But when we got to the column, we saw something that made us shudder in fright. The Ayatollah and I stared, not daring to believe our eyes.

Before us danced a tiny one-inch ad, "Driver needed for Boston, Massachusetts." We grabbed the paper and raced for the pay phone.

Tollah spoke to the owner, who said he'd already received four calls that morning and had told them all that the first person to get to his house could take the car. The house was about ten miles away straight down the highway. I looked to Tollah. "You better take the Italian," I said. He nodded and rushed off to grab her and together they raced to the highway, and raised their thumbs high.

Two hours later, Tollah and Carmella returned in a two-door Accord hatchback.

"How the hell are we supposed to fit in that thing all the way to school?" Zach asked. But somehow we did. The backseat was a tiny shelf, not big enough to squeeze the family poodle into, but in rotation, three of us sat there all the way back to Massachusetts. We played local radio most of the way. Frank and I didn't speak to each other.

We made the drive in a straight shot, stopping only for gas and fast food. Thirty or so hours later, we drove onto the campus, still blotched with patches of snow. Mercifully, there was no one around to ask how the trip had gone as we parked outside Prescott House dorm.

"You going to do anything tonight?" I asked the others. "There's probably a party. . . ."

"I think I'm going to pass," Zach said. Everyone nodded and grabbed their bags out of the car. Muttering terse good-byes, we slunk back to our rooms to sleep.

Frank and I never repaired our friendship after that trip. Pre-trip, on campus, I'd always appreciated his Man of the Road routine, seeing it as a charming eccentricity. I couldn't have imagined that one day it would annoy me so much it would drive a wedge between us. Nor could I imagine that a fight over a pillow would be the last real conversation we'd ever have, its wounds never quite healing, as life sent us down separate paths until, finally, we never spoke to each other again.

But before we headed down those roads, two more months of Hampshire loomed. Spring Break may have kicked some of the fight out of us, but the rest of campus returned, eager and licking their chops, to pick up where they had left off. Unfinished business would be attended to before anyone got out of there alive.

CHAPTER FIFTEEN

Twilight of the Gods

We crawled back from Spring Break bloodied, broken, and bowed. But while we came creeping in like a quintet of very exhausted lambs, the rest of the school roared back to campus eager to resume the battle and deliver the coup de grâce to intolerance, imperialism, and all other ills that had kept humanity in bondage for so long.

Within days, hours even, of returning to campus we were warned anew that oppression was still lurking in every corner. Vigilance was the order of the day. With all those eyes on the lookout, it didn't take long for oppression to reveal itself. In short order, the Community Council itself was rocked by a scandal involving one of its own elected members. Council Member Alex had been an active, if somewhat low-key, supporter of the demonstrations and occupation. Unfortunately for him, however, he had the habit of dabbling as an amateur cartoonist. He also had the extremely poor judgment to bring his talent to bear upon his elective duties. Feeling whimsical at a marathon Council meeting, Alex doodled and distributed a cartoon satirizing the meetings, in what he thought was a gentle, loving homage. Seconds after the copies left his hand, he found himself summoned before a special session, accused of an act of racial and gender hatred thrown in the very face of the Council. The problem with Alex's cartoon, he was told, was its portrayal of the Council president, Cynthia, an African-American woman. Although she was depicted as something of a heroine in the cartoon's text, the rendering of her had drawn on bigoted stereotypes; specifically Alex had drawn Cynthia with breasts that were disproportionately large—an ancient means of mocking the African-American woman.

There followed a lengthy Council session in which the flesh-and-blood proportions of Cynthia's breasts were compared to the cartoon version of Cynthia's breasts. While it was agreed that real Cynthia's breasts were large, it was argued, they were not so ridiculously large as their hateful cartoon depiction. Alex urged, realizing that he was sinking in quicksand with every word he spoke, that he had intended the objects in question to be realistically large, not comically large. At the meeting's end, he was duly removed from office as a Community Council member.

Meanwhile, the deliberations over the Ayatollah's case were renewed. Shortly after Spring Break the school's Judicial Council—comprised of a mix of elected students, faculty, and administrators—decided to impose four sanctions on Tollah and the other alleged offenders in the late graffiti incident (pending expulsion, which was above the powers of the Council). First, they were ordered to write a letter of apology to the community. Second, they would undergo racial sensitivity training. Third, they would perform some hundreds of hours of community service for the school; and fourth, they would make financial restitution for the property damaged.

They immediately appealed these to the college president, who they were told would not be able to meet with them for several weeks. Pending that meeting, however, they were ordered to write their apology to the campus at once—the campus's need to hear their contrition was so overwhelming that it could not wait until the president got around to considering whether the punishments were just. Warned more or less at gunpoint that the direst consequences would fall upon them if they refused to comply, the three wrote and signed a letter expressing regret for all disturbances to the community and their commitment to fighting oppression with every remaining ounce of breath. A copy of the letter was delivered to every student and faculty member's mailbox and was roundly considered to have gone not nearly far enough to repay all the damage they had done.

In the week after Spring Break I received some jarring news. One afternoon at the snack bar I ran into my friend Emily, who was part of Elizabeth's circle. Delicately, trying not to show my hand, I asked her how Elizabeth was doing.

"You don't know?" she said. "Elizabeth is gone."

"What do you mean?"

"Her father came and took her home."

"Is she coming back?"

"I don't think so. Not this year."

"What happened?"

Emily sighed. "Things have gotten really bad out there. Nobody's been outside for weeks. And Elizabeth was kinda out there to start with. She just got crazy. I think she lost it completely."

I tried to sort out how this made me feel but came away confused. Was I relieved I wouldn't have to deal with the two-year-old Elizabeth question anymore, or sad that it had never been resolved? Should I have said more to her, or not said anything at all? Should I have pulled her out and rescued her from her drift into chaos this year? Or, more romantic-sounding at the time, should I have joined her in it?

Although I knew she had left and wasn't coming back anytime soon, it was inconceivable that there wouldn't be another chance for me to be with Elizabeth, that she could actually disappear from my life. For the next few years I heard drips of information about Elizabeth—that she had moved to San Francisco and then away from the city, that she was working on farms somehow—and then eventually I stopped hearing anything at all. Little could I have imagined then, at age nineteen, that it would be another twenty years, more years than I had lived at that point, before I spoke to her again.

We had come to a place where we dared not move a muscle. After two years, it had gotten through my thick skull that Hampshire was not a place to "try anything." With the campus under siege, with people watching their words in the dining hall, with Tollah and the others under permanent interrogation, with glares of open hatred greeting us down every hallway, it was time to take off-campus what scraps of energy and pride we still had left. And so we dedicated our attentions to our neighboring schools.

No one expects trouble to come in the form of an a cappella group.

Sometime in March, Tollah and a few others were roving the Smith College campus during Spring Weekend—a two-day festival of parties, teas, and formal dances all across the school. Any Spring Weekend house party worth its weight in taffeta would host a performance by *at least* one Ivy League a cappella group. Each year, the Whiffenpoofs, the Katzenjammers, the Krokodiloes, the Counterparts, and the Din and Tonics descend upon Smith for two days of overdressed revelry. On the second night outside a party, Tollah and some others got in a scuffle with the Princeton Tigertones, which somehow led to Tollah shouting in their coach's face that "Hampshire a cappella could kick your ass any day of the week," and challenging them to a face-off in the Smith quad against the celebrated—and nonexistent—Hampshire Happy Notes.

At midnight, responding to the emergency summons from the Ayatollah, six of our friends threw on their best flea market blazers and raced to Smith, where they stood on a lawn waiting for hours for the Tigertones, who never arrived. But no matter— the Hampshire Happy Notes were born.

The next weekend a dozen of us, including Nathan and Roger, piled into Janet's van. Somehow the specter of us got up in blazers and cheap ties seemed more ghastly than our usual day dress of mohair sweaters and wool hunting coats. We set a course for Hampshire's closest neighbor, the cloistered Mount Holyoke College, where we had been tipped off that a formal tea was under way. In the van on the way over we tried to think of some songs that we all knew the words to; Beatles songs and TV show themes seemed to be our entire common frame of reference.

Piling out of the van on Mount Holyoke's foreboding Gothic campus, we were momentarily awed and hushed. Finding our way to the right house, we poured through the doorway, all twelve of us spilling into a candlelit room where a hundred or so students in dresses, pearls, blue blazers, and rep ties tittered quietly with glasses of white wine in hand. As we entered, the girl at the door, checking names against a guest list, gasped in alarm. "Excuse me, can I help you?"

"Hey, no problem," Tollah glibly replied, glancing at his watch. "We're the Happy Notes and looks like we're a little late. But we'll just go right ahead and get set up."

We flooded in as panic spread across the girl's face. "The Happy Notes? Who did you talk to?"

"I forget her name. . . . The activities chair? Naomi, maybe?"

"Harriet?"

"Exactly, Harriet. Now you'll want to stand back, we're gonna go ahead and get started." He called out to the room. "Hey, everybody, the Happy Notes are here! Come gather round!" Exchanging quizzical looks, the crowd dutifully assembled, many taking seats on the floor in front of where we stood in a single-file line. If you ever have to rob Fort Knox, do it disguised as an a cappella group. When an a cappella group is announced, society's defense mechanisms crumble. Nothing in humanity's training teaches it to be suspicious of traveling a cappella groups, even if the head of the social committee hasn't been properly notified by the activities chair.

The Ayatollah took the center stage. "Hi, everyone. As I'm sure you know, we're the Hampshire Happy Notes here to do a few of our most treasured hits for you. We want to start out now with a little number that will take you back, way back before the Cold War to the dark days of World War Two, the big one. Close your eyes now and picture yourself in a simpler time. You're a colonel in the U.S. Army. You've been captured behind enemy lines. And you're taken to a magical place called Stalag Seventeen. That's right, join in if you know the words, this is 'Hogan's Heroes'."

We broke into a vocalized version of the instrumental theme. "Ba-ba-ba-ba-ba-be-ba-bep-ba. Bop-be-bop-be-baaa-bop-be-bop-be-baaa." Our first time through the verse the crowd amazingly was with us, laughing and clapping along. The second time, we still drew polite smiles. By the fourth round, people were shifting restlessly. Mercifully, Tollah shut it down after eight verses. Somewhere in the middle of the next song—a bizarrely out-of-tune rendition of "You're So Vain" where two-thirds of the group mumbled through the unknown lyrics of the verses—the crowd began to give each other nervous looks, the first hints of recognition that something *terrible* was happening here. The mixer had been hijacked and none of its planners knew how to respond, nor what ghastliness lay ahead.

Tollah introduced a song by "those lovable mop-tops" and led us into "Helter Skelter" complete with a mad, chaotic medley at the end. As we launched into "Kumbaya" we could see, at the back of the room, our hostesses conferring and racing for the phone. The group had agreed that we wouldn't leave the stage until security came, but nineteen verses into "Kumbaya" and Tollah was struggling for more verbs ("Someone's *fishing*, Lord; Someone's *walking*, Lord; someone's *whittling*, Lord"). When security finally showed up, it felt to us, at least, like they had arrived in the nick of time to save us before our voices collapsed completely.

"What the hell took you guys? We were dying up there," Nathan complained, and they manhandled us toward the door.

Over the next weeks we filled out our repertoire, adding the *Hawaii Five-O* theme, the Beatles' "All My Loving," "California Dreamin'," pieces of "You're So Vain" (mostly the chorus), and the national anthem. With practice, we put together a very tight ten- to-seventy-five-minute set, complete with skits and encores. The Hampshire Happy Notes toured New England, doing impromptu shows and being chased off half the liberal arts campuses in the region. On the road with the Notes, we momentarily revived a bit of the enthusiasm that seemed to have been drained from the glum Hampshire campus. It was, however, during this tour that I sustained the one college injury that would follow me for the rest of my days. One of our skits at Williams concluded with a shoving match, the band degenerating at the end into a giant dog pile. I was trapped at the bottom of the dog pile with my back bent at such a harsh angle, I screamed and feared it would break. Twenty years later, I still feel the pain at times and beg off strenuous activities, citing my old a cappella singing injuries.

Back on campus, the Ayatollah's case finally came before the college president, whose primary interest seemed to be getting the

whole matter out of her life in the quickest way possible. There-
fore, after being told that Tollah and the others were fighting the
remaining sanctions and refusing to comply, with a harrumph she
said she was willing to overturn the sanctions and let it go at that,
gambling, no doubt, that by this time the campus had moved on
and the matter could safely be brushed under the table.

However, the Ayatollah shocked her by throwing in a new element. Pointing out that his entire semester had been consumed
in disciplinary hearings, himself held hostage in his mod, expecting to be expelled at any moment, and further pointing out that
his parents were not remotely rich and had worked hard and saved
their money to help finance his time here, the Ayatollah demanded
that his semester's tuition be refunded. An angry face-off followed, with some heated words exchanged, at the end of which
the president announced she had to leave in a few days as part of
a delegation that was visiting the Soviet Union and that she didn't
have time to deal with this silliness. When she returned, she declared ominously, she would straighten all this out. Whether his
money would be refunded or whether he would now, after all, be
expelled was left hanging in the balance awaiting an opening in
the president's schedule. And there the matter was left to sit, un-
resolved for the rest of the semester.

One evening shortly after this, as Tollah and I loafed around
the 89 living room, a question occurred to me that I had never
thought to ask. "Tell me, Ayatollah," I said, "what did that damn
graffiti say, anyway?"

"How would I know?" he answered without blinking. "Is my
name Henry?"

"Of course not. Of course. But did he tell any of you that
night what it was he might've written?"

Tollah looked at me sideways. "Well, I saw it. They're keeping
the sign in the dean's office."

"So what did it say?"

The Ayatollah drew a deep breath. "What it said was, 'Lesbians, third world students, and cripples: Suck our tits.'"

I took that in and thought back on the turmoil of the past semester, pausing to note that the accused trio included one lesbian and one third-world student. I looked at him and thought about what he had endured and the uncertainty still ahead. "I guess that says it all," I said.

"Put it on my tombstone." Tollah nodded.

Despite all the adventures of the past two years, as spring semester wound down, the campus had become a lonely place. The Ayatollah was under virtual lockdown in our mod. Since Spring Break, Frank and I remained on distant terms, generally avoiding each other. After spending a few months milling around Northampton, Jon had largely decamped to New York, where Ox and Tim Fall had rented a ramshackle studio space in Alphabet City, accessible through a vacant lot dotted with cast-off syringes.

Zach's path had taken him in an unexpected direction. Early in the semester, he and I had made friends with Lori, a girl who lived in a mod next to mine. Our friendship had blossomed when we learned that she was a diehard Bruce Springsteen fan, a species unknown in postpunk/pregrunge Hampshire. Intrigued, we told Lori that we, too, were devoted to the Boss and began a club reviewing the complete oeuvre. Each day we convened in Lori's room and listened to one song, working our way chronologically from *Greetings from Asbury Park* all the way to *Tunnel of Love;* discussing the day's song at length after we listened. Armed with two years' worth of assimilated critical theory jargon, Zach and I held forth on the mythopoetic archetypes in Springsteen's narratives, on the use of narrative as an instrument of control, and the subtle subversion of the sense of the other in songs like "Thunder

Road." Through the spring our friendship with Lori grew until one day, as I got a bit too expansive on the subject of "My Hometown," she suddenly screamed.

"Wait a second!" Lori hollered. "You guys are joking! You've been joking this whole time!"

Grabbing a broom, she chased us out of her mod and down the stairs, refusing to speak to or acknowledge us for a week after. Somehow, apologies were made and eventually accepted and the club resumed, albeit with a more restrained dialogue. Shortly thereafter, Lori broke the news to me one afternoon that she and Zach had been "hanging out." Theirs became the first relationship I had seen up close in my life and perhaps because it was such a defiance of gravity in those days, it lasted all throughout college and on to today, where their marriage and children persist as perhaps the one bright relic of that lost age. More importantly for me, in the meantime, their "hanging out," whatever that was, meant more nights wandering the campus alone.

Steve Shavel and Nathan spent the semester in a desperate fight to save their philosophy professor. In past years, Hampshire might have smiled benignly on their activism, however misguided it was judged to be. In this day and age, however, their fight on behalf of europhallocentric studies could no longer be tolerated. Not only would their protests not save the professor's job, but they found themselves in the crosshairs for having caused an outcry. In May, Nathan learned that his financial aid had been withdrawn and he thus would not be able to return to Hampshire. For Steve, however, the punishment was something once considered unthinkable—after a decade as a fixture of Hampshire College, he would be handed a diploma and sent into the world.

With Elizabeth gone, my attentions and interests were aimlessly scattered around. I spent many nights in underlit Prescott House stairwells, trying to make myself heard by scowling girls over the roar of guitar-clatter echoing off the cinder-block walls, and more and more learning, simultaneously, to look as though I didn't care if they heard me or not. Meanwhile, the clatter and drone coming out of the tape decks and at SAGA concerts was sounding increasingly familiar, more and more like the dissonant sounds once produced here by my now departed friends.

One night at a party, Meg and I discovered we both were carrying jars of pills. In those days the campus health service office was notoriously free about dispensing prescriptions to whoever showed up reporting the most tenuous of symptoms. I had made the trip the day before and complained of headaches, for which I had been prescribed Darvon. Meg had been experiencing a bit of back pain and had been given some muscle relaxers. We traded a couple pills each and washed them down with the Jack Daniel's I carried in my overcoat pocket. A few others standing nearby noticed our exchange and produced a few bottles of their own, offering to trade. In the end we pooled our supplies, mixed them in one big pile, and each took out a handful that we chased down with more Jack Daniel's.

A few minutes later, I sat in a corner on the couch, surveying the spinning room. Meg and a few others of my friends thrashed against each other to a particularly angsty Sonic Youth song. I saw Nathan come in and wave; we'd had plans for a grand celebration of his final days at Hampshire. Against the far wall stood a first-year girl with a knot of black hair and a black leather jacket whom I'd talked to on the beer line about how she hated that in the warm weather everyone had to pretend they were happy. I noticed her glance, and when she saw me still looking at her, she sneered in contempt, looked away, then looked back again. The room dipped and dived around her and I wondered how she stayed on her feet without holding on to anything. *She's very good,* I thought, and I wanted to ask her how she did it.

I leaned forward to stand up. When I tried to wave to them I realized I couldn't move my hand. I looked to my left at the pair of punks sitting on the couch next to me and tried to tell them that I was stuck but I realized I couldn't speak.

I sank back into the couch and watched the room spin around me; Meg slammed her elbow into a guy's jaw on the dance floor and he fell to the floor in pain; Nathan and a friend did shots of something at the kitchen counter; the girl in the leather jacket sneered at me some more. I could feel nothing, not my limbs, not my frozen face; even the sense of anxiousness that had plagued me more or less since I'd gotten to Hampshire, the sense of imminent doom, floated just beyond my reach. Paralyzed and trapped in my head, I looked out at my friends and wished this moment could last forever.

May 1991

My father raised his glass, beaming. "We thought you'd never make it, but nothing can stop you now!"

The rest of the family joined in the toast. My mother hugged me and we all clinked glasses. I thought as I lifted the glass to my lips, *Don't count your eggs before they shake hands with the president.*

At last, the family had arrived to celebrate closing the breach in their financial levees that had been my college career. However, as we sat, jubilant, at the Aqua Vitae Restaurant, there was a nagging awareness at the front of my mind that, less than twenty-four hours before graduation, three of my comrades were waiting for a meeting with the college president, where their fates, as well as mine, hung in the balance.

It impressed even me that having come so far, and being so close to actually graduating, I still hadn't managed to leave well enough alone. After five years, one last piece of poorly planned spectacular idiocy just had to happen.

During my last year, I had finally drifted out of mainstream Hampshire life to the point where the administration no longer even knew my name. After that fateful second year when I saw the removal of most of my friends from school, I had barely even been a Hampshire student—living in apartments in Northampton, taking my classes at Smith and Amherst, going for weeks at a time without setting foot on Hampshire soil.

After the mad year of '87–'88 the campus settled down into relative normalcy, with only the occasional halfhearted takeover disrupting the normal schedule. The message had been sent and it was reiterated in a steady drum roll of teach-ins, seminars, and impromptu lectures on the lawn. Few expulsions were needed to enforce the new era, and it would have taken someone even dumber than me to fight the times.

In 1990 the Berlin Wall came down, but at Hampshire the walls had gone up to stay. By my fifth and final year Halloween was rung in with a smallish party at SAGA, where a few dozen hippies kept the Trip or Treat flame burning while the rest of campus focused on schoolwork. The Tavern was shut down. Campus security began appearing at parties and asking students with cups of beer in their hand for ID. At the library it became hard to get a table; terminals in the computer room were reserved days in advance. Slowly but surely terms like *exercise, motivation, goals, GRE,* and *relationship* wormed their way into the vocabulary. People worked out, went on dates, and planned for their futures, and these remaining few of us who remembered the old days felt very much alone.

When I stopped by, I walked the campus like something of a ghost, my old comrades gone. New students, if asked whether they had heard of the Supreme Dicks, went completely blank; all traces of the legend washed away in just a few years. Only the graffiti in the library toilet stall lingered on, still bellowing, "Supreme Dicks Rule OK!" and below, "NO THEY DON'T," and then "Go back to your fucking spoiled mothers you fascists!"

At Amherst College, I stumbled into a Gothic architecture class. In the first session, the professor projected a slide of a sculpture carved into one of the towers of Chartres Cathedral: a depiction of a cat, twisted and clinging desperately to a crevice, its eyes fixed with horror at the ground hundreds of feet below. Its mouth contorted in a terrible scream. "That," the professor explained, "according to the Gothic world, is the human condition."

I became an art history student at once and to my shock found myself attending classes and writing actual papers and, in my time, starting a Div III on the predictably cheery topic of "Images of Death in Art of the French Revolution." At the beginning of the year, I had no idea how I would pull off writing an entire major paper, but in a mind-altering series of all-nighters in the library computer room, I managed to hammer one out that, to my astonishment, my committee accepted. And to my astonishment, I found myself ringing the bell that Steve Shavel had once nearly given his life to destroy.

So maybe it was my past calling out that made me listen the week before graduation when Patrick, a new acquaintance, laid out his plan to paint over the giant Hampshire sign at the main gates to make it read "Dartmouth College." Somehow, twenty-four hours later, I found myself stationed inside the campus windmill in the middle of the night with a walkie-talkie, calling in the movements of security to the team at work desecrating the sign. And it was a happy reminder of my Golden Age when every part of the plan fell to pieces—the walkie-talkies didn't work, the stencil wouldn't fit. As I realized it had all gone wrong and fled through the woods to get off-campus, three of my comrades were nabbed and called before the president, the night before graduation.

Ultimately, I was allowed to graduate on the condition that I sign a confession the moment after I accepted my diploma, pledging to pay for damage to the sign. Since we'd used indelible paint (so they couldn't paint over it) the bill ended up being fairly substantial; in my time after Hampshire I had no means of paying, which thus led to my transcript being withheld for years to come until the whole thing seemed, one day, to have been entirely forgotten.

Meanwhile, after a few years in Northampton and New York, Jon, Ox, and eventually Steve Shavel relocated out west to Seattle, where the Dicks were on the brink of being signed to the burgeoning Sub Pop Records for years. Sometime after they arrived, a movement that became known as "Grunge" swept out of Seattle and took America by storm. This emergent demographic was famed for their depressive, decadent lifestyle, their nihilistic refusal to champion any agenda or cause, and their devotion to completely unmotivated, ironic negativity-driven "slacking." The living room couch became the totem of a new age. The Supreme Dicks never played again at Hampshire College and Mod 21 was gone, but our long nights of trying to decide whether we should get up and get dinner would light the world for years to come.

Explanations and Acknowledgments

Impossible though it is to believe that so many spectacular adventures could have happened in the life of one mere mortal, I can attest that they did. For readers of this newfangled genre known as memoirs it can be a chore sorting out the "That really happened" from the "He just made that up." But I am here to say that everything in here actually occurred—or at least, this is how I remember everything having happened, and I have, in the course of writing this book, attempted to verify all these stray bits of memory whenever possible with others who were there. To the best of my recollection and reporting, every conversation recorded here actually happened pretty much as depicted. The words are reconstructed as best I can reconstruct them and shaped into dramatic form, but the gist of every conversation, the critical takeaways, I insist are as described. Every event described here within—from expulsions to stairwell parties—actually took place pretty much as recorded.

The only element I have deliberately fudged is in the names of the characters in the book, which have been changed, with critical details in order to mask their identities. The three heroes of this book—Jon Shere, Dan Oxenberg, and Steve Shavel—are by their consent depicted by their real names. As is Her Majesty, the queen of Amherst punkdom, Ramona Clifton, whose proper place I felt it was important that history accurately record. Other than those, however, the characters have been assimilated, combined, and rearranged to ensure that no one depicted in this book is meant to represent any actual person who shared those days with me. In particular, I have taken care that the characters of the administrators—from my advisor to the college president—are in no way meant to represent the characters of actual people who held any of those jobs. What is depicted of their official duties, however, from warnings to conferences, all actually happened.

It has been a long road bringing the tale of these epic days to the masses and I have been carried on some very tall shoulders. First of all, I want to thank my agent, Daniel Greenberg, whose idea this whole thing was in the first place and who stood by it through thick and thin. A million hosannahs also be upon Monika Verma at his firm, who saw our little project through. At Gotham, thanks to the brilliant Jessica Sindler for getting me in shape and steering me through to the light and to William Shinker and Brett Valley for bringing me in from the cold. Over the decade I've spent writing this book, I've sprung out of the past to badger many of my old comrades, scraping their memories for glimpses of what was in their tape decks and on their dorm walls. Especially thanks to the gentlemen of the Supreme Dicks mentioned above as well as Tim Wilson, Colin Logins, Rachel Schaal, and Nelly Reifler for sharing with me.

Before the band plays me off—thanks as always to Karen, Len, and Ali Rushfield for their support, Stacey Grenrock Woods and the Memoirists Club, and to Rob Barrett and Meredith Artley at the *L.A. Times* for giving me some time and space to knock this out, and to the world's greatest Web team—Joseph Kapsch, Lora Victorio, Jevon Phillips, Rebecca Snavely, Patrick Day, Denise Martin, and Stephanie Lysaght—for holding me up through it all.

And mostly thanks to Hampshire College. For all the rocky miles we've been down, you provided the most memorable years of my life, years that made me who I am today, and without them, there would have been no memoir.

ABOUT THE AUTHOR

Journalist **Richard Rushfield** is a contributing editor at *Vanity Fair*, where he coauthors the popular infotainment feature "The Intelligence Report." He is the Entertainment Editor of latimes .com and the author of *On Spec: A Novel of Young Hollywood*. His writing has also appeared in many other venues, including *The New York Times, Variety*, and *Los Angeles Magazine*. He lives in Venice, California.